The Silk Industry in America.

A HISTORY:

PREPARED FOR THE CENTENNIAL EXPOSITION,

BY

L. P. BROCKETT, M. D.

1876.

George F. Nesbitt & Co.,
PRINTERS,
Cor. Pearl and Pine Sts., N.Y

PREFACE.

The little treatise herewith offered to the public can make but slight pretension to original thought, or literary merit; though its preparation has required extensive and somewhat protracted research in fields seldom explored by literary men, and not often by those specially interested in the silk industry.

The writer desires to acknowledge his deep obligations to Franklin Allen, Esq., the Secretary of the Silk Association of America, not only for placing at his disposal the Association's large collection of works on silk and silk culture, which comprises most of the literature of the subject, but in a still higher measure for his free permission to use and transcribe the greater part of his "Chronological Record of the Silk Industry in America," prepared with great labor for the forthcoming volume of the U. S. Industrial Directory; and for tables of statistics, which add greatly to the permanent value of this volume. Without such coöperation, the production of this work would have been impossible. Grateful acknowledgments are also due to A. T. Lilly, Esq., the author of a history of the silk industry in Connecticut; John Ryle, Esq., of Paterson., N. J., and other manufacturers, who have also communicated important facts for the work.

For whatever of good or use there is in this little volume, the credit is largely due to these kind friends; for its errors and shortcomings, if such there be, the writer must alone bear the responsibility; but the burden will be lighter, if his readers will do him the justice to believe, that he has sought, to the best of his ability, to honor American Industry, and to set forth the achievements of American enterprise and perseverance.

This work is published under the auspices of the Silk Association of America. The privilege of its sale at the International Exhibition at Philadelphia, has been accorded by A. T. Goshorn, Esq., Director-General of the U. S. Centennial Commission.

L. P. B.

BROOKLYN, N. Y., *June*, 1876.

TABLE OF CONTENTS.

THE SILK INDUSTRY IN AMERICA.

FOURTH ANNUAL REPORT OF THE SILK ASSOCIATION OF AMERICA.

Illustrations.

INTRODUCTORY CHAPTER.

When our mother Eve draped herself in the broad leaves of the banian fig, just before leaving Paradise, and when just after the expulsion from that pleasant abode, the fallen pair were clothed in "coats of skin," their rude garments were, all unconsciously to themselves, the types of the textile fabrics which were to form the raiment of their descendants for all coming time. The leaf of the banian fig, with its soft and silky fibres, was the food of several species of silk-worm, and the source from whence was obtained the material for those delicate filaments which constitute our silken tissues; it was also the type of those other vegetable fibres, which have furnished so large a portion of the clothing of the world; while the skins of animals slain for propitiatory sacrifice were the prototyes of the karosses, haiks, and other garments of sheepskin, fur, or wool, goat's hair and camel's hair.

The progress of civilization at every stage has been marked by some improvement in the fabrics which constituted the clothing and drapery of the human body. The skins, fur, wool and hair of animals were early laid under contribution for this purpose, and in the warmer climates, the fibres of flax, grass, cotton, the inner bark of trees, and somewhat later the exquisite and glossy filaments spun by the silk-worm were appropriated for the same purpose. It was not until a comparatively high state of civilization had been attained, that the art of spinning and weaving these into fabrics of wonderful beauty and grace was discovered, and every step of subsequent progress in the fabrication and ornamentation of silken tissues has marked a stage of æsthetic culture and advancement.

It is our object to trace briefly the history of this progress in the manufacture of what has been throughout all the past an article of luxury, and which so lately as the third century of our own era commanded a price so great as to be beyond an emperor's wealth to purchase for his empress; but in our own time has come to be within the means and ability of the great masses of our people, and a necessity instead of a luxury. We do not propose to make this history exhaustive—many volumes would be required for that purpose—but only to review briefly the course of the silk manufacture in other lands and countries, and somewhat more fully the struggles of our own people to attain to the position which they now hold of competing on fair and equal terms with the manufacturers of the Old World.

We deem the hundredth year of our national existence, and this Centennial Exposition in which we place the products of our own looms, spindles, and forges by the side of those of all the nations of the world, a fitting time and place to record, with proper modesty and in no boastful spirit, the efforts through which we have attained our present measure of excellence, and to indicate to those who may come after us that it is by continuous effort and toil alone that further honors can be gained. It is alone, as the old Latin poet has well said, "by rough ways that we can reach the stars."

SILK INDUSTRY IN AMERICA.

I.

The Derivation of Silk.

GARDNER, and some other philological writers, tells us that *Se*, or, as it was corruptly pronounced, *Ser*, was the original name of silk in Eastern Asia; and that hence, the people who first produced silk were called *Seres;* whence, after the silk fabrics became known to the Greeks, came the Greek word *serikon*, and the Latin *sericum*, and by the substitution in the languages of Western Europe of *l* for *r*—a very common, and almost universal practice—*sericum* became *selicum*, *selic*, and at last *silk*. This is very plausible and possible; but it seems to us more probable, that the *se* or *ser*, has been reduced by analysis from *seres*, than that there should have been any authentic evidence of its previous existence. The name given to the original silk producers—Seres—was not one which they ever recognized, but one applied to them by the Greeks, Syrians, or Persians. A more probable origin of the word seems to be, that, as from the earliest times, that portion of Eastern Asia which now constitutes Chinese Tartary, and China was called *Sinim* (only receiving the name of China, or "Cheen," from a military tribe or caste called *Chinas*, or *Cheenos*, who penetrated thither from India, after the death of Gautama Buddha, and introduced Buddhism there)—and the inhabitants, *Sinerim;* and, as these were the earliest silk producers, the Greeks formed the adjective and noun expressive of this fact, from their names, thus, *Sinerikos—Sinerikon*, which, in time, would be abridged to *Serikos* and *Serikon*. Yet some doubt is thrown on this derivation by the uncertainty whether the name applied to the people was *Sinim* or *Sinerim;* the later Latin names, *Sinæ* and *Sinensis*, would seem to favor *Sinim*. The subsequent transformation into *selicum*, *selic* and *silk*, is matter of undoubted history.

Aristotle, as the result of the observations of some of the more intelligent of the scholars who accompanied Alexander the Great in his expedition to India, gave a tolerably accurate description of the silk-worm, speaking of it as a horned insect, which passed through successive transformations, and produced *bombykia.** Pliny, nearly four hundred years later, was acquainted with the silk-worm, which he described; but knew nothing of its connection with the production of silk, which, he affirmed, was a woolly substance, combed from the leaves of trees, and spun to form the threads used in making silk by the Seres. For twelve or fifteen hundred years after silk fabrics had become known in Western Asia and Eastern Europe, the prevalent opinion was, that it was either a fleece which grew upon a tree (thus confounding it with cotton), or the fibre obtained from the inner bark of some tree or shrub; while some, deceived by the glossy and silky fibres of the seed vessels of the *Asclepias Syriaca* (our milk or silk weed), and the still longer and more beautiful product of the silk-cotton tree (*Bombax*), believed that it was the product of some plant or flower of the Asclepias or Bombax family. A few had come so near the truth, as to conjecture that it was spun by a spider or beetle. So carefully did the Orientals keep their secret, that it was not exposed until the sixth century after Christ, when two Nestorian monks, who had been engaged in missionary labors in China, solved the mystery, by bringing to Constantinople a small quantity of silk-worm eggs, concealed in the hollow of their palmer staves. This knowledge, thus made public, soon spread over the world, and though the vast production of silk by the Chinese was not diminished, that of Europe and Western Asia was greatly developed in the centuries that followed.

The nature of silk may here be stated. It is a liquid, gummy substance secreted by certain insects, from their food, at different stages of their growth; it is contained in cells or tubes on each side of their bodies, and, at their volition, is drawn out through the minute orifices of the organs called spinnerets. From two to six of these threads being united as they are drawn out, they harden and strengthen to form a fine but remarkably

---

* See note, page 12.

strong thread. This thread is used by the insects themselves for a variety of purposes; the spiders, of which one large family are spinners, use their threads as a means of locomotion, and in the formation of a trap for catching their prey, themselves remaining concealed in a little chamber of silk at the centre, or at one angle of their web; and some species also spin a little cocoon or egg-case to protect their eggs from injury. Of the caterpillars, some, like the tent-caterpillar, spin extensive and closely-woven nets or tents, from the fibres of the leaves they have devoured, and, drawing these partly round them as a protection, pass into the chrysalis state; others, like the measuring worm, use the threads they have spun almost entirely for the purpose of locomotion; while the larvæ of the *Bombycidæ*, or silk-worm family, and of some others, do not attempt to spin until they are ready to pass into the chrysalis condition, and then enshroud themselves in a silken cocoon of their own spinning. In all these cases the product is the same; viz., silk, but silk which requires to be reeled or carded, spun, doubled and redoubled, cleaned, twisted, and otherwise manipulated, before it is fit for use.

The number of larval and perfect insects that produce silk is very large; it includes many genera, and probably not less than a hundred species of the spider family; a considerable number of spinning caterpillars whose tents, webs, or threads are not of practical value, though they may consist of a fine quality of silk; and lastly, the larvæ or caterpillars of ten or twelve genera, and not less than fifty species of the family *Bombycidæ*, all of which spin silk cocoons. Yet of these 200 or more species of insects, comparatively few are of service to mankind. The spider family, though producing silk of the most exquisite quality, which has repeatedly been used for making small articles of silk, must be rejected from the list of practical workers, on account of the uncertainty of their tempers, the small amount of their product, and the impracticability of maintaining a continuous industry on the part of the insects for a sufficient time to draw forth their supply.* It

* Prof. Burt G. Wilder has made many experiments with several species of these spiders, and was so far successful with the *nephila plumipes*, one of the most promising of the family, as to obtain a sufficient quantity of silk to manufacture a number of small articles; but his experiments give no good reason for hoping that spiders' silk can be used on an extensive scale.

would be well if the tent-caterpillars and measuring worms could be put to some use; but there seems to be no hope of it; and they are now a nuisance which is being abated by the sparrows, which, in their turn, may require to be abated. Even among the *Bombycidæ*,* all of which produce silk cocoons, there are not more than four genera and fourteen or fifteen species whose cocoons are available for commercial purposes. Some make a cocoon which cannot be reeled; some make soft and dark-colored cocoons; some feed in their wild state upon the leaves of trees which make their silk of inferior quality; while some will not thrive under culture. The best silk-worms are those of the genus *Bombyx*, most of which feed, in preference, on the leaves of the white mulberry (*morus alba*), though some of them may be reared on the leaves of other species of the mulberry, as the *M. multicaulis*, *M. morettiana*, and to a smaller extent *M. nigra*, the common black or American mulberry. One or two species of *Bombyx*, as well as some of the other genera, feed on the leaves of the ailantus, and of the castor-oil plant (*Ricinus communis*), but these make an inferior quality of silk; and some of those whose cocoons are not used, eat of the leaves of the oak, weeping willow, osier, kilmarnock willow, and peepul, mango, &c.

The Tussah or Tussur Moth, from whose egg comes the Tussah caterpillar, is a wild genus, of which there are seven or eight species, as *Anthæra paphia*, &c. It inhabits the jungles of India, Burmah, and Assam, feeding on the jujube, the silk-cotton tree and the Indian almond; and its cocoons, which are with difficulty reeled, are of the color of the bark of the trees to which they are attached, and are not readily discovered. The *Anthæra Assama*, or moonga, an Assamese moth, which feeds upon the mango as well as the mulberry, and whose larva produces a large, fine, and easily reeled cocoon, though not of very light color, is perhaps the best of the wild varieties. The *Attacus cynthia*, better known as the "Eria," or "Arrindy" silk-worm, feeds on the *Palma Christi*, or castor-oil plant, and is now found in Nepaul, Mussooree, Java, and to some extent

* *Bombykia*, (Greek *Bombukia*) from *Bombux* (Bombyx) a caterpillar, the name since restricted to the genus of silk-worms best known, and its derivative *Bombycidæ* to the whole silk-worm family.

in Southern Europe. Its silk is of fair quality, but is not easily reeled, and is used for carding and spinning. The silk manufactured from these cocoons is coarse, but very durable. The silk-worms of China and Japan are mostly of the genus *Bombyx*, as are the greater part of those produced in Southern Europe and Asia. Reared in different climates, they assume different colors, and vary considerably in size. The most of the Japanese cocoons are of a pale green color, those of China usually white or yellow, varying from a pure white to a pale lemon color. The French, Italian and Spanish cocoons are of a white or yellow color, or occasionally tinged with a pale green. Those of Broussa and Adrianople—the best silk districts of Turkey—are a pure white.

The Asiatic cocoons and some of the European differ in another respect. The best breeds of silk-worms go through their changes but once a year. They yield large cocoons, and are less troublesome to the silk grower; but there are breeds, apparently of the same species, certainly of the same genus, which go through these changes two, three, four, or even eight times a year, and of course yield as many crops of cocoons. These are called polyvoltines, and are subdivided into bivoltines, yielding two crops of cocoons yearly; trivoltines, three crops, &c. The silk-worm yielding eight crops is found in Bengal, and is there called *dacey*.

The changes which the silk-worm undergoes are those which are common to all caterpillars of lepidopterous insects. The moth, miller, or perfect insect, which, after a longer or shorter time, according to the genus, the climate and the temperature, works its way out of the cocoon, has but a brief life, not exceeding a week in any case, and usually of only two or three days. In this time, the female moth lays about 400 or 500 eggs, whitish or yellowish, and about the size of a mustard seed. These usually, though not always, adhere by a gum analogous to silk, to the leaves, paper, or other surface on which they are laid. In the annual varieties they may be kept without hatching, in a cool place, for seven or eight months, and may even make the circuit of the globe. When their food is ready for them they are hatched, and at first the worm does not exceed one-twelfth of an inch in length. Under favorable circumstances of food, warmth, &c., they go through their various changes in from 20 to 56 days, moulting or casting their skin four times. When they have attained their full growth, they are about three inches in length, and have increased in weight from $\frac{1}{100}$ of a grain to 80 or 90 grains. At this time they seek a place to spin their cocoons, which are generally finished in from three to six days. In the cocoon they assume the chrysalis condition; and, in a period varying from twenty to forty days, the perfect insect emerges from the cocoon to pursue the same round again. The engraving exhibits the perfect insect, or moth, the eggs, the silk-worm, the chrysalis, and the cocoons of different forms.

II.

Early Production of Silk in Asia, Europe and Africa.

IF we can place any dependence upon Chinese records, silk, in point of time, stands about midway among textile fabrics: wool and flax, or linen, having preceded it; while cotton, hemp, and other fibrous plants, and paper, followed it somewhat closely. The exact date when its use was first discovered is uncertain. The Chinese in their records claim that it was about 2,700 years B. C., and point to the calculations of eclipses, made by Jesuit missionaries for the emperors, and fitted to each event, as their proof. But the record of the length of the reign of the early emperors, and the incidents which occurred during their reigns, offer a much safer means of calculation. From these we deduce the conclusion that Hoang-ti, the third of the Chinese emperors, and the first of silk culturists, must have been the contemporary of Joseph, the son of Jacob, and have commenced his reign about 1703 B. C. This would give to China almost 3,600 years of silk culture and production.

The Chinese legend is as follows:* "This great prince, Hoang-ti, was desirous that Si-ling-chi, his legitimate wife, should contribute to the happiness of his people. He charged her to examine the silk-worms, and to test the practicability of using the thread. Si-ling-chi had a large quantity of these insects collected, which she fed herself, in a place prepared solely for that purpose, and discovered not only the means of raising them, but also the manner of reeling the silk, and of employing it to make garments." . . . . "It is through gratitude for so great a benefit that posterity has deified Si-ling-chi, and rendered her particular honors under the name

* From the "Summary of the principal Chinese Treatises upon the Culture of the Mulberry and the rearing of Silk-Worms," compiled and translated from M. Stanislas Julien's French edition of the Chinese Treatises. Washington, D. C., 1838.

of 'The Goddess of Silk-Worms.' To the present time, it is said, that the empresses of China, on a certain day of the year, go through the ceremony of feeding the silk-worms, and rendering homage to Si-ling-chi, as 'Goddess of Silk-Worms.'" It would seem from this legend that there were forests of the mulberry, or some other tree, which furnished food for silk-worms, and that the worms themselves existed in great numbers in a wild state, and attached their cocoons to the trees. Perhaps the fact of cocoons being composed of silken threads had already been discovered, since Hoang-ti directed Si-ling-chi—not to examine the cocoons and ascertain their structure—but "to test the practicability of using the thread." Yet all honor is due to this Chinese empress, whose quick eye discovered the possibility of reeling the silk, and who not only fed the worms with her own hands, but herself led the way to reeling, doubling, twisting, and preparing the silk to be made into garments. Silk production extended at a very early period to the adjacent nations. In China, silk culture was mainly successful between the parallels of 23° and 42° North latitude. Among the agricultural Tartar tribes, in the lower part of what has been known in our times as Chinese and Independent Tartary, large quantities of silk were made for several centuries before the Christian era; and some writers, after careful investigation, though on perhaps insufficient grounds, contend that the country of the *Seres*, or silk producers known to Persian, Scythian, Egyptian and Greek adventurers, was Bucharia, or Bokhara. However this may be, the Tartar caravans carried loads of silk which were sold to the Persian and Arabian merchants. The greatest expansion of the silk culture and manufacture was eastward, southward, and eventually southwestward. Whether the original inhabitants of Japan attempted the culture of silk, is uncertain; but the race now dominant there, who have occupied the country since the seventh century before Christ, very early engaged in silk production, and it has been ever since one of their principal industries.

In Annam, Cochin China, and Cambodia, especially the more mountainous part, as well as in Pegu, Burmah and

Northern India, which abounded in wild species of the silk-worm, the production of silk became a recognized employment centuries before the Christian era. The India silk has always been of poorer quality than that from China; but has had a recognized and peculiar character which adapted it to certain uses.

It is often said, by writers on silk, that it is only mentioned in the Scriptures in Revelations, xviii. 10, among the luxurious merchandise of mystic Babylon, and that the two instances, in which our translators have rendered the Hebrew words by our word, *silk*, in the Old Testament, are cases of incorrect translation. The two passages are, Prov. xxxi. 22, where our English version reads: "Her clothing is silk and purple." The word used is elsewhere translated "fine linen." Ezek. xvi. 10 and 13: "I girded thee about with fine linen, and I covered thee with silk," . . . "and thy raiment was of fine linen, and silk and broidered work." This is supposed by some to refer to garments wrought of camel's hair, or other animal fibre; but there is certainly no impossibility that it refers to silk, as the Hebrew word, *meshi*, comes from a root signifying "to draw out," as the silken threads are drawn from the cocoon. It has been urged that silk was not known in Europe till the time of Aristotle, in the fourth century before Christ, and that, as he was the first Greek writer who mentioned silk, it was impossible that Ezekiel, two hundred years earlier, should have any knowledge of it. Such reasoning is, however, fallacious. Many arguments might be brought against it. Obviously, the commerce of Syria and Palestine with the far East long preceded the age of Aristotle, whether we consider the maritime trade recorded during Solomon's reign, or the overland traffic for nearly a thousand years before Christ, by means of caravans, between Persia, China, and the countries intervening.

Before the time of Aristotle, according to Theophanes and Zenaras, the raw silk had been imported into Persia, Tyre, Berytus (the modern Beirut), and perhaps also into some of the cities of the Grecian Archipelago, where it was manufactured into garments and robes for kings and princes. In Cos (not Ceos, as Chateaubriand states)—according to Aristotle, followed by Tibullus, Horace and others—the nymph Pamphila, procuring the silk fabrics from the East, unravelled them, and, by splitting or separating the filaments of the thread and spinning them anew, wove them into a transparent gauze so fine and thin that it was named *woven wind.* The production of this silken gauze was continued at Cos for several centuries. As we have said, the Oriental nations kept the process of producing the silk a close secret for many centuries, and hence the cities of Greece and Syria, which imported the raw silk, were compelled to pay so high a price for it that their silk fabrics were sold ounce for ounce for their weight in gold. They were in demand in Rome, even at this price, by the wealthy; but the Emperor Tiberius prohibited their being worn by men, declaring that it was a mark of effeminacy, and the Roman satirists inveighed against the wearing of the transparent tissues of Cos by either sex, on the ground of indecency. In A. D. 222, the profligate Heliogabalus scandalized his people by appearing in a garment made wholly of silk. In A. D. 273, the Emperor Aurelian refused to procure his empress a silk robe on the grounds of its enormous expense, and the bad example of such reckless extravagance.

But even these high prices were liable to be greatly increased by any interruption to the carrying trade, since no one in the Roman Empire knew how to produce silk. The Emperor Justinian found this to his cost, when, between A. D. 529 and 549, a war occurred with the Persians, who had for several centuries been the principal carriers of raw silk between the Chinese and the cities of Greece, Rome and Egypt. Two of the Arabian princes offered to supply his demand, but failed completely, and Justinian placed a prohibitory duty on the importations through the Phœnician manufacturers. The traffic in silk throughout the Roman Empire was, for the time, at an end. The Emperor had, about this time, manifested his decided sympathy for the Nestorians, whom his predecessors had opposed and persecuted; and it was perhaps in gratitude for this sympathy that two Nestorian monks, who had been for some years missionaries in China, where the Nestorians had a most numerous following, came at the peril of their lives across the Asiatic continent, and presenting themselves before the Emperor, in A. D. 555, showed him a quantity of silk-worm eggs which they had brought, concealed in the hollow of their palmer's or pilgrim staves, from China; and revealed to him the entire process of silk culture which they had carefully observed.

III.

Silk Culture and the Manufacture of Silk in Europe.

JUSTINIAN gave the control of the silk industry, thus newly established, to his own treasurer. The Nestorian monks were charged with the direction of the silk culture; and weavers, brought from Tyre and Berytus, were employed to manufacture the silks; the whole production being a close monopoly, and the Emperor fixing its prices. Under this management the cost of silks became eight times as great as before, and the royal purple was twenty-four times its former price. The imperial treasury was soon filled by this management; but Justinian died in 565, and at his death the monopoly ceased. All over what is now European Turkey, as well as in Asia Minor, the culture of the mulberry and the rearing of silk-worms became a favorite employment. While the looms of Byzantium or Constantinople, and those of Athens, Thebes, Corinth and the Peloponnesus, consumed the greater part of the silk which was raised, the importation from China became smaller and smaller. In 877, the rebel chief Baichu captured Canfu, the centre of the Chinese foreign silk trade, put to death all its inhabitants, among whom were 120,000 merchants, destroyed all the mulberry trees and silk-worms of the region, and put heavy and cruel exactions on all foreign trade, annihilating for more than sixty years the foreign commerce of China. But the silk production was then so well established in Western Asia and Eastern Europe, that this wholesale destruction hardly affected the price of silks in the civilized world. The Byzantine manufacturers of silk were accustomed to adorn their finest goods with rich embroideries, often of sacred or religious subjects; following in this respect the example of the Persians, whose fabrics had usually upon them the *homa* or "tree of life" of the Zend-avesta and the figures of the cheetah or leopard, and of their genii and devs, or good and evil spirits. Much of the Byzantine silk was used for ecclesiastical purposes, such as dalmatics and other vestments, copes, altar cloths, palls, &c., &c. Many of these were richly embroidered. The Byzantine looms declined in the amount and excellence of their production in the 8th and 9th centuries; but those of Thebes and the other Grecian cities, as well as those of Syria, increased their production, and introduced material improvements in their manufacture, though the latter copied somewhat servilely the Persian designs.

Until the downfall of the Eastern or Greek Empire, in the twelfth century, the Greeks maintained their superiority in silk production; but the Arabs and the Saracen princes, who derived their knowledge of the manufacture from the Persians, carried it with them to Northern Africa, to Spain and Portugal (then Saracenic kingdoms), and to Sicily. The silk production of Spain and Sicily was very considerable as early as the tenth and eleventh centuries; and in the twelfth century, when the Normans had conquered Sicily, and the Genoese had taken some of the largest cities of Spain and Portugal from the Saracens, the first thought of the conquerors was the encouragement of this important manufacture. For this purpose King Roger, the first of the Norman kings of Sicily, after his return from his second crusade, in 1146, invaded Greece, carried off the silk treasures of Athens, Thebes and Corinth, and took captive a large number of silk weavers, whom he constrained to settle in Palermo and Calabria, and to teach his people the Greek methods of silk culture. This produced a marked change in the character and designs of the Sicilian silks, which had previously been exclusively Saracenic. In the beginning of the 13th century, the Venetians and Genoese, having the opportunity of following the example of King Roger in regard to some of the Greek provinces which had come into their possession, transferred many Greek and Syrian silk-growers to Venice and Genoa. In both States, the Governments gave every encouragement to this industry, and ennobled the successful silk producers, as, about the same time, Venice did the skillful glass-workers of Murano. At the beginning of the 14th century, Florence and Modena were largely engaged in the production of silk, and it had already become a source of considerable revenue to them. Bologna was for the next two centuries the principal seat of the machinery for the work of the silk throwsters. The production of velvets at Genoa, Florence and Lucca, and a little later in Flanders, belonged to the 14th century, though a few pieces probably from China or Persia had made their appearance in Europe as early as the 13th century. Canon Rock, in his valuable little work on Textiles in the South Kensington Museum, speaks of a velvet vestment mentioned in the inventory of St. Paul's Cathedral, in 1295. In Italy, as in Spain and Flanders, both the culture and manufacture of silk received the protection and encouragement of the rulers. In France, as in Italy and Greece, the manufacture of silk long preceded all serious attempts at silk culture. There were beginnings of the manufacture at Tours and perhaps at Lyons certainly in the 13th century, and, if some of the writers of the Middle Ages are to be believed, even before the close of the 12th century. It is asserted that the first white mulberry tree ever planted in France was brought from Syria by Guipape de St. Aubon, on his return from the Second Crusade (about 1147), and planted three leagues from Montmeliart; and it is further stated, that this tree was the parent of the greater part of the white mulberry trees in France. It was still standing in 1810, and was carefully guarded by its owner. But neither this tree nor the silk factories of Tours contributed for a long period to any considerable development of the silk trade in France; though most of its kings, from Charlemagne onward, as well as many of its nobles, appeared in vestments of silk and velvet. These were generally brought from Greece, and later from Italy; but some of those worn by Charles VI., Charles VII., and Louis IX., may have been from the looms of Tours. The manufactory at Tours was greatly enlarged by Louis IX., in 1480, who sent thither weavers and other workers in silk whom he had brought from Genoa, Venice and Florence. He also made some attempts to introduce the culture of the mulberry and the rearing of silk-worms, but with very slight success. Charles VIII. renewed the attempt in 1494, and with somewhat better results, for the provinces along the Rhone raised a considerable quantity of cocoons. About 1521, Francis I. undertook to foster both silk manufacture and silk culture. He transported a large number of skilled silk workers from Milan (which was then held by the French) to Lyons, established extensive silk manufactories there, supplying them with raw silk from Italy, and then attempted to introduce silk culture into the provinces of Lyons, Avignon and Provence. More than forty years later (in 1564), we find that Fraucat, a gardener of Nismes, founded the first nursery of white mulberry trees in France, which, in a few years, supplied the southern provinces with that valuable tree. But it was not until 1603, during the reign of Henry IV. (Henry of Navarre), that the silk culture was fairly and fully established in France.

He called to his aid a skillful and philanthropic agriculturist, Ollivier de Serres, and after considerable deliberation ordered the planting of large groves of mulberry trees around Paris, distributed lavishly the eggs of the silk-worm, and offered bounties for silk and for the most productive trees. In this first experiment he was too hasty. The people were not fully instructed; the trees did not thrive; the worms died by tens of thousands, and of the few that did make cocoons the moths were allowed to pierce the cocoons, and their eggs were wasted. Vexed with their want of success, where they had cherished such anticipations of profit, the people rooted up the trees, destroyed the few remaining worms and eggs, and abandoned the business in disgust. But Henri IV. persisted in his determination. Selecting a very large orange orchard of his ancestral estates, he ordered it cleared and stocked with mulberry trees, procured an ample supply of silk-worm eggs, and a skillful silk-grower to manage them, and presently he had an abundance of silk. Ashamed of their former petulance, the people began to work again, this time under skilled instructors; and their efforts were crowned with success. The experiment cost the king a million and a half of livres. But the money was well expended, securing as it did the prosperity of the nation. In the reign of Louis XIV., his great minister, Colbert, continued to care for the silk manufacture. The Huguenots were largely engaged in this business, and when the *Grand Monarque* sought to atone by an old age of fanaticism for a sinful life, and revoked the Edict of Nantes, nearly 400,000 Huguenots, most of them dependent directly or indirectly on the silk industry for their living, were driven into exile, and almost as many more perished or were slain. This nearly annihilated the silk manufacture of France; the 18,000 looms of Lyons were reduced to 4,000, and weavers could not be found even for those; the 11,000 looms of Tours were diminished to 1,200, and its 800 mills to 70. Of the Huguenot refugees, more than 100,000 fled to England, and established the silk manufacture there on a firm basis. All attempts at silk culture in that country failed, the climate being unfavorable to the silk-worm; but after the introduction of the Italian method of throwing or twisting the silk in 1718, through the daring enterprise of Mr. John Lombe—then a mere youth—the manufacture in England received a new impulse, and English silks largely replaced the French in the European markets. It was long before France recovered the prestige which she had lost through the folly and wickedness of Louis XIV.; and when it was partially restored, it was again almost destroyed by the Revolution of 1793, and only recovered under the protection afforded by the stringent tariff of Napoleon I., which was afterwards maintained by the Bourbons and Louis Philippe.

In England, laboring under the disadvantage of being obliged to buy raw silk in the open market, after the failure of repeated efforts at silk culture, it was only by the most rigid protective measures that the silk manufactories were sustained; and while it might have been supposed that, with all the improvements in machinery and the vast amount of capital invested in the silk industry, her manufacturers would have been able to maintain their position, it is an admitted fact that the commercial treaty of 1860, which admitted French silks duty free, proved fatal to many branches of the silk manufacture of Great Britain, and reduced the silk weavers of Manchester and Macclesfield to beggary. These great seats of the English silk manufacture formerly competed with Lyons for the American trade; but since that treaty went into effect the competition has ceased, and the English mills are closed.

Switzerland and Germany profited by the misfortunes and mismanagement of France, and are at the present time largely engaged in the manufacture of silk. The raw material is, in part, produced within their own boundaries.

Belgium and Holland have been for several centuries largely engaged in silk production, and the velvets and satins of Flanders are quite as old and of as good quality as those of the Italian cities.

The manufactured silks of China, Japan and India, have a character of their own, and for some purposes are in demand, but they do not compete to any considerable extent with European silks, though so-called Japanese and India silks are largely manufactured in Europe.

IV.

Silk Production in America.

SILK CULTURE was attempted in the early infancy of the American Colonies, and it is worthy of notice that the first, as well as several of the subsequent efforts to promote it, grew out of the selfish desire of English kings to keep the colonies dependent on the mother country, and to make them serve its interests, even at the expense of their own.

James I. of England, while one of the most pedantic, was also one of the most willful and stubborn of English kings. He was almost insane on two subjects, viz.: his hatred of tobacco, against which he wrote a most absurd book, called "The Counterblast Against Tobacco;" and his sanguine conviction that silk-worms could be reared in England in sufficient quantities to supply the increasing demand for raw silk for the English manufactories. In 1608, he commenced his attempts to compel the raising of silk-worms, but fourteen years of successive and costly failures finally convinced even him, that there was no hope of success in that direction. Meanwhile, a colony had been planted in Virginia, and was becoming moderately prosperous. This colony was cultivating the hated tobacco tos uch an extent, that it had become its currency; everything was reckoned at so many pounds of tobacco, from the salary of the rector to the price of a pair of shoes. Here James I. found opportunity to gratify two master-passions; he could, he believed, cut up, root and branch, the culture of tobacco, and in the genial climate of Virginia he could employ the colonists in cultivating the mulberry and rearing silk-worms; not, be it observed, to encourage them in the manufacture, but to compel them to supply the cocoons, or the raw silk, to his manufactories in England, which was to be their only market for this product. Whether this would inure to the growth and prosperity of the colony, was not a question which troubled him; it was sufficient for his purpose that it would injure the tobacco culture, and make the colonists dependent on England for a market for their products. The orders he gave were peremptory. The culture of tobacco must be abandoned. The mulberry must be cultivated, and silk-worms reared. He sent over the mulberry trees and the silk-worm eggs, and directed the company who were managing the colony to follow up his orders by suitable legislation. They did so, imposing a fine of ten pounds of tobacco on every planter who did not cultivate at least ten mulberry trees for every 100 acres of his estate. This was in 1623, and for some time the business went on well. The raw silk was made in small quantities and sent to England, and Parliament once or twice offered premiums for larger quantities; but the Civil War came on, and the Stuarts for the time disappeared. Cromwell was too busy with other matters to find time to attend to the culture of silk in a distant colony. Moreover, the tobacco trade was prosperous and profitable, notwithstanding King James' counterblast. In 1656 and 1657, the silk culture was moderately thriving, but the Colonial Assembly thought it needed encouragement. Mr. Walker, one of the members of the Assembly, said he had 70,000 mulberry trees on his estate, but did not tell how much silk he made. The Assembly offered 10,000 pounds of tobacco to any planter who should export £200 worth of raw silk or cocoons in a single year; 5,000 pounds of tobacco to the producer of 1,000 pounds of raw silk; and 4,000 pounds of tobacco to any planter who would remain in the country to devote himself exclusively to silk culture. We have no evidence that these premiums were ever earned. Some silk was produced and sent to England, and there is a tradition that either Charles I. or Charles II. had a robe made of it. In 1666, these offers of premiums were withdrawn, the Legislature alleging that the culture was so well established that there was no need of further encouragement; but it was renewed for a year in 1669. From this period it seems to have fallen off rapidly; and though the mulberry trees were sufficiently abundant, and the silk-worms thrived when they received attention, the production of silk had ceased to be profitable—especially as compared with tobacco—and was virtually abandoned. We find instances, occasionally, during the next hundred years, of some delegate to the Colonial Assembly coming thither with a silk waistcoat or handkerchiefs, made from silk of his own raising, and woven in his own house; or of some grand lady appearing at a reception of the Colonial Governor or in a public assembly, clad in a gown woven from native-grown silk. In either case, the fabrics were greatly praised; yet it must be confessed that, as compared with the silks of our own time, they were very imperfect goods, and would be scouted by our belles and beaux as unworthy to be worn. This imperfection was due to four or five causes: bad reeling, imperfect twisting or throwing of the silk (the art of the throwster being very little understood at that time, even in England), insufficient cleaning, and ignorance in regard to weaving and finishing the goods. Those home-made silks were fuzzy as well as stiff; the colors did not stand well, and they were defective in lustre.

In 1732, a piece of ground was allotted by the Colonial Government of Georgia as a nursery plantation of white mulberry trees. Lands were granted to settlers on the condition that they should plant 100 white mulberry trees on every ten acres, when cleared, and ten years were allowed for their cultivation. Mulberry trees and seed, and the eggs of the silk-worm, were sent over by the colonial trustees. An Episcopal clergyman, who was versed in silk-culture, and a native of Piedmont, who was an expert silk-reeler, were engaged to instruct the people. So early as 1735, eight pounds of raw silk were sent from Savannah to England, where it was woven, and presented to the Queen. To encourage the culture, the British Parliament passed, in 1749, an Act exempting from duty all raw silk which was certified to be the production of Georgia or Carolina. The same year a bounty was also offered for the production of silk, and an Italian gentleman, Signor Ortolengi, was engaged to proceed to Georgia to instruct the colonists in the Italian methods of sericulture. Twelve years later, viz., in 1761, we learn from the Rev. Dr.

Jared Elliott's Essays, that the London Society for the Encouragement of Arts, Manufactures, and Commerce, had offered a premium of three pence per pound for good single cocoons, which was nearly equivalent to three shillings sterling per pound for raw silk. The cocoons were to be brought to the filature at Savannah under the direction of Signor Ortolengi. The establishment of this filature—for reeling, doubling, cleaning and twisting, or throwing silk—is an added testimony to what we learn from other sources, that the silk culture had come to be an important business in that colony. Dr. Elliott states that in 1759 the export of raw silk to England for that year, from Georgia alone, already exceeded 10,000 pounds, and that it was of such excellent quality that it sold in London at from two to three shillings a pound more than that from any other part of the world. In 1758, a fire in the filature and storehouse consumed a considerable amount of raw silk and 8,000 pounds of cocoons. The year 1759 seems to have been the culminating year in the silk culture in Georgia; for, though the exportation continued until 1772, it was in decreasing amounts. The introduction of cotton culture seems to have been, in part, the cause for this; for, though, of course, the export trade was wholly cut off by the Revolutionary War, there does not seem to have been any silk to export. There is recorded in the 18th century but one lot of silk exported from Savannah after the Revolution. In 1790, two hundred pounds of raw silk were purchased there for exportation at prices ranging from 18 to 26 shillings per pound. For the next thirty-five or forty years there was very little silk produced in Georgia.

The silk culture and trade in South Carolina commenced about the same time as in Georgia, and though much less was produced there than in the sister colony, its quality was said by Sir Thomas Lombe, the most eminent silk manufacturer in England, to have been equal or superior to any of the Italian. In 1755 Mrs. Pinckney, a lady of great distinction and wealth in South Carolina, took with her to England a quantity of excellent silk which she had raised and spun in the vicinity of Charleston, and had enough of it woven to make three dresses, one of which she presented to the Princess Dowager of Wales, and another to Lord Chesterfield, keeping the third for her own use. This silk was pronounced in England equal to any imported into that country. The dress she had reserved for her own use was in Charleston as late as 1809, in possession of Mrs. Pinckney's daughter, and was even then remarkable for its beauty, firmness, and strength.* The silk business began to decline in South Carolina at about the same time, and probably from the same cause, as in Georgia. It is stated, on the authority of Thomas McCall, in the Report on the Growth and Manufacture of Silk, made to Congress in 1828, under the direction of the Hon. Richard Rush, then Secretary of the Treasury, that the colonists at New Bordeaux—a French settlement on the Savannah river, about 70 miles above Augusta—manufactured sewing-silk during the Revolutionary War, in such quantities as to supply the high country (probably Georgia, and the western parts of South and North Carolina).

Connecticut was the next colony to engage in the silk industry, though the culture of the white mulberry had commenced on Long Island as early as 1755 or 1756. Dr. N. Aspinwall, who had a large nursery of these trees on the Island, planted considerable numbers at New Haven, and about the same time at Mansfield, Windham County. He also introduced in both places, as early as 1762, silk-worm eggs, and in 1763, with the aid of the Rev. Dr. Stiles, afterwards President of Yale College, succeeded in obtaining from the Legislature of the colony an Act, offering ten shillings bounty or premium for every hundred trees which should be planted and preserved in a thrifty condition for three years, and three pence per ounce for all raw silk which the owners of trees should produce from cocoons of their own raising within the State. This bounty was continued for some years, and when the cultivation of the mulberry had become so general that the act was found unnecessary, a small bounty on raw silk manufactured within

* "Ramsay's History of South Carolina," Vol. I., p. 221.

the State was substituted for it for some years longer.* Barber, in his Historical Collections of Connecticut, states that in 1766 a half-ounce of mulberry seed was sent to every parish in the colony. The date is probably three years later than it should be. Mr. A. T. Lilly, in a very interesting pamphlet on the "Silk Industry of the United States, from 1766 to 1874," which is mainly confined to an account of that industry in New England, and for the first half of the 108 years to Connecticut, says that "Mansfield seems to have been the only locality where raising silk became a fixed industry." While this statement is probably true of the period between 1810 and 1844, it hardly does justice to other portions of the State at an earlier period. The Rev. Dr. Stiles became an enthusiast on the subject of silk culture from the first; he reared many silk-worms. Their product was reeled after the rude fashion of those days, wound, spun or twisted, dyed and woven, and his official robes were made from this silk. It was undoubtedly a very durable, though perhaps not as compared with the manufactures of the present day, an elegant silk. But President Stiles did more than this; he kept a diary of his experiences in silk culture, from 1763 to 1790, and his observations in regard to the climate, temperature, amount of food for each age, and the provision of suitable facilities for spinning, as well as concerning the preservation of the cocoons, the care of the silk-worm eggs, &c., are very interesting to the silk culturist. This manuscript diary, in a thick quarto volume, fastened with a silken cord, is still in the library of Yale College; and is one of about twenty volumes of his manuscript observations, preserved there. The domestic culture of silk was very general, both in the eastern and western parts of the State, during and subsequent to the Revolution, and even as late as 1820 or 1825. Many persons now living have a vivid recollection of having seen small groves of white mulberries, and rude cocooneries built of rough boards or shingled, in which the women of the generation immediately following the Revolution used to feed silk-worms.

* Gov. Wolcott's reply to the Silk Circular of the Secretary of the Treasury, in 1828.

The cocooneries were to be found all over New Haven, Fairfield, Middlesex, Tolland, New London and Windham Counties. There is no question of the excellence of the cocoons which were thus raised; but the reeling was very poor. The threads, when wound, spun, twisted and dyed, were uneven and gummy; and, for the most part, though of better material than the imported silk, bore no comparison to it in evenness, color and finish. This was particularly true of the sewing silk, which could be sold only in barter, and at prices greatly below the imported article. There was also an enormous waste of silk from this imperfect reeling. Jonathan H. Cobb, in his "Manual," 4th edition, pages 123 and 124, states that the loss was one-half the weight, although the goods were manufactured from the best silk, while Italian sewing-silk was manufactured from the lower grades. The Hon. Peter S. Duponçeau, President of the American Philosophical Society, and a most zealous silk culturist, in a letter to Mr. Cobb, of October 21, 1831, says very forcibly, "this comes from bad reeling. This shows that our Connecticut women in 70 years have not improved their knowledge in the art of reeling."

The culture of silk, mainly in the domestic way, though with some improvements in spinning and reeling, which made the product a little more marketable, was continued in Mansfield and in Tolland Co., Conn., and did not quite cease until 1844. It was not unprofitable; the outlay was slight, and the reeling and spinning were performed in those leisure hours of which our grandmothers had so many more than their granddaughters. Mr. Lilly estimates that, in the town of Mansfield alone, the silk-growers received, from 1820 to 1830, mainly in barter, about $50,000 per annum for their silk. Under other circumstances, the business, if followed as a means of livelihood, might have proved a failure. When the raw silk, properly reeled, came to have a definite cash value, the wasteful processes which had hitherto characterized its production must cease; but this would require skilled labor, the result of long and careful training, and commanding a high price. It would have been difficult to have educated American women, accustomed from childhood to the careless ways of reeling practised here for seventy years, to the patient, slow, and skilful methods of the Chinese, Italian, or French women, who do well if they produce a pound and a half or two pounds of perfectly reeled silk in a week. But the children might have been educated to the work. Improvements in the machinery of reeling have since been made, which would much simplify the problem to the present generation, if the culture of silk should again be attempted here.

At no time did silk culture make any great progress in the New England States, except in Connecticut. Considerable efforts were made to promote it, but only with temporary success. The next State or colony which engaged in silk culture after Connecticut was Pennsylvania. Dr. Aspinwall, a resident of New Haven, and the pioneer in the culture of the white mulberry in Connecticut, was the first to introduce that tree into Pennsylvania. This must have been in 1767 or 1768. The rearing of silk-worms probably commenced about the same time, or possibly a little earlier. These may have been fed at first on the leaves of the wild or black mulberry. John Clarke, a silk culturist of 1830–1844 states, in his Treatise on the "Mulberry and Silk-worm," page 114 (though he does not give his authority), that in 1770, Mrs. Susanna Wright, at Columbia, Lancaster County, made a piece of mantua, sixty yards in length, from her own cocoons, and that it was afterwards worn as a court dress by the Queen of Great Britain. About this time Grace Fisher made a considerable quantity of silk stuffs, and a piece of these was presented by Governor Dickenson to the celebrated Catharine Macauley. He also says: "We learn that many ladies before the Revolution wore silk dresses of their own fabrication." The American Philosophical Society, at Philadelphia, had taken much interest in the subject of silk culture. Mr. D'Homergue, in his "Essays," states that a filature of raw silk was established in Philadelphia in 1769; the *Genesee Farmer* adds, after correcting the date of establishment to 1770, that in the following year, 2,300 pounds of cocoons were brought there to reel.

From Secretary Rush's report, which gives the dates somewhat differently, it appears that the establishment of a filature, and other efforts with respect to silk culture, resulted from a public subscription amounting to £875, 14*s.* colonial currency (about $2,627). This subscription was raised by the efforts of the American Philosophical Society, which had been aroused by a letter from Dr. Benjamin Franklin, then residing in England as Agent of the Colony. The letter replied to one on the subject from Dr. Cadwallader Evans. Dr. Franklin also sent the Society a work by the Abbé Sauvage on the raising of silk-worms. Thus stimulated, the industry attained a fair prosperity in Pennsylvania, and many of the older families still possess the silk garments made by their ancestors. But the war of the Revolution checked these labors, and they were only partially resumed on the return of peace. The publication of a paper by the Philosophical Society (Transactions, Vol. II), on the mode of rearing silk-worms and winding silk, proved of conspicuous service.

The culture of silk was attempted in the latter part of the eighteenth century in New Jersey and New York, but did not attain any great magnitude in either State. It was also commenced on a moderate scale in Delaware and Maryland, and was maintained in the vicinity of Baltimore for many years. Secretary Rush's report states that the French colonists in Illinois had very early commenced raising silk-worms. Similar attempts were made in Massachusetts, Vermont and New Hampshire, and even in Maine, though in the last three States with no great success.

V.

Efforts to Revive and Extend Silk Culture —1780–1844.

DURING the period from 1780 to 1820 or 1824, the amount of silk made in the United States was not very great: it had become a domestic manufacture. In some considerable districts, many families made their five, ten, twenty, thirty, or fifty pounds of silk annually; and very rarely an enthusiastic worker brought her product up to 80 or 100 pounds. This domestic production and manufacture was perhaps more common in Connecticut than elsewhere, though there were numerous instances in New Jersey, Pennsylvania, and in parts of New York, Delaware, Maryland and Virginia. The silk was reeled on the ordinary hand-reel—very badly, as we have seen. It was spun upon the ordinary large wheel used for spinning wool; though in 1800, in Windham County, Horace Hanks invented a double wheel-head which greatly facilitated the labor of spinning cotton, woollen or silk. A part of this silk was dyed, doubled, twisted, and made into sewing-silk, as already described. A part was made into domestic silks, which were somewhat uneven in texture—comparing with our present silks very much as the old-fashioned homespun cloths would with the best broadcloth. The floss and waste, and probably the pierced and imperfect cocoons also, were carded and spun, and being mixed with wool, cotton, or flax, made very durable, though not very elegant, stuffs for every-day wear. In 1810, according to the "Statement" of Tench Coxe, the value of the sewing-silk and raw silk, made in the three counties of New London, Windham and Tolland, Conn., was $28,503; while the fabrics made from the refuse silk were estimated at about half of that sum. During the War of 1812–15, Samuel Chidsey, of Cayuga Co., N. Y., sold sewing-silk of his own manufacture to the amount of $600 per annum. Silk culture had been commenced about this time in Ohio, Kentucky and Tennessee. In the first State it was in the hands of emigrants from England; in Kentucky, the Moravians or United Brethren were introducing it; and in Tennessee, it was probably undertaken by some of the Georgia or South Carolina silk-growers who had emigrated thither.

Meanwhile the importations of silk goods were increasing in a fearful ratio, and our exports of breadstuffs—which at that time were a staple commodity—were decreasing in more than an equal degree. A committee of the national House of Representatives, in May, 1826, made a report showing that in 1821 we imported $4,486,924 worth of silk goods; in 1823, $6,713,771; and in 1825, $10,271,527; on the other hand, in 1817 we exported breadstuffs to the amount of $20,374,000; in 1818, to $15,388,000; in 1824, to $6,799,246; in 1825, to $5,417,997, or about one-half the value of the silks imported. This entire amount of imports, and indeed much more, it was contended, we should have produced on our own soil; and it was said that we were going to ruin because we had not done so. Twenty-four years before, an eminent New York agriculturist, Peter Delabigarre, had said in an address on this very subject, to the New York State Agricultural Society:* "Gentlemen, you have in your hands all the means requisite for success, and for enriching yourselves by the culture of silk. It remains with you to compare and judge your many attempts in it, and *discover wherein they have been defective.*" At the period of which we are speaking—1825–1844—everybody seemed to have started out on this voyage of discovery. Committee after committee was raised in Congress to see what could be done to help the silk business. It was at this time that the Secretary of the Treasury produced a goodly octavo report on the subject. Such men as the Hon. Peter S. Duponceau, the friend and countryman of Lafayette, and at that time President of the American Philosophical So-

* Vol. I., Agricultural Transactions of the State of New York, 1801.

ciety; his protegé and friend, J. D'Homergue; Gov. Lincoln of Massachusetts, and Gov. Wolcott of Connecticut; the Hon. Jonathan H. Cobb of Dedham, Mass.; the Hon. Gideon B. Smith of Baltimore; the Hon. Andrew T. Judson, then a member of Congress, and afterward one of the Supreme Court Judges of Connecticut; the Hon. Zalmon Storrs of Mansfield, Conn.; Dr. Felix Pascalis of New York; Samuel Whitmarsh and Dr. Stebbins of Northampton, Mass.; the Rev. I. R. Barbour of Oxford, Mass.; and in the latter part of the period the brothers Charles and Ward Cheney, all appeared in print with their "discoveries" of the best methods of reviving and enlarging the domain of the silk industry.

VI.

The Morus Multicaulis Mania.

ONE after another of the experimenters in silk culture began to advocate the *Morus multicaulis*, and recommend their friends to cultivate the trees, and raise silk if they could; but at all events to raise *multicaulis* trees. Grave doctors of medicine and doctors of divinity, men learned in the law, agriculturists, mechanics, and merchants, and women as well as men, seemed to be infected with a strange frenzy in regard to this mulberry tree. They met in solemn conclaves over bundles of *Morus multicaulis* twigs, discussing seriously the glorious time, when, in the not distant future, every farm should be a nursery for the young trees, every house should have its cocooneries attached, its silk-worms of the bivoltine, trivoltine, or polyvoltine breeds yielding two, three or four crops of cocoons per year. The farmers' wives and daughters, when not engaged in feeding the worms, were to reel the silk, and perhaps to spin and twist it, till silk should become as cheap as cotton, and every matron and maid rejoice in the possession of at least a dozen silk dresses. It does not clearly appear where and on what occasions they were to wear these dresses, while their whole time was to be occupied with the care of the silk-worms and cocoons.

Gideon B. Smith, of Baltimore, is said to have owned the first *multicaulis* tree in the United States, which was planted in 1826; but Dr. Felix Pascalis, of New York, was the first to make known to the public the remarkably rapid growth, and supposed excellent qualities, of the tree; and so may be said to have opened this Pandora's box, from which so many evils escaped. The excitement in regard to the *Morus multicaulis* grew steadily; slowly, indeed, at first, but increasing with a geometrical progression until 1839, when it culminated in utter ruin to the cultivators. The shrewdest and wariest operators, men who did not believe in its loudly heralded virtues, were fairly carried off their feet by the surging tide of speculation. The young trees or cuttings, which were sold in 1834 or 1835 for $3 or $5 a hundred, came soon to be worth $25, $50, $100, $200, and even $500 a hundred. The writer well recollects being in Northampton in the Spring of 1839, when Mr. Whitmarsh and Dr. Stebbins were rejoicing over the purchase of a dozen *multicaulis* cuttings, not more than two feet long and of the thickness of a pipe-stem, for $25. "They are worth $60," exclaimed the Doctor, in his enthusiasm. It is said that a florist and nursery-man, on Long Island, who was one of the first to introduce the tree into the country, though he had no particular faith in it, devised a plan for enhancing its price. He had sold small quantities to nursery-men in Providence and Newport, and several of the Massachusetts cities and large towns; and one day, in 1835, while at work in his nursery, he determined to make a bold push for a speculation. Hastily returning to his house and putting up a change of apparel, he mounted his sulky, drove into New York, and on board the Providence boat. Arriving at Newport, he landed, drove to the first nursery there, and asked, in an excited way, "Have you any *multicaulis* trees?" "A few," was the reply. "I will give you fifty cents apiece for all you have," said the Long Islander. The nursery-man thought a moment. "If," he said to himself, "Mr. —— is willing to give that price for them, it is because he knows they are worth more." He raised his head, "I don't think I want to sell what few I have, Mr. ——." "Very well," was the reply. "I presume I can get them for that," and he drove off. Every nursery-man who was known to have any trees in Newport, Providence, Worcester, Boston, or the towns adjacent, Springfield, Northampton, &c., was visited, the same offer made, and the same answer returned. "I came back," said Mr. ——, "without any trees; but you could not have bought *multicaulis* trees, in any of the towns I had visited, for a dollar apiece, although a week before they would have been fully satisfied to have obtained twenty-five cents apiece for them." Yet this very man, shrewd as he was, was carried off his feet by the greatness of the demand which followed. He imported large quantities from France, multiplied his cuttings by all the devices known to his profession; and at last, so enormous were his sales, that, in the Winter of 1838-9, he sent an agent to France with $80,000 in hand, with orders to purchase one million or more trees, to be delivered in the Summer and Fall. Before the whole of his purchase had arrived, the crisis had come. The nursery-man had failed for so large a sum that he could never reckon up his indebtedness; and the next Spring his *multicaulis* trees were offered in vain to the neighboring farmers at a dollar a hundred, for pea-brush.

Another incident related of the speculation was, that after the crash came at the East, some of the largest holders of the trees, in their desire to get them off their hands, chartered a vessel notoriously unseaworthy, loaded her with the *multicaulis* shrubs, and sent the cargo by way of New Orleans to Indiana, insuring it in one of the marine companies at a high price. Greatly to their disappointment the vessel reached New Orleans safely, and the cargo was transshipped at an enormous expense to river boats, and when the trees reached Indiana they found no one who was willing to take them as a gift. This discreditable adventure cost the shippers a large sum of money.

The times were rife with speculation. The great panic and disaster of 1837 had thrown to the surface many restless, unscrupulous spirits, who were willing to embark in any enterprise, however daring or doubtful its character, which seemed to promise the slightest opportunity of regaining the fortunes they had lost. Numbers of these plunged into the *multicaulis* speculation, and made it more disastrous in its results than it otherwise would have been; but there is this ground of consolation in regard to them, that not one of them escaped the ruin they helped to bring upon others.

VII.

Workers in Silk Culture, from 1825 *to* 1844.

IN the earlier years of this epoch there were many men of honorable and patriotic character, who honestly believed that by some of the measures proposed, the culture and production of silk might become a national industry, and who demonstrated their faith by their works. Some of them were men of moderate or large fortune, who expended considerable sums to promote this enterprise, without thought of personal gain, and only for the furtherance of the national prosperity. Among these the Hon. Peter S. Duponceau deserves, perhaps, the first place. Having found a Frenchman, J. D'Homergue, who was an intelligent, skilful and competent silk manufacturer, Mr. Duponceau took him under his care, and aided him in the publication of a series of essays on silk culture. Afterwards, by dint of his personal influence, and at a great cost of time and labor, Mr. Duponceau brought the matter before Congress at two or three successive sessions, asking for an appropriation of about $40,000 to establish a normal filature in Philadelphia, with M. D'Homergue at its head, to instruct persons in the art of reeling silk, who might afterwards instruct others. A favorable report was obtained in Congress, and but for some untoward events the bill would have been carried through both houses. Failing in this, Mr. Duponceau established in Philadelphia, mostly at his own expense, a temporary filature, where he produced some very creditable specimens of silk, even under unfavorable circumstances; and for several years carried on an extensive correspondence with other persons interested in silk culture, and not infrequently wrote for the reviews, periodicals and newspapers, articles of remarkable ability and vigor upon different phases of the subject. Mr. Duponceau was born in 1760, and consequently was already past seventy years of age when he engaged in this enterprise, and his life had been one of great activity. He expended some thousands of dollars in the promotion of the silk culture and reeling of silk, and continued his efforts to that end till 1836 or 1837, when, finding his plans a failure—in part from the prevalent folly in regard to the *multicaulis*, in which he took but little interest—he withdrew from his silk enterprises, and gave up his filature and cocooneries. Mr. Duponceau opposed the views of those who desired to see manufactories established at once. "To do this," he said in a letter to Mr. Cobb, "would necessitate the importation of raw silk from France, Italy, or China. It is better for us to wait for twenty years if necessary, till we can make a perfect raw silk, and export it for some years to Europe, than to commence manufacturing too soon. It will be longer than that, I fear, before we can make silk enough to supply our manufactories, should we start them." Mr. Duponceau's views were diametrically opposed to those of our manufacturers of the present day; but it is interesting to observe how, from points of view so diverse, they recognized the same invincible obstacle to the production of American raw silk. The successful reeling of the silk, which he felt to be the greatest difficulty in the American production of silk, has continued to be an obstacle for the forty-five years and more, which have elapsed since that letter was written; and while the silk manufacture has become a necessity, our American silk-growers are no better able to supply the demand for the silk mills now than they were then.

In any history of the silk industry in America in the present century, the name of Jonathan H. Cobb, of Dedham, must come into prominence. He has been for many years past Probate Judge of the District which includes his birthplace. Judge Cobb had not Mr. Duponceau's ample fortune, nor perhaps his scholarship and peculiar literary abilities; but in his way he contributed as much or more than any other man to the development of the silk culture. He had been engaged in rearing silk-worms and the production of raw silk on a small scale, certainly as early as 1828. He had invented a reel, which was very much better than that previously used in Connecticut, though perhaps not equal to some which were devised a few years later. He had also been in correspondence with Mr. Duponceau, and with others interested in silk culture, for several years. His success had attracted considerable attention in Massachusetts. In December, 1830, Governor Lincoln called the attention of the Legislature to the development of the silk culture, and suggested that the State should encourage it. The Committee on Agriculture reported in favor of having a manual prepared for the instruction of silk-growers; and, the Legislature concurring, Gov. Lincoln appointed Mr. Cobb to prepare such a manual. The Legislature soon afterward offered liberal bounties for the production of raw silk. The Manual appeared at the close of 1831, and passed through a number of editions, being repeatedly enlarged. Meantime its author was becoming more and more interested in silk culture. He not only extended his cocooneries and reeling apparatus, and spent much time in lecturing on the mulberry and the rearing of silk-worms, but in 1835, with the participation of some friends, he formed the New England Silk Company, and built a mill at Dedham capable of making 200 pounds of sewing-silk per week, and manufacturing also some silk and cotton goods. He also assisted in establishing the Connecticut Silk Company, at Hartford, of which Christopher Colt was president. By the bursting of the *multicaulis* bubble, in 1839, he was a heavy loser, and the subsequent depression in the silk and all other manufactures led to his bankruptcy in 1840. He, however, recovered his position in part, and though he had resolved to have nothing more to do with the silk business for the remainder of his life, he was for a time connected with a silk-manufacturing company, which occupied his old mill at Dedham, under the management of C. Colt, Jr., in 1843. But on the destruction of the mill by fire in 1845, Judge Cobb abandoned all farther connection with the silk industry, in which for twenty years he had borne an active and distinguished part. Other men whose names deserve to be embalmed in this record, for their unwearied efforts to promote an industry which they believed essential to the prosperity of the country, were: Dr. Felix Pascalis, an eminent scientist in New York City; the Hon. Andrew Judson of Canterbury, Conn., already alluded to; the Hon. Gideon B. Smith and the Hon. John S. Skinner, both of Baltimore; the Rev. J. R. Barbour of Oxford, Mass.; Samuel Whitmarsh and Dr. Daniel Stebbins of Northampton, Mass.; Judge F. G. Comstock of Hartford, editor of the *Silk Culturist;* the brothers Cheney, of South Manchester, Conn.; Edmund Morris, editor of the *Silk Record*, and afterward well known as an author; John Clarke of Philadelphia, William Kenrick of Newton, Mass., Zalmon Storrs, of Mansfield, Conn., and perhaps some others.

Reference should here be made to the silk-growers of Windham and Tolland Counties, Conn.; and especially to those of Mansfield, where, for a longer period than anywhere else in the United States, the silk culture was persistently carried on. Mr. Lilly, in his historical essay, already referred to, has given so full an account of both the culture and manufacture in Mansfield, that there is little occasion to add to his narrative. The white mulberry had been so thoroughly tested at Mansfield, that the extravagant expectations of silk-growers elsewhere from the *multicaulis* were not entertained there, except by a few. Yet the extravagant prices at which the cuttings were sold were entirely prohibitory of their use to feed silk-worms, since the cost of the tree was more than all the silk that could be made from it would be worth. Thence resulted heavy losses to purchasers of the trees. Nor did the evil end here. After the bursting of the *multicaulis* bubble, attention was directed to the other and really valuable species of the mulberry, more hardy than the *multicaulis* or even the whites, such as the Alpine and the Brussia or Broussa, and speculation became rife in these. Mr. Lilly gives an instance which came within his own knowledge, occurring in August, 1842, where two trees of one season's growth, in North Windham, Conn., were sold at auction, as they stood in the nursery, the first bringing $106 and the second $100; the remainder of the lot was withdrawn because the bidding was not sufficiently spirited!

This spirit of speculation was really prejudicial to the true interests of silk culture; and when, in 1844, a general blight affected all the mulberry trees, the rearing of silk-worms was abandoned throughout the United States; and in Mansfield, where for more than eighty years silk culture had been the principal business of the town, there were no more cocoons of native growth to be had. The mulberry is by no means an uncommon tree in the Atlantic and Central States, most of the species being hardy, except in very severe winters. The *Morus multicaulis* does not bear the New England or Northern New York climate well; but this is of little consequence, as experience has demonstrated that it is the least valuable of the mulberry family.

VIII.

Later Efforts at Silk Culture.

SINCE 1844, no effort has been made in the Atlantic States to rear silk-worms on a large scale. There have, however, not been wanting advocates of the lost art who have urged its restoration with much of the old enthusiasm and a formidable array of argument and figures. Among these advocates, in recent years, Dr. Samuel Chamberlaine, of Bryn Mawr, Montgomery County, Pa., deserves a word of praise for the careful collection of facts bearing on the subject, in his Essay on Silk Culture and Home Industry, read before the Social Science Association, at its meeting in 1875. From 1860 to the present time, some attention has been paid to the business in a few of the Southern States and in California, but without great success. In the South there has been no market for cocoons, and little possibility of reeling the silk well. In the vicinity of New Orleans, mulberry trees abound, and there are many in the city itself. They were planted by the early colonists, and probably under French Government instruction or protection. In these trees the cocoons of the wild insect are somewhat plentiful. From 1871 to 1874 an Italian named Roca made a business of rearing silk-worms and shipping the eggs and cocoons to Italy. His invoices, passed by the Italian consul at New Orleans, during 1873-4, are said to have been of a value of $10,000. The cocoons were adjudged at Milan superior to those of that part of Italy, and three crops of cocoons per year were obtained from the American insect, while only two were yielded by the Italian. With a market for the cocoons, it might not be difficult to encourage silk culture in Louisiana, though some practical observers have pronounced the climate too damp for success. In California, the demand has been so large for silk-worm eggs, mainly for exportation, that only a little silk has been made. Louis Prevost, a botanist from Normandy, France, commenced planting mulberry trees in San Jose, in 1856, and attempted to procure silk-worm eggs soon afterward. Meeting with no encouragement (the people being so fully occupied in gold mining), he abandoned it for a time; but in 1860 or 1861 procured silk-worm eggs and entered in earnest upon the culture of silk. He raised three species of mulberry trees, the *Morus alba*, or white, the *M. multicaulis*, and the *M. moretta*. Of these he gave the preference, as most of the Californians do, to the white mulberry. A. M. Müller, of San Jose, also entered upon the business, in 1861, in connection with M. Prevost. They made no silk of any consequence in 1865, there being a constant demand for the eggs. Having friends who were familiar with all the processes of silk culture, M. Prevost succeeded in reeling his silk very well, and sent samples of the raw silk to Europe, where they were favorably received. In 1866, Joseph Neumann, a German silk-weaver, commenced raising silk-worms and manufacturing silk in the vicinity of San Francisco; and soon afterward, Felix Gillet, also a French silk-grower, entered upon the business at Nevada City. M. Neumann raised, in 1869, enough cocoons to make 130 pounds of raw silk, from which he wove two very beautiful United States flags, one of which he presented to the United States Government, and the other to the State of California. He also made many smaller articles. One of these flags forms part of M. Neumann's display at the Centennial Exhibition; a display which includes all the processes of silk culture, and even the live insects. California voted a bounty of $250 for every 5,000 mulberry trees planted, and also for every 100,000 cocoons produced in the State. But these provisions were so greatly perverted by speculators who planted millions of the worthless *multicaulis* trees, that the bounty was repealed the next year. M. Prevost died in 1869. The demand for silk-worm eggs was checked during the Franco-German War, but has since revived, and is now so large that, though there are several silk-mills in California, they are entirely supplied with imported raw silk, while the export of silk-worm eggs amounts to a value of many thousands of dollars annually.

A promising enterprise has been undertaken at Silkville, Franklin County, Kansas, by E. de Boissière, a French gentleman of means, who has set his heart upon surrounding his chosen home with a colony of operatives employed in silk culture and manufacture. Details concerning his factory will be given in another chapter. He designs raising his own silk; and with that view planted mulberry seed during the Spring of 1870, and in the following year set out also ten thousand young mulberry trees obtained from France; so that now he has abundant material for feeding silk-worms. In respect to the insects themselves he has not been so fortunate. His earlier ventures in silk-worm eggs procured from France developed insects suffering probably from *pebrine*, and they did not produce a supply of good cocoons. Experiments with smaller lots of Japanese eggs gave better results; but as yet M. de Boissière has not made the culture a success. He is, however, very hopeful, and while he has temporarily given his villagers employment in other pursuits, he is not among those who fear that the high price of labor at the West cannot be counteracted by economy and ingenious device. He still believes that the silk which shall supply his mill will be raised in and around Silkville. Some of the more sanguine silk-growers of California have proposed to employ Chinese labor in reeling, winding, cleaning, doubling and throwing the silk. But even this labor is too dear to compete with that of China and Japan, or perhaps with the peasant labor of France or Italy, in a business in which machinery cannot take the place of trained and skilled hand-labor. In China or Japan, the skilled labor of the artisan, inherited through more than thirty centuries of the same kind of toil, is amply repaid by from five to ten cents a day: a sum which provides a daily abundance of food for a large family. A good reeler there will reel perfectly from one and a-half to two pounds of silk in a week, and is satisfied with receiving eight or ten cents a day. Here, even the poorest Chinese reeler would demand from 75 cents to $1 a day. None of our Yankee girls would be willing to undertake it, though perfectly ignorant of the process, for less than a dollar a day. The waste from incompetent help would be very much larger than from the reeling of a skilled artisan.

There is at least one alternative. Our friends who are determined to raise silk-worms can do so profitably in one way, and only in one, at present. There is a good market, and is likely to be for years to come, if it is not glutted, for silk-worm eggs in France and Italy, where for some years a contagious disease has made sad havoc with the native worms. The needs of that market will furnish employment for a reasonable number of silk-growers, who can meantime also supply the home demand for these eggs, while the pierced cocoons will find a ready sale, though at a lower price, to our manufacturers who are producing spun silk. The time may come, and probably will, when that market will be fully supplied; but by that time there may be such changes in the value of the raw silk, or such improvements in automatic machinery, that raw silk can be produced here at a profit.

Our description of silk culture in America would be incomplete without a notice, however brief, of its development in Brazil. A fair conception of what is accomplished in that empire in the way of producing silk, may be obtained by visitors to the Centennial Exhibition, from the display of Luis de Resende, a producer and exhibitor of raw silk, and the representative of the Society of "The Union of Exhibitors of Brazil." M. de Resende has presented the industry in a most attractive form, showing the 100,000 mulberry trees that constitute his plantation, and exhibiting the silk-insect in all stages of its growth and labors. More interesting, however, than even this display, is the lively interest which M. de Resende takes in all matters pertaining to the care and cultivation of the insect and its food, and the intelligent observation which he brings to bear upon the subject.

IX.

Organized Silk Manufacture in America.

WE HAVE SAID, perhaps, as much as is appropriate concerning the domestic manufacture of silk, in our account of its early culture. The rulers of Mexico, in the early years of the present century, introduced both the culture of silk and the manufacture of an excellent article of sewing-silk into that country, procuring skilled manufacturers and culturists from France to instruct the natives. In the frequent revolutions and political disturbances with which that unhappy country has since been afflicted, both the culture and manufacture have probably been abandoned; though no region in the world, except perhaps California, is better adapted by climate and temperature to make it profitable, than some portions of Mexico.

Aside from some special cases of weaving or manufacturing silk goods as samples of American products, there was probably no other than the domestic manufacture of anything in the way of silk, until 1810, when Rodney and Horatio Hanks, the latter the inventor of the double wheel-head already mentioned, erected at Mansfield, Connecticut, the first silk mill on this continent. They attempted the manufacture of sewing-silk and twist by means of machinery made by themselves, and propelled by water-power. The mill was a very small affair; its size was 12 by 12 feet. In 1814, these two enterprising mechanics having associated with themselves Harrison Holland and John Gilbert, built a larger mill at Gurleyville, Connecticut; but the new mill failed of any considerable success, and was finally given up. In 1821 Rodney Hanks built another sewing-silk mill at Mansfield, and associated his son George R. Hanks with him. This mill was maintained till 1828, when it

Mills of Wm. H. Horstmann & Sons, Fifth and Cherry Streets, Philadelphia. Established 1815.

was finally abandoned; the failure of this and the preceding enterprises being due to the crudeness of the machinery and the imperfect appliances for reeling.

The next effort in the way of silk manufacture was made by William H. Horstmann, a native of Cassel, Germany, who came to America in 1815. He established himself at Philadelphia, in the manufacture of trimmings wholly or partially of silk, to which were subsequently added narrow goods, belt and other ribbons, plaited and braided goods, fringes, military and naval sashes, epaulets, &c. Mr. Horstmann had learned the art of silk weaving in France; and after coming to this country he added machinery for plaiting, braiding and fringe-cutting. Many other machines for different branches of the silk manufacture were invented by him. He was the first manufacturer in this country to introduce the Jacquard loom, of which he made use as early as 1824. In 1837–38 his son, William J. Horstmann, manufactured power-looms of his own designing, and introduced power-loom weaving for narrow textile fabrics, simultaneously with its adoption in Switzerland. W. H. Horstmann had married the daughter of Mr. Hoeckly, a German manufacturer, who was established, as early as 1793, at Philadelphia, as a maker of coach lace, fringe and tassels. Mr. Horstmann died in 1852, leaving his business to his sons, Wm. J. & Sigmund H. Horstmann. Wm. H. Horstmann & Sons are the oldest and one of the largest silk manufacturing houses now existing in this country. Their warehouses and salesrooms in Philadelphia are of great extent, and filled with valuable and beautiful goods. It is impossible to present, without an extended catalogue, any clear notion of the number and variety of the manufactures of this firm; the whole range of narrow textile fabrics is included. At the exhibitions of the Franklin and of the American Institute, the displays of Wm. H. Horstmann & Sons have justly won the highest commendations and awards; their bindings, braids, fringes and dress trimmings called forth complimentary notices; and the specialties of the firm, such as coach laces, tassel cords, undertakers' and upholsterers' trimmings, deserved and obtained substantial praise. Besides the articles we have named, the firm produces all sorts of military equipments and trappings, the regalia of societies, and theatrical goods, including hundreds of things to which the silk that adorns them may be a mere adjunct; since among them are crowns, jewelry, weapons, ornaments, masks, fancy costumes, and all the glittering paraphernalia of the lodge-room and the stage.

In 1829 a manufactory of silk ribbons from American silks was started in Baltimore, but had only a brief existence. In 1827-8 the Mansfield (Conn.) Silk Company was formed. This vigorous undertaking aroused, far and near, an interest in the industry, both as to culture and manufacture. It stimulated the efforts of the other pioneers in the business, and made a permanent impression as to the solid reality of the silk manufacture in this country. The partners were Alfred Lilly, Joseph Conant, William A. Fisk, William Atwood, Storrs Hovey and Jesse Bingham. We shall meet nearly all of these names in subsequent pages of this history, for they have been identified in one way or another with numerous enterprises in the silk manufacture. The Company was incorporated by the Connecticut Legislature in 1829. While it was a part of the Company's purpose to encourage the production of silk, its efforts were especially directed to the improvement of the methods and machinery for reeling and "throwing," and to the manufacture of a better article of sewing-silk. Its first successful machinery was made by Mr. Lilly, in accordance with the descriptions and rude drawings of Edmund Golding, a young English "throwster," who came to this country at the age of seventeen, expecting to find employment in his particular branch of the business. The great difficulty was in reeling. It was not until a year or more after the concern had started in business that, by the advice and instruction of Mr. Brown, an English silk manufacturer who had just commenced business in Boston, they were able to construct a reel which did its work satisfactorily. It was worked by water-power, and not by hand, like the reels of Messrs. Cobb, Gideon Smith, Morris, Duponceau, and others. The reeling was successful, and

Mill at Gurleyville, Conn., occupied in 1828 by the Mansfield Silk Company.

"the Company advertised their willingness to purchase all the cocoons that might be offered, and their purchases were large." . . . "The native silk was found to be of superior quality and strength, winding and doubling with greater facility and less waste than China or Brutia silk."* Encouraged by their success, and the demand which now sprung up for American sewing-silk, though the colors and evenness of it were not yet perfect, the Company committed a very natural, but, as the event proved, a very grave error. They sought to become silk culturists on a large scale, as well as silk manufacturers. They leased land at numerous points in Connecticut and adjacent States, planted large mulberry orchards, and entrusted to their agents the rearing of silk-worms. They also applied to the Legislature, in 1832, asking State aid for encouraging the culture and manufacture of silk. A bounty of $1,500 was granted to the Company, and premiums were offered for raising mulberry trees and for reeling silk. They soon attempted silk weaving, but their machinery was not well adapted to the work. An ingenious mechanic in Mansfield, Nathan Rixford, had already made improvements in the machinery for winding, doubling, and spinning, which were eagerly purchased by competing companies, and which distanced theirs. Their capital was too small, and the experiments they made in the culture of silk were unwise and expensive. Mr. Lilly, the originator of the Company, withdrew from it in 1835, and three of the other five partners in 1839; and the Company dissolved the same year, though they let their establishment to others, who carried on the silk manufacture for a time. Notwithstanding the misfortunes which closed their career, the Mansfield Silk Company is fairly entitled to the credit of having built the first mill in this country in which the manufacture of silk was practically successful. We present on an adjoining page an engraving, giving a view of this mill (at Gurleyville). The original of the engraving is a water-color picture by C. C. Burleigh, Jr., an artist of distinction. It is not in the least a fancy sketch, its truthfulness being vouched for.

---

* Mr. A. T. Lilly's "Silk Industry of the United States, from 1766 to 1874."

In 1829 or 1830, two Frenchmen exhibited at North Mansfield, Conn., what they called a Piedmont silk reel, and, in the presence of a considerable number of people, reeled silk upon it from cocoons. Soon afterward, a similar reel was started at Shubael Dimock's cocoonery, in North Mansfield. Eliphalet Snow made and patented an improvement on this reel in Mansfield soon afterward, and sold a number of reels, but Nathan Rixford (see above) produced a still better one which was largely sold; and some years later, as we shall see further on, some of his reels were sent to China for introduction and use. Improvements were also made in the Piedmont reel by Gideon B. Smith, of Baltimore, and J. H. Cobb, of Dedham, Mass., of whom more will be said by-and-by. Mr. Rixford, in 1838, made also great improvements in machinery for spinning silk in his "Friction Roller Mill," built for Ralph Cheney, of Cheney Brothers, and for Aaron Mitchell, of Nantucket. Two silk banners, each twelve feet long and six feet wide, woven from Pennsylvania silk, by J. D'Homergue, and some other silk goods of the same silk, were exhibited at the Fair of the Franklin Institute, in 1830.

Without adhering very closely to a chronological arrangement, we may conveniently refer to manufacturing enterprises in the order of their inception. We find that John McRae commenced, in 1830, the manufacture of silk fringes, tassels, &c., in New York City. In 1852, the firm was changed to Thomas C. McRae & Co., and silk ribbons, silk braids, and elastic cords, were added to their manufactures. They continued in business till 1866.

At least a hundred years ago, near Northampton, Mass., then an agricultural village of historic fame in struggles with the Indians, a building was erected which was ever afterwards known as "the old oil mill." The village of Florence, now containing 3,000 inhabitants, which has since grown up around the mill, had then no existence. Its site is on the Mill River, a stream made memorable in 1874 by the bursting of the Williamsburgh reservoir. The engraving of the "Old Oil Mill" which we present, is (as well as that of the mill at Gurleyville, Conn.) reproduced from a painting by Mr. Burleigh. The

THE "OLD OIL MILL," AT FLORENCE, MASS., OCCUPIED IN 1834 BY THE NEW YORK & NORTHAMPTON SILK COMPANY.

millstones still remaining by the roadside are a record of the early uses of the building, which, after doing good service in its original capacity, was for some years occupied as a grist-mill. About 1832, under the direction of Samuel Whitmarsh, this building was put in order for receiving silk machinery, made by Nathan Rixford, who has been already mentioned in this history. Mr. Whitmarsh at this period outran all his compeers in enthusiasm concerning silk culture and manufacture. He had accumulated about $25,000 in New York city, while in partnership with Mr. St. John, in the tailoring business, in Broadway, opposite the old City Hotel. He went to Northampton, in 1830, bought land there and built a mansion, now owned by Edward Lyman, of the firm of A. A. Low & Bros. Attached to this building were two hot-houses, each 100 feet long, for raising mulberry trees in winter. Such was Mr. Whitmarsh's faith in the scheme that he spent all the money he had upon it.

Mr. Whitmarsh succeeded in impressing his own enthusiasm upon others, and induced several gentlemen of Middletown, Conn., to take stock in his new enterprise, "the New York and Northampton Silk Company." Among these investors were Augustus and Samuel Russell, who had established in China the firm of Russell & Co., the leading American house in that empire. The New York and Northampton Silk Company was formed in 1833-4. They erected a brick building, to supersede the old oil mill. Broad plantations were stocked with mulberry trees, and extensive preparations made for a large supply of raw silk. The supply was, however, always deficient. Some specimens of watch ribbons, satin vests, &c., were made by this concern. Henry Clay, Daniel Webster and A. A. Lawrence were each presented with a heavy black satin vest pattern, and they evinced a lively interest in the success of the enterprise. Samuel Whitmarsh was the leader in this undertaking; he became President of the Company in 1835. He went to Europe in the following years, to obtain information respecting silk culture; and early in 1839 published, through the press of J. H. Butler, of Northampton, a work entitled, "Eight Years' Experience and Observation in the Culture of the Mulberry Tree and in the Care of the Silk-worm; with Remarks adapted to the American System of Producing Raw Silk for Exportation. By Samuel Whitmarsh."

The crash came soon after the collapse of the *multicaulis* speculation. "I shall make this year two hundred and fifty thousand dollars, before next Winter:" so said Mr. Whitmarsh, in the Summer of 1839, to John Ryle, (now of Paterson, N. J.,) then a weaver in his employ. Before that Winter was past, Mr. Whitmarsh had neither cash nor credit enough to buy a barrel of flour. The Company, however, eventually paid all its debts, having sunk not less than $100,000.

Mr. Whitmarsh had undiminished faith in the silk industry, even after the failure of the Company. He then went to the West Indies, and on the island of Jamaica had iron buildings, sent thither from London, erected as a factory. A mulberry plantation of 300 acres was set out; but a great disaster overtook Mr. Whitmarsh. He had invested the larger part of his fortune in silk-worm eggs, and by the carelessness of the consignees at Kingston the whole invoice was destroyed after safe arrival on the island. The want of raw silk prevented the realization of his hopes, although he demonstrated the practicability of both the culture and the manufacture by negro labor. He had fifty reels ready to run by steam, but never got silk enough for more than two of them. Some of the product of these reels was submitted, by a Committee of the British House of Commons, to the Board of Trade, and was by the latter pronounced equal to Barcelona silk. Mr. Whitmarsh lost money in silk enterprises, but never faith; and shortly before his death, in 1875, was seriously considering a project for silk culture in California.

The period from 1831 to 1839 was prolific in the formation of silk manufacturing companies—some of them started by speculators—which had with few exceptions a brief existence. Among the new concerns were the Connecticut Silk Manufacturing Company, incorporated at Hartford, in 1835, which received a bonus of about $11,000 net, from a bank charter; it was managed by Christopher Colt and J. H. Hayden. The

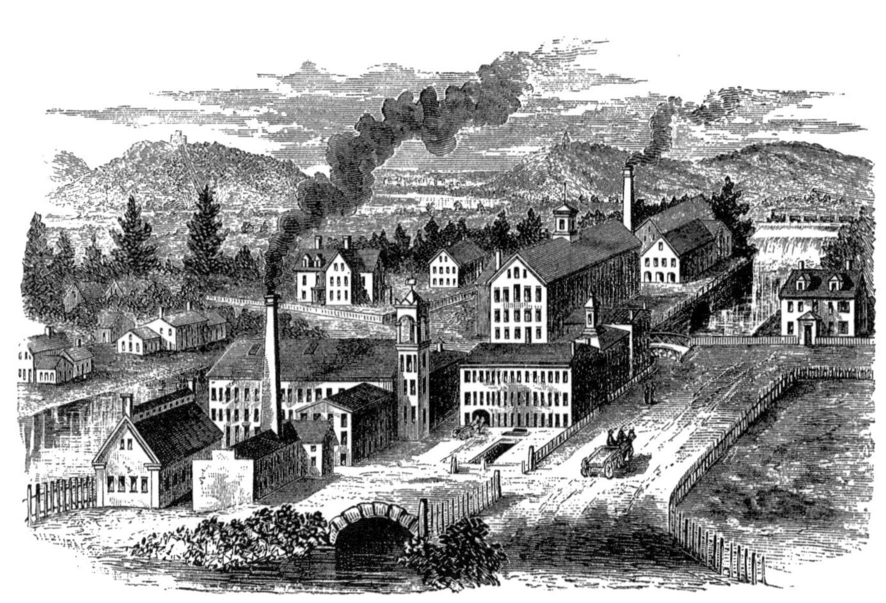

Mills of the Nonotuck Silk Company, Florence, Mass.

former being the largest stockholder, was President and Agent; the latter became book-keeper and general assistant. The business was not fortunately managed after Mr. Hayden left it, and it collapsed in 1838, having sunk its entire capital. Mr. Hayden in 1838, in partnership with Mr. Haskell, established a silk mill at Windsor Locks, Conn. The business continues to the present, and is now in the name of J. H. Hayden and Son. The Atlantic Silk Company, of Nantucket, and the Poughkeepsie Silk Company, of Poughkeepsie, went down in 1839, having completely sunk their capital. Mr. Cobb's silk mill at Dedham, the New York and Northampton Company, the Morodendron Silk Company of Philadelphia, and one or two companies in Mansfield, formed part of the list of those that failed in 1840 or 1841; but several other companies, which had begun in a small way in 1836–1840, grew up, and some of them entered into the labors of the pioneer companies with advantage.

After the withdrawal of Samuel Whitmarsh from the New York and Northampton Silk Company, that concern obtained the services of Captain Joseph Conant to manage their mills at Northampton and Florence. Captain Conant's connection with the business of silk manufacturing dated from 1827–8; after the failure of the Mansfield Silk Co. he was associated with William Atwood and Harvey Crane in making sewing-silk and twist; when leaving them to go to Northampton, he took with him their foreman, Dwight Swift. By the end of 1840 the effort to keep the Northampton and Florence concerns going, even under Capt. Conant's management, was evidently hopeless. The Company decided to sell out and close.

Captain Conant then associated himself with S. L. Hill, George W. Benson and William Adams, whom he interested in the project, and these four bought the property; the conveyance was made in the Fall of 1841. The real estate was a farm of 300 acres, mill buildings, water-power, &c., at what is now Florence. In the following Spring the purchasers organized as the Northampton Association or Community, and undertook to carry out a communistic system at table; in farming; in silk culture and manufacture; and as to the ownership of property. This experiment proved a financial failure. In 1844 they sold what remained of the property to S. L. Hill, who thus became sole proprietor.

Mr. Hill offered the land at Florence to all who were willing to settle there on homesteads, reserving only sufficient of the real estate, water-power and buildings, to carry on the silk manufacture. He also interested S. L. Hinckley, a capitalist of Northampton, as a silent partner in a new undertaking, based on the ruins; it was known as the "Nonotuck Steam Mill," S. L. Hill, Agent. Nonotuck was the Indian name for Northampton. Subsequently others joined the enterprise and the Nonotuck Silk Company was formed, Mr. Hinckley being President and Mr. Hill, Treasurer. The business of this Company has steadily increased, and new buildings have been erected from time to time, till they now form the group shown in the engraving on an adjoining page. The floor space which these cover is nearly 60,000 feet. They are wholly occupied in the manufacture of sewing-silk and twist. The "Corticelli" brand of sewing-silk is famous. This Company succeeded, after repeated trials, in manufacturing the first machine-twist produced. Sales were made to I. M. Singer, the inventor of the Singer sewing-machine, as early as February, 1852. At present 600 operatives are employed by the Company, and 100,000 pounds of raw silk are annually consumed. The officers are Ira Dimock, President, A. T. Lilly, Treasurer.

Another prosperous house which grew from these earlier undertakings is the present firm of O. S. Chaffee & Son, the senior Mr. Chaffee being Capt. Joseph Conant's son-in-law, and having taken an interest in the business as early as 1838, at Mansfield, Conn. After the Community experiment, Capt. Conant built and started the mill situated between Florence and Northampton, now owned by Warner & Lathrop. Capt. Conant's firm was then J. Conant & Co., Dwight Swift and O. S. Chaffee forming the Company. In 1852, Capt. Conant built the "Conant Mill," at Conantville, Conn. For nearly half a century Capt. Conant's name was prominent in silk

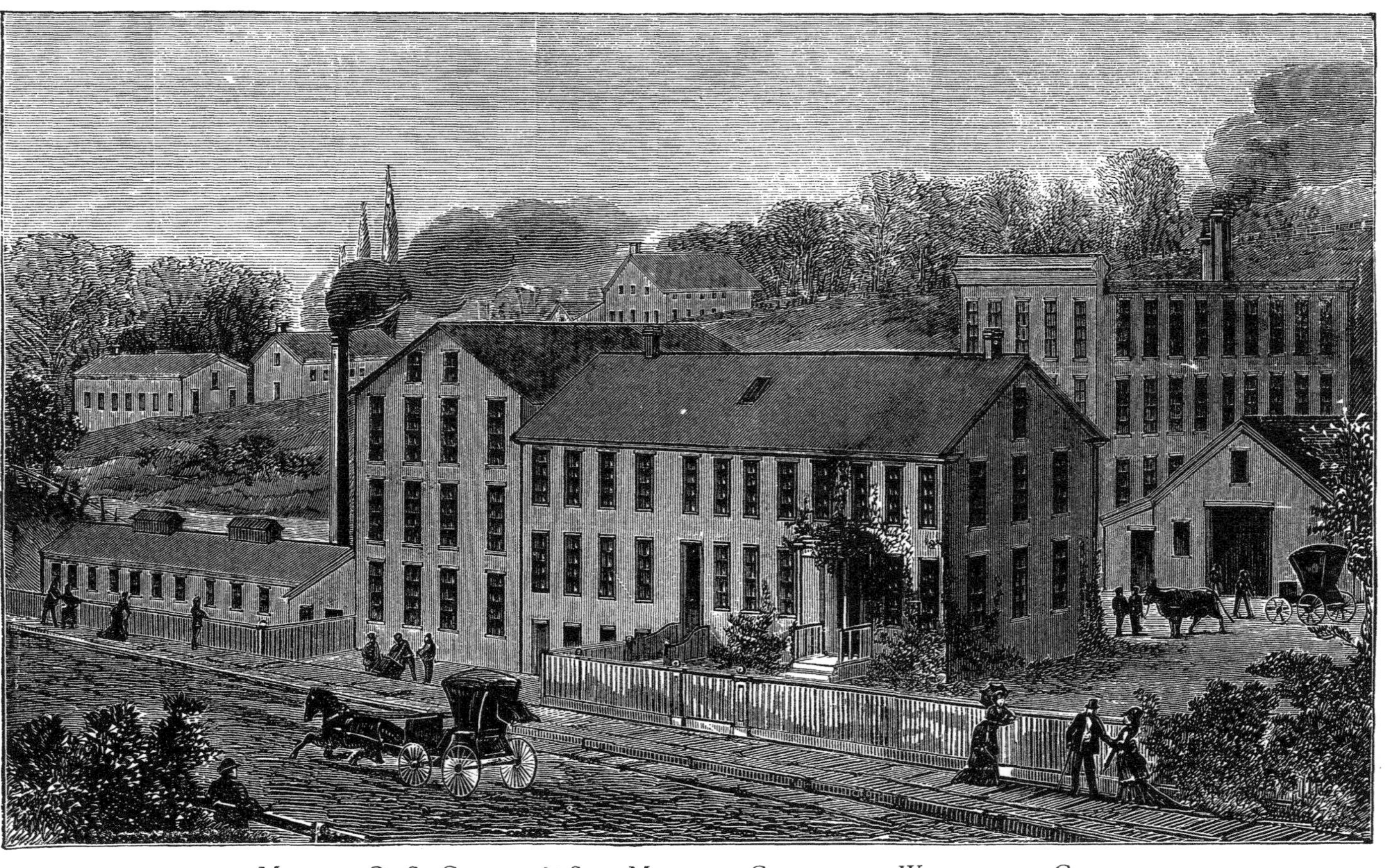

Mills of O. S. Chaffee & Son, Mansfield Centre, and Willimantic, Conn.

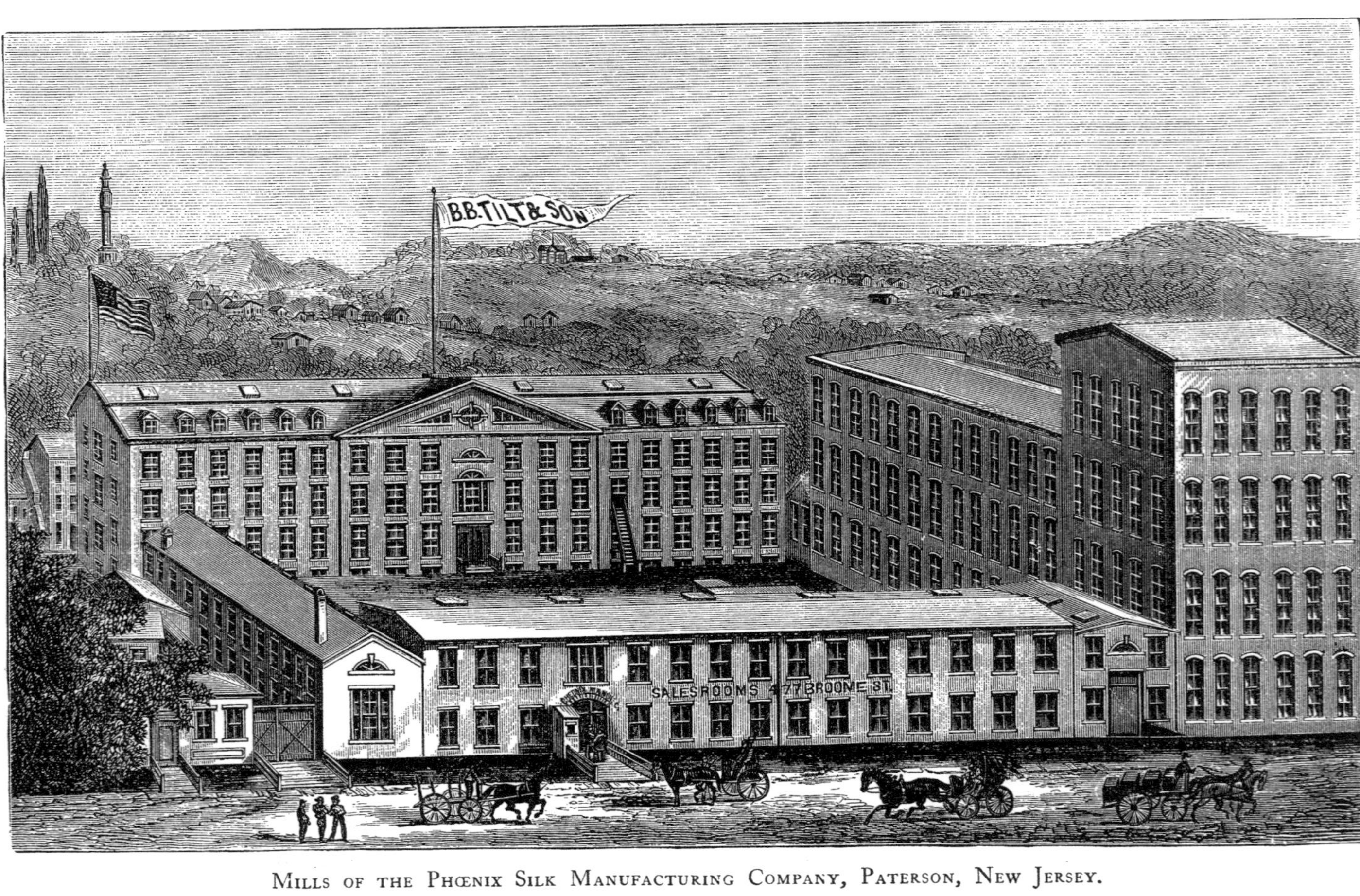

Mills of the Phœnix Silk Manufacturing Company, Paterson, New Jersey.

interests, and he took an active share in urging the protection of the manufacture by a suitable tariff. O. S. Chaffee is one of the oldest of silk manufacturers actively engaged in the business. The goods of his firm have always been distinguished for uniform excellence.

Mr. Dale and Mr. Hayden, subsequently distinguished as manufacturers, took their first lessons in the art under the Connecticut Silk Manufacturing Company. In 1834, B. B. Tilt, who has since occupied so prominent a place in connection with the manufacture of silk, first took an active part in it by commencing the manufacturing of ladies' dress trimmings in Boston. The firm was soon changed to B. B. Tilt & Co., and later to Tilt & Dexter. In 1855, Mr. Dexter and his associates bought out Mr. Tilt's interest, and organized the house of Dexter, Lambert & Co., at first at Boston, from whence they removed to Paterson, N. J., in 1867. This house is still largely engaged in the manufacture of dress trimmings and ribbons. Mr. Tilt organized, in 1862 or 1863, the Phœnix Silk Manufacturing Company, at Paterson, of which he is President. This has been one of the largest silk manufactories in the country, producing silk piece-goods, handkerchiefs, ribbons, trams, organzines, &c., &c.

X.

The Growth of a Manufacturing Village.

IT was in the midst of the wild speculation of the *multicaulis* fever, and the disasters which followed the bursting of that stupendous bubble, that the largest and most celebrated of our manufactories of silk goods had its birth. The brothers Cheney, the sons of a farmer in South Manchester, Connecticut, had cultivated a few mulberry trees and reared some silk-worms, in their boyhood; but as they grew up they scattered, after the manner of New England boys. Two became artists of rare skill and genius, another was a merchant in Providence, and had presently called one of his younger brothers to assist him; others were engaged in farming, and some of the younger sons remained on the old homestead with their parents. There must have been something unusually attractive about that old homestead, for we find that, in the very prime of life, these sons, *not* after the manner of New England boys, came drifting back to it, one after another; not from any want of thrift or enterprise, for they were young men self-poised and energetic in all business matters; but because it was to them the dearest spot in all the world. Even the traveled artists, Seth and John Cheney, found no skies so bright, no landscapes so lovely, no residence so delightful, as at that farm-house in South Manchester.

In January, 1838, Ward, Rush, Frank and Ralph Cheney, started, at South Manchester, the Mount Nebo Silk Mills. They had been for four or five years previous raising silk-worms and producing some silk, like their neighbors. The mills were closed for a time, when Ward, Rush, and Frank removed temporarily to Burlington, N. J. They established there mulberry orchards, cocooneries, &c., and conducted and published from July, 1838, to July, 1840, the magazine known as the "Silk Growers' Manual." Other members of the family established mulberry plantations near Augusta, Ga., in Florida, and at Mt. Healthy, Ohio. In 1841 they returned to South Manchester heavy losers by the failure of the *Morus multicaulis*. They reopened the Mount Nebo Silk Mill, and with new machinery, commenced the manufacture of sewing-silk and twist, using mostly imported raw silk, as the supply of American-grown silk was too scanty to supply their needs. They added, after a time, ribbons, handkerchiefs, and eventually broad goods to their manufacture. They made their first experiments in the production of spun silk from the pierced cocoons, floss, silk waste, and whatever silk cannot be reeled. This, by carding, spinning and weaving, by machinery especially adapted for preparing it, is now made into substantial and durable goods, somewhat wanting in lustre, but admirable for their wearing qualities. It required more than five years of patient and costly experiments before they were able to utilize successfully this material. At first the spun silk was made into pongees and handkerchiefs, and subsequently was used for filling, foulard silks, &c. Eventually they perfected processes by which it was woven into broad goods and ribbons, and these are now widely known as the cheapest and most serviceable silks of their grade in the market. Prior to the late civil war, however, the Messrs. Cheney as well as other American manufacturers, found themselves unable, in the production of most descriptions of broad goods, to compete successfully with European manufacturers.

The war, which compelled the government to levy heavy duties on all articles of luxury, proved of great benefit to the silk manufacturers; the tariff of August, 1861, raising the duty on most classes of imported silk goods to 40 per cent., and that of June 30, 1864, to 60 per cent., at which rate it has since remained. The importation of raw silk largely increased, while that of silk goods decreased continuously. The competition in the manufacture of most silk goods brought the prices to a lower point (the quality being taken into account) than at any previous period, notwithstanding the tariff. The goods of Cheney Brothers have been constantly improving in quality, durability and color; and both their spun and reeled silks have for the past two or three years confessedly excelled, in all respects, the best imported silks of their class. Meantime the Brothers Cheney have not been less mindful of the interests and comfort of their employés than of their own profit. Their two great manufacturing establishments at Hartford and South Manchester are models of convenience and ventilation; and their manufacturing village at South Manchester has not been surpassed in this country in its abundant appliances for the health, comfort, instruction and enjoyment of their operatives. The cottages for the married employés have ample room, water and gas, and a pleasant garden-plot for each. There are no fences throughout the village. Commodious boarding-houses are erected for those who are single or prefer not to keep house. There is a fine hall, library and reading-room, to the support of which the employés contribute a little, though the greater part of the expense comes out of the pockets of the proprietors. A first-class school, an armory for the military company, and ample accommodations for religious worship are also provided. The work is not severe nor the hours long, while the pay is fairly liberal.

Charles Cheney, the third son of George Cheney, was born at South Manchester, Conn., in 1804, and died there, June 20th, 1874. Ward Cheney, the sixth son of George Cheney, was born at South Manchester, in 1813, and died there, March 22d, 1876. These brothers were two of eight, all of whom have been interested in the business first of silk culture, and later of silk manufacture. They were brought up to the practical work of a farm, and received such an education as the little New England district school of those days supplied. This would have been but a meagre training, had not the stirring and potent thought of the neighborhood and the family circle made such an atmosphere about them as to quicken every faculty into full activity.

Charles Cheney left the home and farm at the age of fourteen; and as clerk in a country store in Tolland, Conn., received his business training, and acquired habits of method and exactness which characterized all his later business life. When about twenty years of age he went to Providence, and with an old friend and neighbor, Solomon Pitkin, began business as a dry-goods merchant. His brother Ward, still a boy, joined him there after a time as a clerk, and remained with him several years. In 1834 the firm failed, and Charles Cheney then removed to a farm at Mt. Healthy, Hamilton County, Ohio. Ward Cheney returned to the old home in South Manchester, and shortly afterward building a little house, became again a farmer. Both brothers had married in Providence.

A year or two later they became interested in the culture of silk, and in common with many others, in raising mulberry trees as a provision for the silk-worm. Charles Cheney, on his farm in Ohio, was much interested in the enterprise. He planted mulberry trees, constructed a small cocoonery, raised silk-worms, and made a few experiments in silk weaving and reeling. This was, however, done on a very small scale, and though one or two pieces of goods were woven on the farm, the processes were only experimental, and the amount of silk produced was not enough to amount to anything in manufacture. Raising *Morus multicaulis* trees, for which there was a ready market, soon became the principal business, and the production of silk was then made a secondary consideration. At the same time, the brothers who remained at home were in like manner busy with experiments in silk culture, but soon became much absorbed in raising the mulberry trees, and gave up for the time a small silk mill, of which the ownership had been incorporated in 1838, under the title of the Mount Nebo Silk Manufacturing Company. In this new business Ward Cheney was soon the pioneer. Assisted by his brothers, he planted in Burlington, N. J., extensive nurseries of the *multicaulis;* importations from France having been made for the purpose by his brothers Frank and Seth. Here he also published a monthly journal called "The American

Silk Grower and Farmers' Manual." For the purpose of securing the protection of a warmer climate, another farm was started in Georgia, and the business of raising the trees for the market was in a most flourishing condition, when suddenly, in 1839, the bubble burst, and the loss was total.

Foiled in this direction, Ward Cheney and his brothers returned to their forsaken mill at South Manchester, and resumed the work of making sewing-silk from the imported raw silk. A very small building, with machinery driven by a water-wheel, was the first mill. It would be difficult for persons acquainted only with factories as they are to be found to-day in the United States, to picture a manufacturing life such as existed in those primitive days in South Manchester. The mill hands were intelligent and well educated American girls, whose relations with their employers were those of unquestioned equality. No unpleasant comparisons between capital and labor had then clouded the atmosphere of work, and made impossible the mutual kindliness which is the ideal relation between employer and employed. In the simplicity of these beginnings is doubtless to be found the root of all that is good in the conditions of working life in South Manchester. Nothing bearing on this point has there been done or planned theoretically. The problem of capital and labor may be solved elsewhere by experiment, or reasoned out. With Ward Cheney and his brothers it has never been a problem at all. A healthy and truly democratic respect for work and workers has been the simple and only source of whatever they have done wisely or well for their employés.

Making slow progress and meeting with many difficulties and discouragements in the development of a new industry, they had however begun to see daylight, when in 1847, Charles Cheney, having sold his farm in Ohio, returned to Connecticut. He had made an attractive home for himself at Mount Healthy, and had been useful and valued both in his own neighborhood and in Cincinnati, where he is not even now forgotten. He was one of the earliest abolitionists, and was a friend of S. P. Chase and other leaders in the anti-slavery movement, who were then regarded as fanatics.

Himself thoroughly radical on this subject, he did much to help fugitive slaves, and made his house a station on the Underground Railroad. Fugitives were often concealed in his house, and he sometimes encountered great difficulties and no small peril in getting them beyond the reach of their pursuers. No events of his career gave him in retrospect so much satisfaction as these. His life in Ohio was saddened by the loss of his wife and three children, and he came back to South Manchester as home, gladly reuniting his life and work to that of his brothers, and giving undoubtedly most valuable aid in the organization and conduct of a business which they had opened with such indomitable energy and ingenuity.

Experience in the processes of manufacture had brought success, and from this time progress was constant and rapid. Buildings were added, new machinery and methods imported and invented, and new branches of manufacture added to that of making sewing-silk. In 1854, a mill was built in Hartford, Charles Cheney removing there to superintend it, and remaining there until 1868, when he again came back to South Manchester, where he ended his days. During these same years, Ward Cheney had been often abroad, uniting to the pleasures of travel a careful study of the silk industry in England and continental Europe, and endeavoring constantly to improve the methods and machinery at home. His active mind was always at work, not only on business matters, but on all the great interests of the world; and his lively interest in people and in things widened continually. His warm sympathies and his habit of taking care of every one made him the father of the place in which he lived; and constantly taking upon himself greater labors, he went on under his load so easily and joyously as never to show that anything was difficult or troublesome to him.

In the fuller and completer years of later life, when the living brothers were all together, each contributing his important part to the work in hand, each one indispensable, it is difficult to point to any one portion of the work and say who did it. They co-operated heartily, and shared all interests.

labors and rewards. They expanded the aims of existence in all directions, patriotically during the war, generously among their people, with taste and simple hospitality in their homes. Frequent illnesses cast a shadow over the last years of Charles Cheney's life, but were powerless to paralyze his enthusiasm, or render him indifferent to the lives and interests of his fellow-beings. With both him and his brother Ward, the shortening days were more than ever crowded with work, and filled with gracious deeds.

In his business career Charles Cheney was most remarkable for carefulness, thoroughness, and exact, methodical habits, while in Ward Cheney was the impulse and inspiring energy which was the mainspring of every enterprise. Each in his own way was full of human impulses, of kindness and courtesy. Cast in very different moulds, they still shared many peculiar traits by which they were known among men. To brotherhood their lives have left an added beauty. Labor is more honored and honorable for their work. Faith in mankind is quickened by their hearty confidence in man.

On May 14, 1873, Ward Cheney was elected President of the Silk Association of America. He took a warm and active interest in its prosperity. His death was felt generally by the members as a personal loss. Appropriate resolutions were drawn, and a committee including several of the more prominent members attended the funeral; but these formal measures feebly represented the genuine sorrow which the Association shared with the wide circle of Ward Cheney's friends—a circle which embraced all with whom he had been brought in contact, whether as an employer, or in business relations, or in private life.

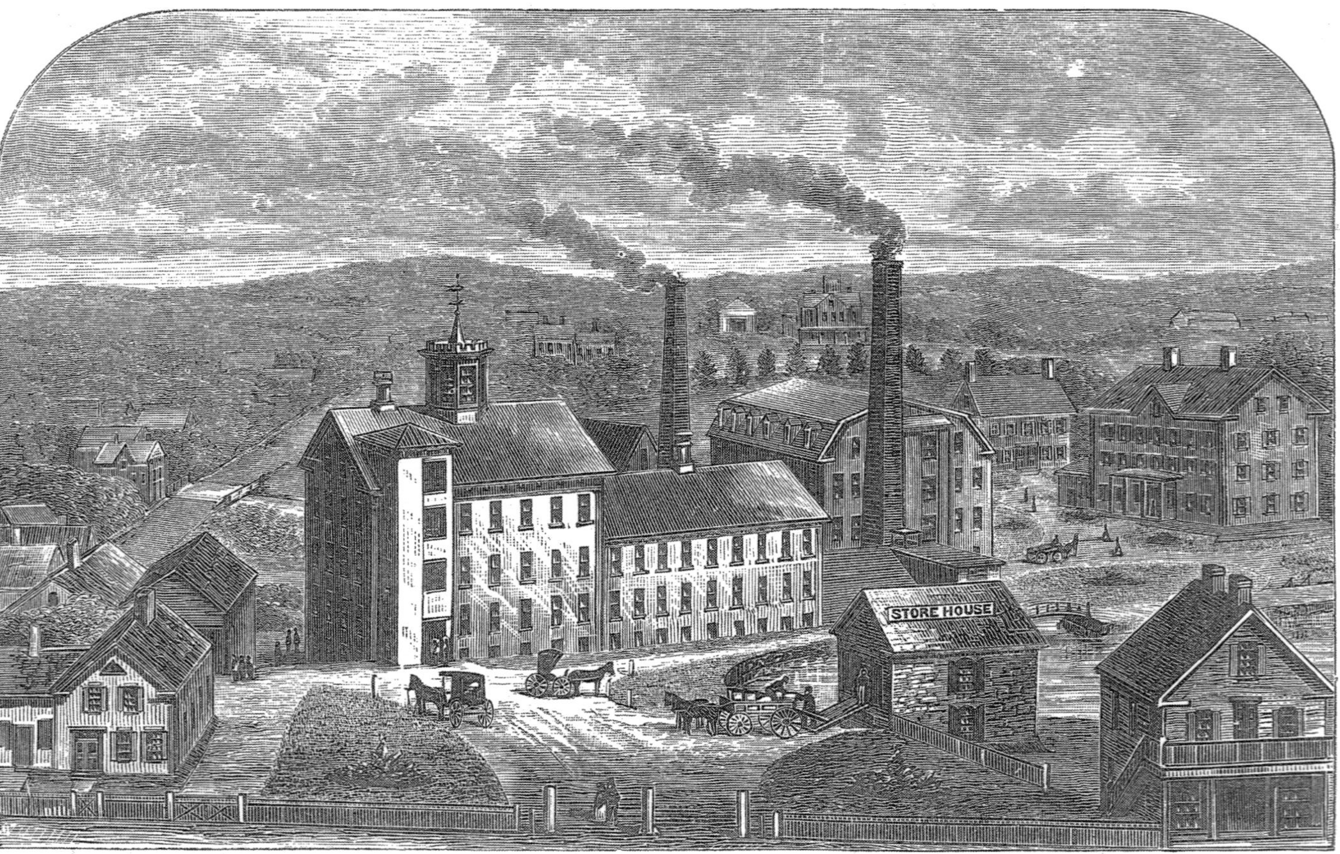

Mills of Seavey, Foster & Bowman, Canton, Mass.

XI.

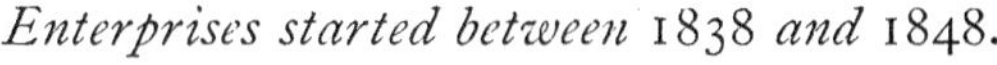

Enterprises started between 1838 *and* 1848.

BUT we must go back with our chronological record to the times which tried the souls of the silk producers and manufacturers. Messrs. Haskell and Hayden (firm name now, J. H. Hayden & Son) began the manufacture of sewing-silks and twist in 1838, at Windsor Locks, Conn., and have continued it uninterruptedly to the present time, using imported raw silks. In 1839, Rixford and Dimock commenced business in the same line in Mansfield; they were quite successful for several years. In 1840, William H. Jones, of North Manchester, Conn., undertook the manufacture of sewing-silk, twist and cord, from American silk. He made excellent silk, which obtained testimonials from the American Institute and at other exhibitions; but the difficulty of procuring American cocoons led him to abandon the business in 1856. B. Hooley, now of the firm of B. Hooley & Son, proprietors of the Keystone Silk Mill, commenced a manufacture of sewing-silk in Philadelphia, in 1840, which has continued uninterruptedly to the present time.

V. J. Messinger started the silk business at Canton, Mass., in 1839; but some months later entered into partnership with Lemuel Cobb, brother of J. H. Cobb, and removed to Needham, where they remained a few years, making sewings, gimps and fringes. About 1844, Mr. Messinger returned to Canton, and in partnership with his brother, V. A. Messinger, established the business there as Messinger & Brother. They continued the manufacture of sewings and twist till 1863, when it was transferred to Charles Foster and J. W. C. Seavey, the latter of whom had been with Messinger & Bro. since 1853. The firm name was J. W. C. Seavey & Co. In 1869 the firm became Seavey, Foster & Bowman. They are now very extensive manufacturers, and their favorite brands, the "Lion" and "Eureka," have a high reputation. The popularity of the Eureka 10-yard button-hole twist has been such as to induce other manufacturers of twist for button-holes to follow the method first adopted with that brand, of putting it on small spools. This improvement was adopted about the year 1870: the 10-yard spool being a convenience to dressmakers, since its quantity of thread is just sufficient for making one dress. The firm have contributed largely to the movement for putting up strictly pure-dye goods, and have also manufactured and introduced measuring and strength-testing machines to enable buyers to inform themselves of the actual quality of the goods they are buying. To the enterprise of this firm consumers are indebted for many im-improvements in the style and quality of twist silks.

The first silk manufactory in Paterson, N. J. (which has now become the chief city of this industry), was started some time previous to 1840, by Christopher Colt, Jr., of Hartford. It was a small affair, and in that year it was purchased by G. W. Murray, of Northampton, who placed John Ryle, an English silk weaver from Macclesfield, Eng., in charge. In 1843, Mr. Ryle was admitted to a partnership, the firm being Murray & Ryle; and in 1846, Mr. Ryle, with the assistance of his two brothers who remained in Macclesfield, bought out Mr. Murray's interest, and the same year attempted weaving dress silks. The silks were of excellent quality, but they could not be made profitably, and for the next thirteen years Mr. Ryle confined himself to the production of tram, organzine,* spool silks and trimmings. In 1859–60, he made another experiment in the production of broad goods, but the times were still unpropitious, and this manufacture was again postponed. In 1872 or 1873, having associated with him his sons, the firm now being John Ryle & Sons, he returned to the manufacture of broad

* These terms, which we shall have frequent occasion to use, may properly be defined here. *Organzine* is the raw silk which has been wound, cleaned and doubled, and thrown or twisted till it is of suitable strength and size for the warp of silk goods. *Tram* (the word means woof) is the silk which has been doubled before twisting, and is used for the woof of silk goods. It may be of a quality of silk inferior to the *Organzine*, but is not so necessarily.

goods the third time, and with gratifying success, the firm being now engaged in the manufacture of twills and fancy silks.

In 1842, Hirsch Heinemann began the manufacture of ladies' belt ribbons wholly of silk, and dress trimmings. Under the names of Hirsch Heinemann, Heinemann & Silbermann, and Silbermann, Heinemann & Co., this enterprise has been continued to the present time. They were the first manufacturers of ladies' belt ribbons in New York. In February, 1876, the partnership expired. Mr. Silbermann continues the ribbon manufacture, and Mr. Heinemann makes a specialty of dress trimmings. In the same year, James Lovett commenced the manufacture of silk twist in Newark, N. J. Under the firm name of Lovett & Standish the business is still maintained, the firm making sewing-silks as well as twist.

Albert A. Conant, the founder of the present firm of A. A. & H. E. Conant, of Willimantic—a kinsman of Capt. Joseph Conant, of the Mansfield Silk Co., and afterward of Northampton and Conantville—commenced in 1843 the manufacture of sewing-silk in the old mill, at Gurleyville, in Mansfield, which had been occupied by the Mansfield Silk Co. The present firm (H. E. Conant having joined it in 1850) are manufacturing sewing-silks and twist. The same year, F. S. Hovey, related to Storrs Hovey, of the Mansfield Silk Co., became connected with the manufacture of sewing-silks in Philadelphia, and still continues the sale of the "Hovacci" and "Vittorelli" brands of silk and twist, which are great favorites with the jobbing trade.

Gurney & Co. started the manufacture of the I X L twist and silk braids, at Newark, N. J., in 1844. We believe they have relinquished the business. A new silk mill, now occupied by E. B. Smith, a sewing-silk manufacturer, was built at Gurleyville, Mansfield, Conn., in 1848, by James Royce.

XII.

Firms established between 1848 *and* 1854.

TOBIAS KOHN, of Hartford, Conn., in 1848, founded a mill for sewing-silks and trimmings, which has since grown into the Novelty Weaving and Braiding Works, of which Mr. Kohn is President. The concern manufactures sewing-silks, gimps, fringes, tassels, braids, and some ribbons. They removed to a larger factory in 1865, and that was enlarged and rebuilt in 1873.

In 1848, William Skinner, of Holyoke, Mass., undertook the manufacture of silk in Northampton, and in 1854 removed to Haydenville, where his "Unquomonk Silk Mills" ranked for twenty years among the largest silk factories in the State. On Saturday morning, May 16, 1874, the Williamsburg Reservoir on Mill River, Hampshire County, Mass., estimated to contain 6,000,000 tons of water as a reserve force to supply numerous mills and factories that lined the river banks, burst its boundaries; 148 human lives and property valued at $1,000,000 were destroyed. Among the severest losers by this catastrophe was William Skinner, who had located on the banks of the river, a few miles from Haydenville. His silk mill and the adjacent homes of his operatives had given the place the local name of Skinnersville. The mill was entirely demolished, and the boiler was carried more than a thousand feet down the river. Mr. Skinner estimated his loss at $200,000. Part of the Nonotuck Silk Company's smaller mill, at Leeds (a few miles above Northampton, on the Mill River), was also swept away. In both these instances, the homes and effects of many of the operatives were destroyed, and they barely escaped with their lives. As the suffering resulting from this calamity became known, and it was manifes

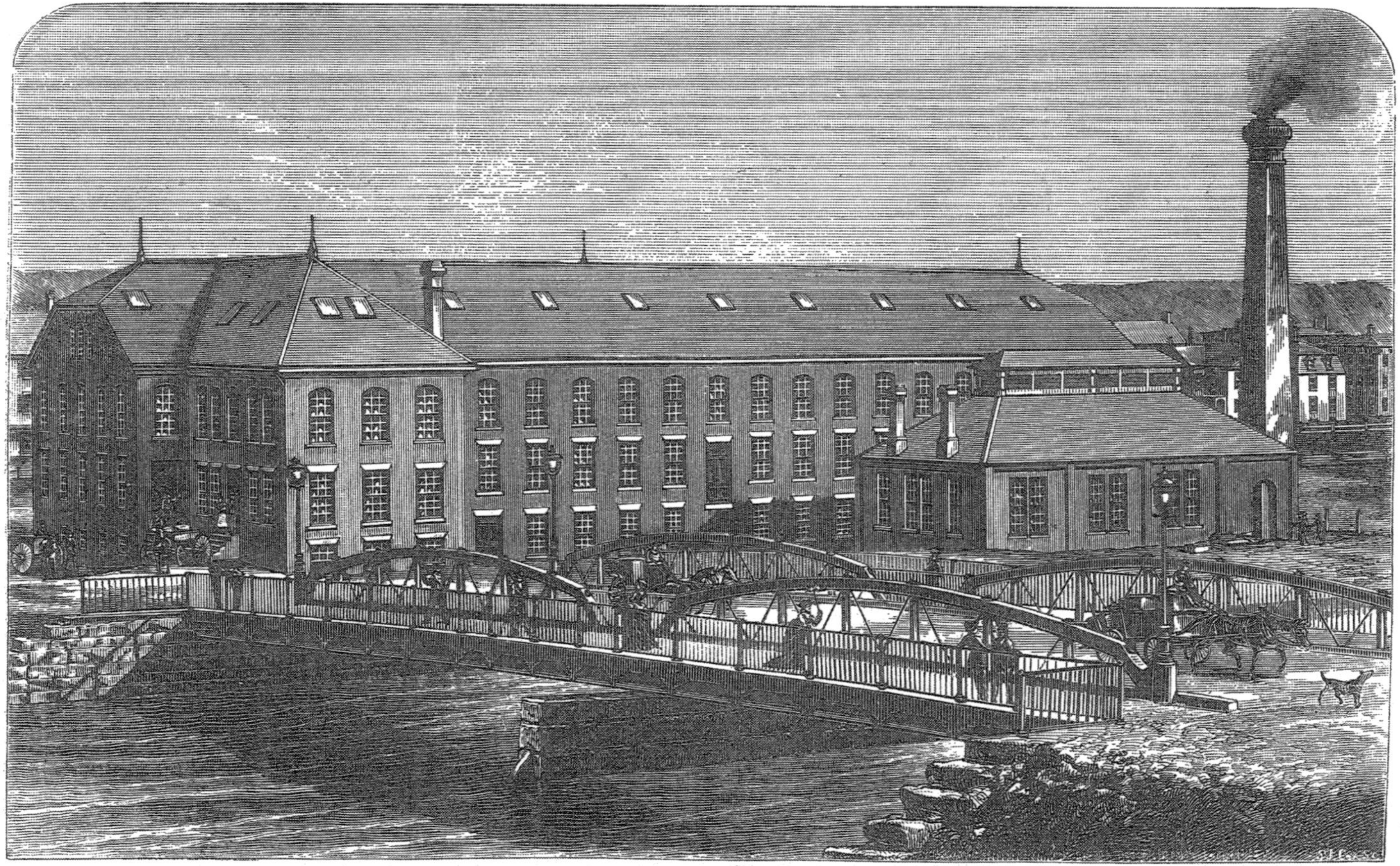

"Unquomonk Silk Mills," of William Skinner, Holyoke, Mass.

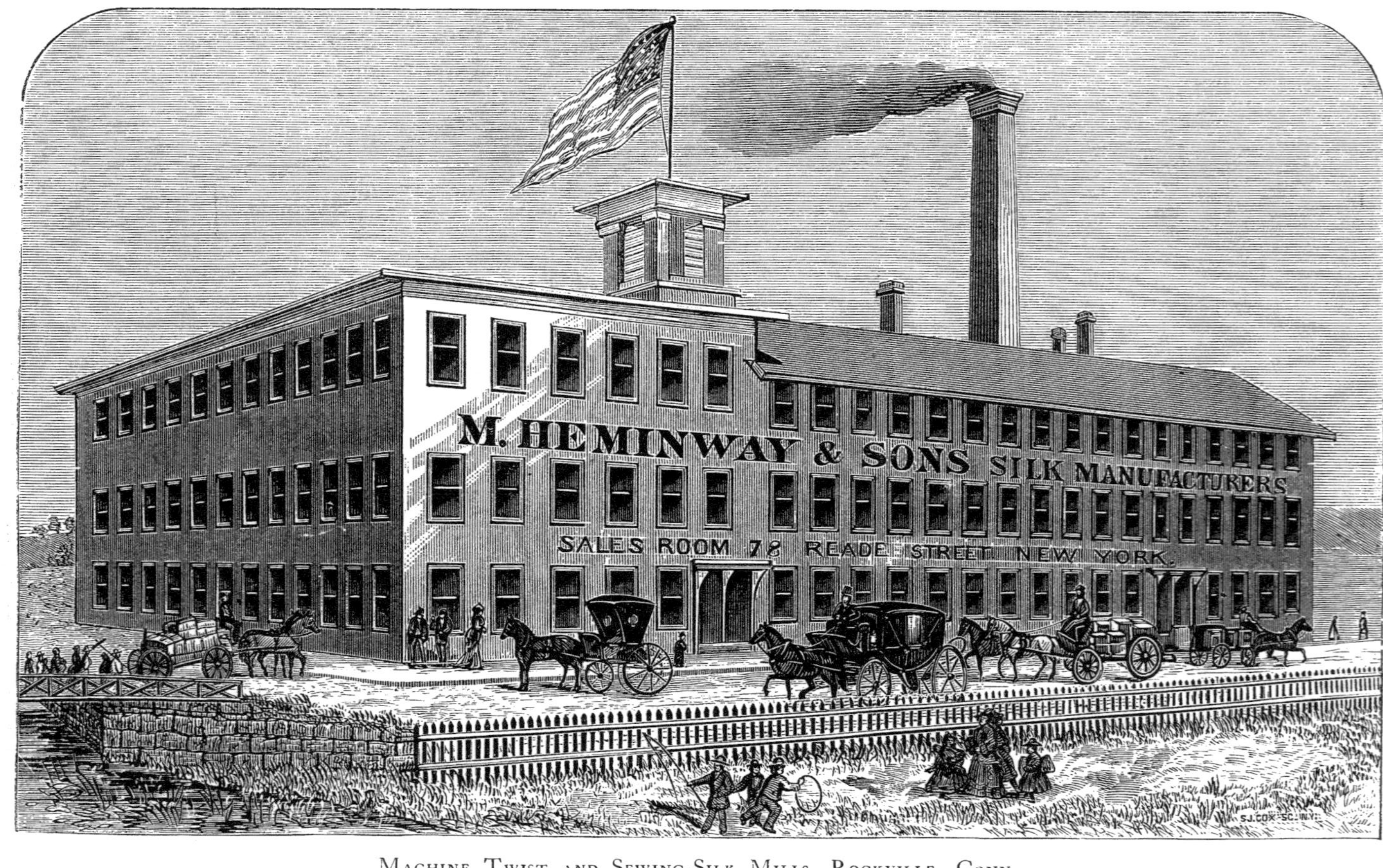

Machine Twist and Sewing-Silk Mills, Rockville, Conn.

that outside assistance was needed for the relief of the destitute operatives, aid was generously extended by money subscriptions among the members of the Silk Association of America; the total contributions from them and from a few other persons making a total of $2,756.* Substantial help was thereby afforded to 43 employés of the silk mills at Skinnersville, and 40 families and employés at Leeds. The remittances to Mr. Skinner in this behalf were by him handed over to the Relief Committee of Northampton, Mass. Girls received one hundred dollars each, and a well-filled trunk of clothing, stockings, shoes, &c.; single men fifty dollars each, and a share of clothing, &c.; men that were tenants three hundred dollars each, and a share of clothing, &c. If householders, they received five hundred dollars each, additional.

Mr. Skinner has since re-established his silk mills at Holyoke, and with new machinery, fine water-power privileges,

---

* The following is a list of the donors :

A. A. Low & Bros	$100 00
A. A. Low	100 00
Wm. H. Fogg & Co	100 00
Wm. H. Smith & Son	100 00
William Ryle	200 00
Hadden & Co	100 00
Hamil & Booth	100 00
Wm. Strange & Co	100 00
Jno. N. Stearns & Co.	100 00
A. Soleliac & Sons	25 00
Silbermann, Heinemann & Co.	25 00
J. Maidhof	25 00
Deppeler & Kammerer	25 00
The Singer Mf'g Co., by I. A. Hopper, Pres.	250 00
C. A. Auffmordt & Co	150 00
B. B. Tilt & Son	100 00
Gossler & Co	100 00
Jno. Caswell & Co	100 00
Belding Bros. & Co	100 00
Jno. H. Draper & Co	50 00
Olyphant & Co., of China	50 00
Jno. T. Walker	$50 00
D. O. Donoghue	50 00
Jones, Underhill & Scudder	25 00
S. M. Meyenberg	25 00
A. L. Mowry	50 00
Arnold, Constable & Co	50 00
Aitken, Son & Co	25 00
Louis Franke	25 00
Jno. Dunlop	25 00
Prall Bros	25 00
Cash	25 00
Thomas N. Dale	50 00
M. W. (Anonymous)	2 00
V	3 00
Wm. H. Copcutt & Co	50 00
Cheney Bros	200 00
C. Greppo	50 00
Cash	1 00
Hensel, Wolff & Co., Philadelphia	25 00
Total	$2,756 00

In addition to the foregoing, cash subscriptions were made on the spot at the time of the disaster by Messrs. George B. Skinner, William Iles and B. Richardson, who immediately visited the scene with proffers of assistance.

Contributions of clothing were received and likewise forwarded from Jno. N. Stearns, 221 East 42d St , and S. McVickar, 123 West 21st St., N. Y.

and indomitable enterprise, is again prospering. He has recently introduced the manufacture of silk braids and bindings at Holyoke.

The name of Joseph Warner first appears in the silk business in 1848, when he was with J. Conant & Co. in the old Conant Mill near Northampton. From that time to this he has not changed his locality or business. He makes the manufacture of sewing-silks a specialty, but occasionally produces some spool twist. J. Harvey Holland was the dyer of Conant & Co. in 1848; in 1849 the firm of Warner, Holland & Co. took the business. Mr. Warner entered into partnership with William Skinner in 1852, but when in 1854 the latter removed to Haydenville, the firm of Warner & Suydam was formed and lasted six years, after which Mr. Warner carried on the business alone for eleven years, and in 1871 took into partnership J. S. Lathrop, of Northampton, forming the present firm of Warner & Lathrop. The sewing-silks of this concern are of merit well known among manufacturers.

In 1849, Col. J. Maidhof, with Mr. Werner, under the firm name of Werner & Maidhof, commenced the manufacture of ladies' dress trimmings at 18 and 20 Liberty Street, New York. In June, 1851, the firm name was changed to Meeker & Maidhof, and in April, 1865, to J. Maidhof, which continued as its designation until January of the present year, when it changed to J. Maidhof & Co. The house still confines itself to ladies' dress trimmings. M. Heminway began the manufacture of sewing-silks at Watertown, Conn., in 1849. If the question should ever be debated as to who was the first to introduce spool silks to take the place of skeins in the market, Mr. Heminway can advance strong claims to that honor. His manufacture of sewing-silk and twist bears high repute, because of its uniform excellence. As the business increased, his four sons and only daughter obtained an interest in it, and it is still continued, under the firm name of M. Heminway & Sons' Silk Co., at the same place.

In 1850, J. C. Graham began the manufacture of dress trimmings and narrow textile fabrics in Philadelphia, and has

525–527 Cherry Street, Philadelphia Pa.

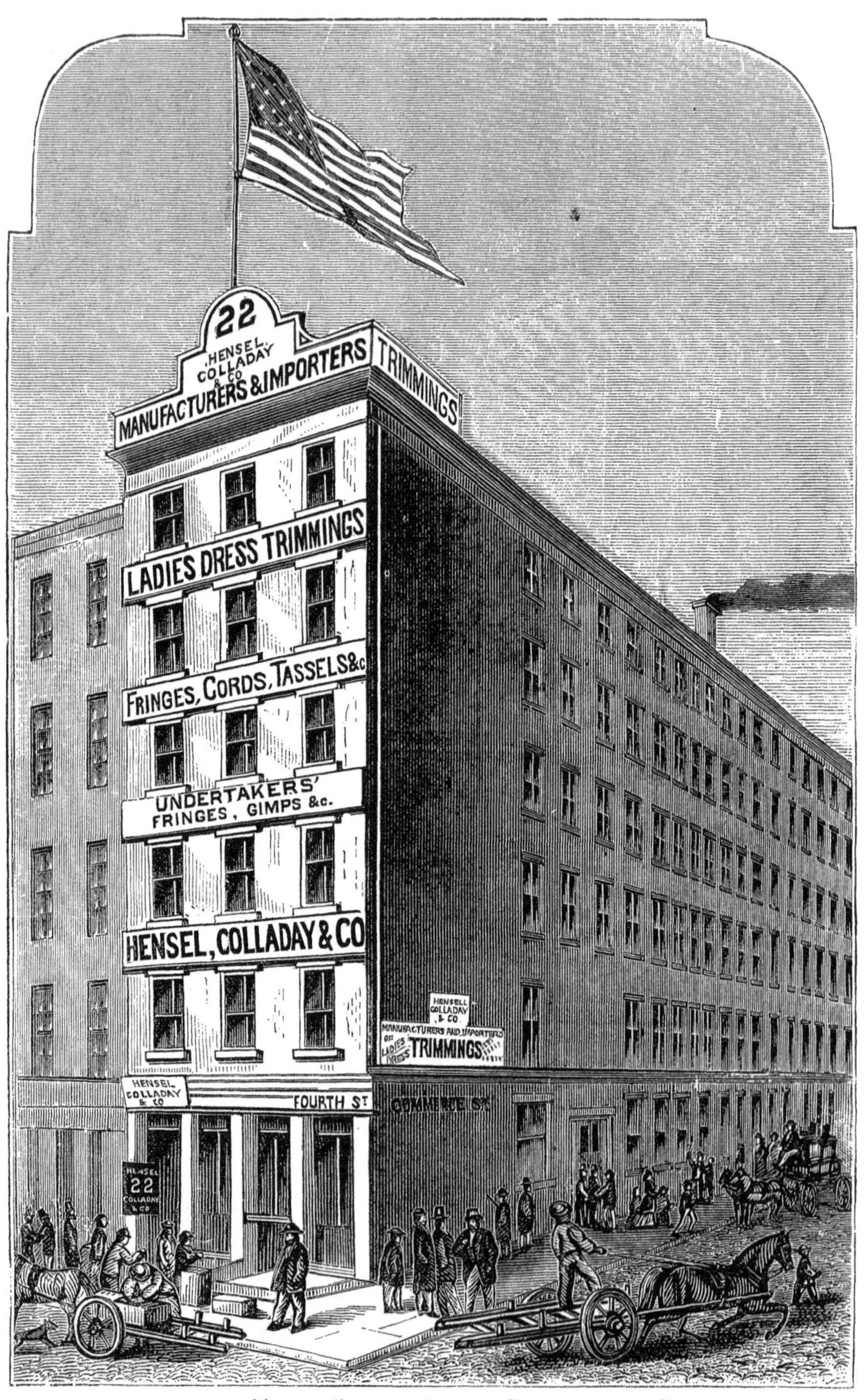

22–24 NORTH FOURTH STREET, PHILADELPHIA, PA.

continued it on an extensive scale to the present time. His manufactory is at 525 Cherry St. He is, after Wm. H. Horstmann & Sons, the oldest manufacturer of dress trimmings in that city. The next year, (1851) Henry W. Hensel founded another house in Philadelphia in the same line of goods. After several changes, the present firm name of this house is Hensel, Colladay & Co. The three large houses of W. H. Horstmann & Sons, J. C. Graham, and Hensel, Colladay & Co. have taken the lead in the manufacture of ladies' dress trimmings at Philadelphia.

L. D. Brown started in the manufacture of skein silk at Gurleyville, Conn., in 1850, in partnership with James Royce, and occupying the mill built by the latter in 1848, which has been referred to. In 1853 Mr. Brown bought the mill then occupied by the Conant Brothers, (already mentioned,) in the same locality, and continued the manufacture of skein silk there until 1865, when he took his son into partnership, sold the mill at Gurleyville to William E. Williams, and bought the William Atwood Mill at Atwoodville. In 1871, L. D. Brown & Son erected a new mill for themselves at Middletown, Conn., and sold the Atwoodville Mill to Macfarlane Brothers. They now manufacture principally machine twist and skein and spool sewing-silk. Their silk has an excellent reputation for strength and purity of dye. In February, 1875, they opened a New York house. Their brands are "L. D. Brown & Son," "Middletown Mills," "Paragon," and "Connecticut Valley." The junior partner, H. L. Brown, has made some inventions of considerable value to the silk industry, including an improvement in winding soft silk, which has been introduced into a number of silk mills, and a new method of silk spooling and weighing.

In 1852 Frederick Baare commenced the manufacture of fringes, galloons and tassels. From 1862 to 1870 he manufactured, at Schoharie, N. Y., the same classes of goods, and also ribbons, foulards, poplins, and other broad goods. Since 1870 he has founded the Baare Silk Manufacturing Company, at Paterson, N. J., which produces plain and fancy silks, ribbons, ladies' dress trimmings, fringes, galloons, &c.

In 1853 George B. Skinner began the manufacture of sewing-silk and twist, at Mansfield, Conn., but subsequently removed to Yonkers, on the Hudson, where he has a large mill, employing 200 or more operatives, in the manufacture of machine twist, tram, organzine and fringe silk. William Iles is in partnership with Mr. Skinner, and superintends the manufacture. In 1854, George R. Hanks—son of Rodney Hanks, already mentioned—erected a mill on Hanks' Hill, Mansfield, Conn., on the site of the mill built by his father in 1821. There he manufactured sewing and twist silk until 1858, when the business passed into the hands of his sons, P. G. and J. S. Hanks, who still continue in it with good success; another of the many instances in this business where, amid all its vicissitudes and disasters, three successive generations have engaged in the manufacture.

Hamil and Booth, now of the "Passaic Silk Works," and the "Hamil Mill," of Paterson, N. J., formed a copartnership in 1854, which has lasted to the present time. They commenced business as "throwsters," with twenty operatives. Increasing their business, and varying its character from time to time, they now give employment to more than five hundred operatives. From 1868 to 1870 they attempted the manufacture of gros-grains and black dress silks, but the condition of the markets, growing out of the effects of the Franco-German war of 1870–1871, led them to suspend operations in those goods for a time, although the perfection of their work had obtained a diploma and medal from the American Institute in 1869. During this period they purchased the Hamil mill, and undertook the manufacture of ribbons and twilled silks. In 1873 they renewed the production of gros-grain and black dress silks, and in 1874 added fringed silks, Jacquard weaving, &c.

Machine Twist and Sewing-Silk Mill, Middletown, Conn.

XIII.

New Firms from 1855 *to* 1863.

THE house of Dexter, Lambert & Co., successors to Tilt & Dexter, to whom reference has been made, was organized in Boston in 1855, and removed to Paterson, N. J., in 1867. In 1874 they added power-loom machinery to their mills, and have since added twilled and figured silk and Jacquard weaving to their previous manufactures of dress trimmings and ribbons. The house of Deppeler & Kammerer was founded in 1855, for the manufacture of dress trimmings, but did not assume their present firm-name until 1866. Their manufactory is now in Grand Street, New York. In 1856, Stelle & Walthall formed a copartnership at Paterson, as throwsters of sewing, fringe and tram silks. Mr. Walthall retired in 1861, and Mr. Stelle associated his two sons with him in the business. In 1873 or 1874 they purchased a mill property at Sauquoit, Oneida Co., N. Y., and have organized as a joint stock company under the style of the Sauquoit Silk Manufacturing Company. They make the throwing of organzine and tram silks a specialty. Mr. Stelle is President of the Company. They have also a branch factory at 319-323 Garden Street, Philadelphia, which is under the superintendence of Richard Rossmässler, the Treasurer of the Company. Samuel Bertschy & Co. commenced, in 1856, the manufacture of narrow goods, hat bands, belt ribbons, and since 1866 as S. Bertschy & Co. have also made bonnet ribbons, neckties, &c., at Tenth Avenue and 46th Street, New York.

C. L. Bottum became connected with the silk manufacture in 1857. He was at first a partner with one of the Conants, at Mansfield Centre, Conn. He removed to Paterson, N. J., in 1858, sold out to Mr. Conant in 1859, and returned to Mansfield, where he formed a partnership with J. H. Holland; and

G. Holland was admitted into the firm a year later. They purchased, in 1859, the Conant mill at Conantville, built by Captain Joseph Conant in 1852, and began the manufacture of sewing and machine twist. One of his partners, G. Holland, with John E. Atwood (another of the Mansfield Silk Co. names), patented an invention known as the stretching machine. It is said that more than 95 per cent. of all the machine twist now made in this country is manufactured on this machine. By its use it is claimed that the cords forming the thread of the twist are drawn into their proper place, making a uniform smooth thread. In the Fall of 1864, Mr. Bottum bought out the manufacturing interest of his partners, holding also one-sixth interest in the stretching machine, and initiated the manufacture of a twist which he calls the "patent machine twist brand." This he makes a specialty. He enlarged his mill to double its former size in 1869, and still continues in the business with G. A. Hammond and C. C. Knowlton as partners, under the firm-name of C. L. Bottum & Co.

In 1861, William P. Towles and Godfrey Tallerman undertook the manufacture of ribbons, scarfs, neckties and trimmings, at Baltimore. Mr. Towles was subsequently a partner in the firms of Towles, Tallerman & Co., Towles Brothers & Co., and after 1870 in the Monumental Silk Works and Silk Manufacturing Company. In the great fire at Baltimore, in 1873, their silk mill was burned, and the Company wound up its affairs. Mr. Tallerman subsequently became the senior of the firm of Tallerman, Hecht & Co. In December, 1873, he withdrew from that firm (who continue business as M. Hecht & Co.) and resumed his old business of ribbons, scarfs, neckties and trimmings, in Frederick Street, Baltimore, the firm being G. Tallerman & Co. The Singer Manufacturing Co. commenced in 1862 the manufacture of machine twist and silk for supplying their sewing machines; their silk factory at Newark, N. J. being the mill formerly occupied by James Lovett & Sons; and have continued it to the present time, selling large amounts at their agencies. John Marr started in the manufacture of silk goods at Trenton, N. J., in 1862, and in 1865 began making hair nets,

BELDING BROTHERS & CO.
SILK MANUFACTORY.
DYE HOUSE
S.J.COX N.Y

to which he added, in 1868, trimming laces and spot nets of silk. He is believed to have been the pioneer in that line of work in this country. Since May, 1870, his factory has been in Centre Street, New York City.

The year 1863 was signalized by the entrance of several large houses into the silk manufacture. Among these were Strange & Brother, who began the manufacture of ribbons at Williamsburgh, L. I., and in 1868 removed to Paterson, where the firm-name was changed to William Strange & Co. This firm have two mills at Paterson, and are the largest silk ribbon manufacturers in the country, employing over 700 operatives. In the same year Belding Brothers & Co. commenced the manufacture of sewing-silks and twist at Rockville, Conn., and have now their warehouses in New York, Philadelphia, Chicago, Cincinnati and St. Louis. They rank among the largest houses in this branch of the silk manufacture, and their goods bear an excellent reputation. Seven prize medals for merit of their goods have been awarded to this firm; two obtained at the Cincinnati exhibitions, three at St. Louis, one at Baltimore and one at Philadelphia. Aub, Hackenburg & Co. also began the manufacture of machine and sewing-silks in Philadelphia, in the same year, and the superiority of their colors and the excellence of their dyeing have caused their goods to be in great demand. They obtained the highest premium at the exhibition of the Franklin Institute in 1874.

XIV.

New Progress from 1863 *to* 1869.

DURING 1863, Louis Franke, in New York City, was enrolled among the manufacturers of fringes, cords and tassels of silk and worsted, and of Angora fringes and tassels. In 1868 he added to these articles, braided cords and silk braids; and in 1870, sash ribbons, marabout trimmings, &c. The business has been successively and largely extended, under the firm-names of Kern & Franke, Louis Franke, Franke & Rost (1865), Louis Franke (again, 1866); and since 1873 H. W. Struss has been a partner. The facilities of this house for manufacture were enlarged in 1868; and within the present year their braiding works—which for eight years previous had been in a separate building from their other factory in New York—have been removed to Paterson, N. J., where also they have established a throwing mill.

In 1864 the Dale Manufacturing Co. was organized, and in 1866 the Dale silk mills were completed at Paterson. The President of the company, Thomas N. Dale, had had long experience as an importer of tailors' trimmings, having for many years resided in Paris as the foreign member of the house of Thos. N. Dale & Co. He turned his attention, in 1864, to the manufacture of tailors' trimmings in this country. The Dale company make a specialty of silk braids and bindings for the tailors' trimmings trade, but they manufacture also tram, organzine, sewing-silk and twist, scarfs and cords. They use the French braiding machinery. Werner Itschner & Co. also commenced the ribbon manufacture in 1864, at Philadelphia, and removed in December, 1865, to Germantown, where they are now carrying on an extensive business. J. H. Booth & Co. began the manufacture of tram and organzine at Paterson the same year (1864), and are still engaged in it.

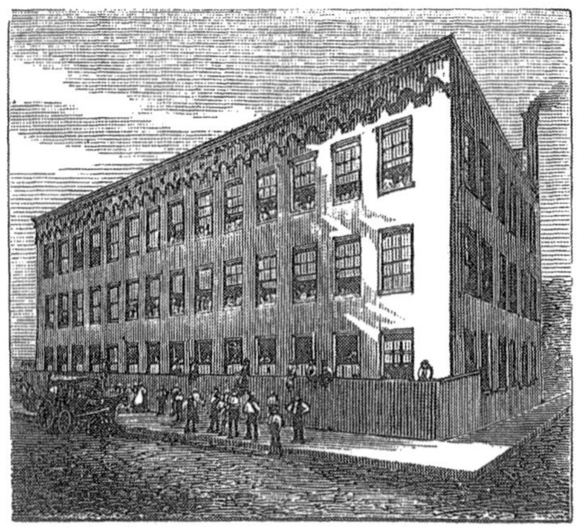

Herman Simon's Silk Mill, Town of Union, N. J.

Mills of Werner Itschner & Co., Tioga Station, Germantown, Pa.

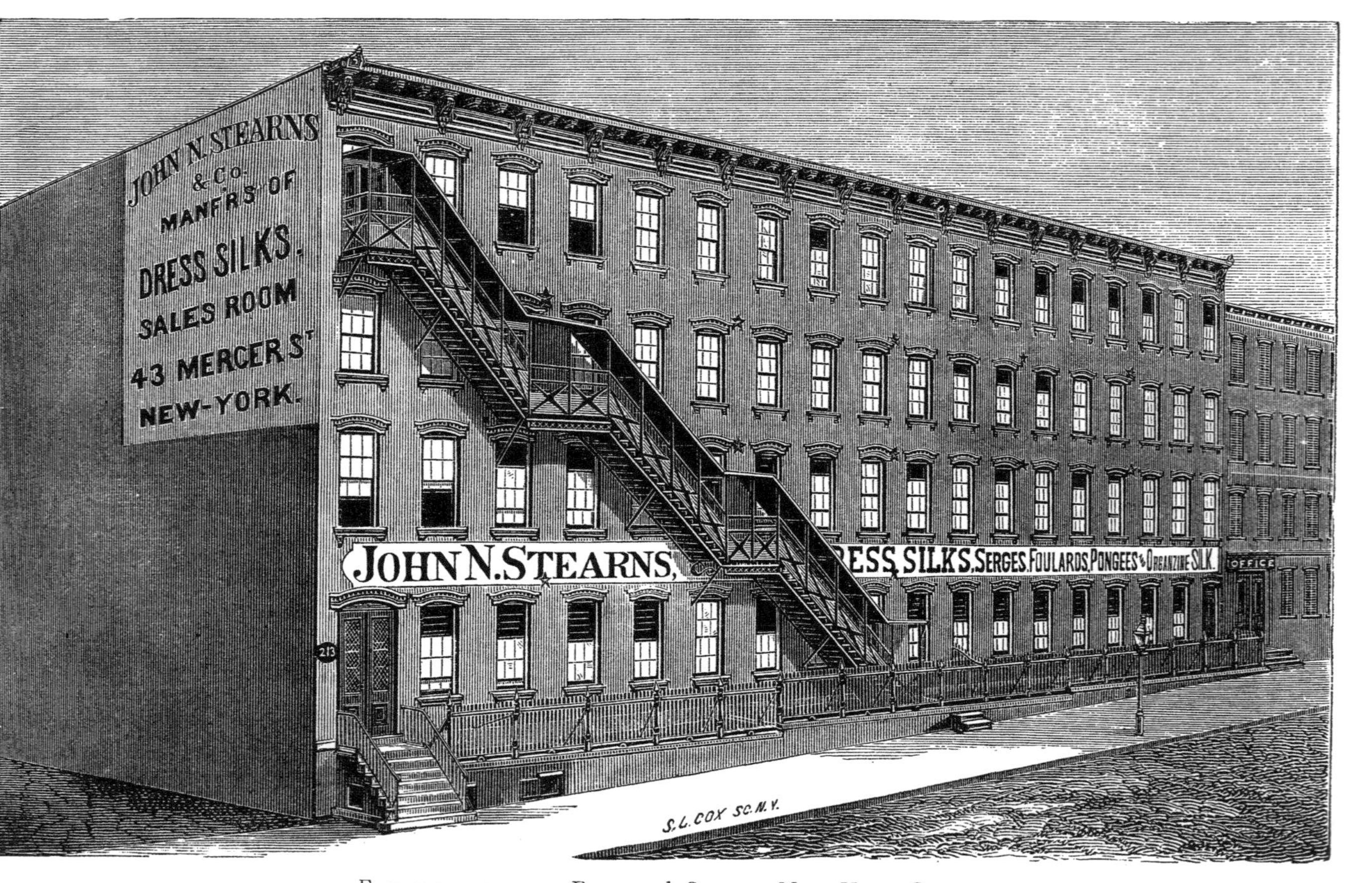

Factory, 213–221 East 42d Street, New York City.

In 1865 another of the leading houses in the manufacture of broad goods started its enterprise. John N. Stearns commenced making fancy silk goods, foulards, handkerchiefs, advancing to Jacquard weaving, and to the production of some varieties of dress silks, all of which are of excellent quality. Stearns & Co.—there are now three partners in the house—have a large factory on East 42d Street, N. Y., and dyeing works on Staten Island. A considerable portion of their spinning machinery was purchased at very low prices from the Manchester (England) silk manufacturers after the Cobden treaty with France had almost annihilated the silk industry in Great Britain.

In 1865–67, two of the largest silk-dyeing establishments in the country were established. Rudolph Klauder, a dyer, and the son of a dyer, organized the Quaker City Dye and Print Works, in Philadelphia, in 1865, and by careful study and investigation of foreign establishments, and the best machinery and processes, has brought the dyeing of silks to the highest perfection. The same year Mr. Greppo (now of Weidmann & Greppo), a nephew of M. Bernaud, one of the most eminent silk dyers of Lyons, France, commenced business as a manufacturer of silk braids at Cranford, N. J., and in 1866–67 started a dyeing establishment at Paterson. Mr. Weidmann, also an experienced and skillful dyer, who in 1873 took charge of the dye-house of the Dale Manufacturing Co., formed a partnership with Mr. Greppo, in January, 1876. Their silk-dyeing works are now the largest in the United States.

J. H. & G. Holland, who had been partners with C. L. Bottum at Conantville, organized, in 1866, a new firm for the manufacture of sewing-silk and machine twist at Willimantic, Conn. J. H. Holland died in 1868, and G. Holland in 1870. The business is now carried on by Mrs. G. Holland, under the name of the Holland Manufacturing Company, of which Ira Dimock is the manager. The company prospered, and in 1872 erected an additional mill. John A. Conant (one of the Mansfield family of Conants) is in charge of the "throwing" department.

Dunlop & Malcolm (John Dunlop since 1873) built a mill at Paterson in 1866, for the manufacture of sewing and machine twist. The Oneida Community also undertook, in 1866, the manufacture of sewing-silk and machine twist at Oneida, and in 1868 established a branch factory at their community in Wallingford, Conn. Their silks have a good reputation.

John D. Cutter started business in the same branch of manufacture at Paterson, in 1866, at first in partnership with D. Beach Grant, afterwards with Benjamin Salter; and since October, 1873, alone. His establishment bears the title of the Excelsior Manufacturing Co. The spool silk of this Company has an established reputation for excellence of material and purity of dye. Their machine-twist and sewing-silk are numbered in sizes corresponding with those of standard spool cotton; a system which facilitates use with similarly numbered sewing-machine needles.

In Jan., 1866, P. G. Givernaud, having associated his three sons with him, brought to this country 60 weavers, and commenced manufacturing silk goods with machinery brought from Lyons, France. Dress silks of the style known as *Grand Cachemire d' Amerique* were his specialty. This house was the first, except Cheney Brothers, to carry on broad silk weaving in plain dress silks on a considerable scale in this country. He employed 150 operatives for the first two or three years. In 1869, this house formed a connection with Benkard & Hutton, under which the business was so much increased that 500 operatives were employed, and an annual production of $600,000 reached. In 1873, this connection with Benkard & Hutton was dissolved; and Givernaud Brothers (the sons of P. G. Givernaud) built a new mill, which was fitted with improved throwing machinery of new American design, constructed by the Danforth Locomotive and Machine Works of Paterson, N. J. This new mill contains all the requisites of a first-class establishment. In the factory, at West Hoboken, there are 100 looms, and in that at Olmstead Station twenty-five looms, now running. The production of dress silks, in 1875, was

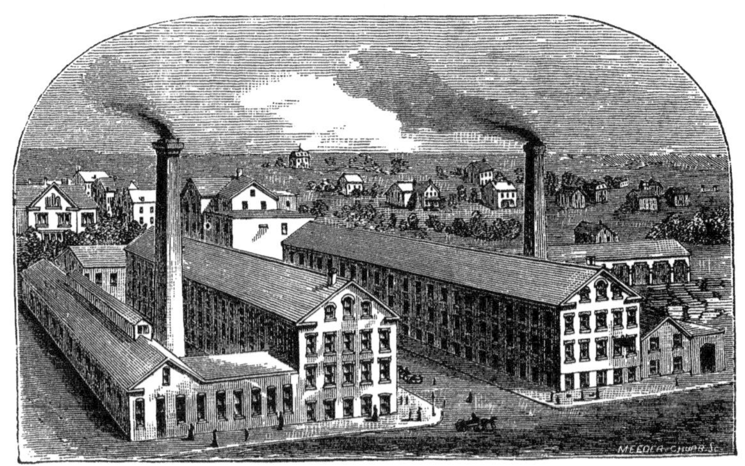

Mills of the Holland Manufacturing Company, Willimantic, Conn.

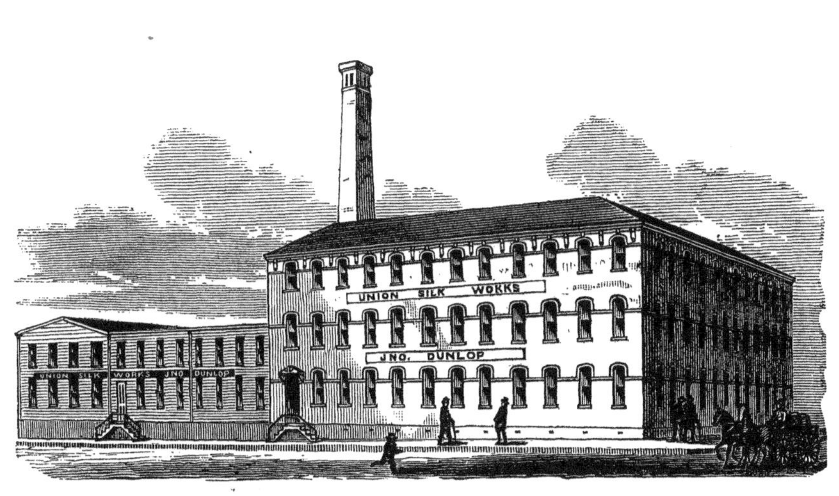

"Union Silk Works," of John Dunlop, Paterson, N. J.

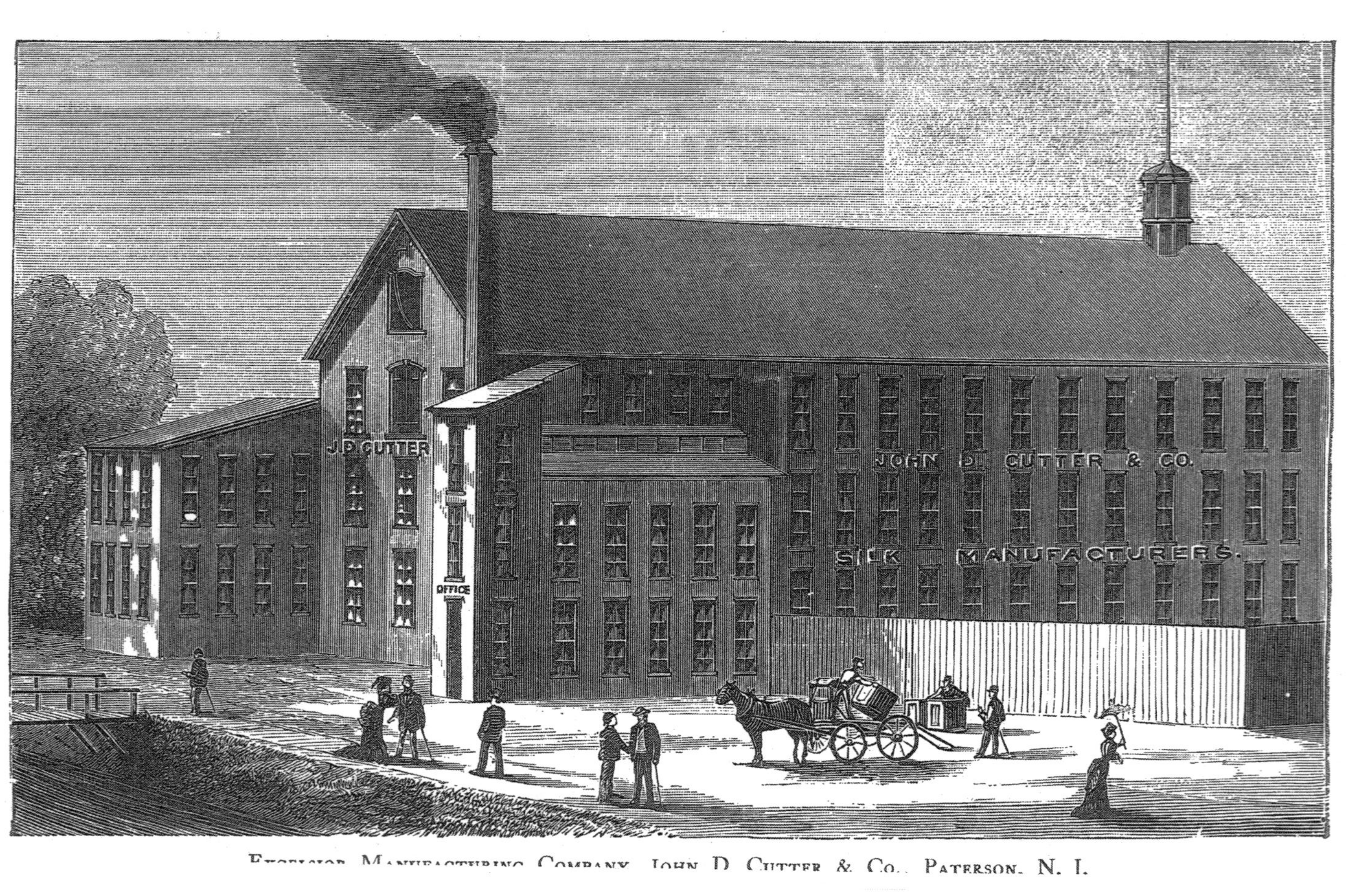

Excelsior Manufacturing Company, John D. Cutter & Co., Paterson, N. J.

valued at $200,000, and that of the present year (1876) is at the rate of $300,000 per annum.

In April, 1866, the firm of Wolfsohn, Meyenberg & Co. was established in New York for the manufacture of silk trimmings and hair nets. It was dissolved in Jan., 1868, and S. M. Meyenberg continued the business alone till October, 1870, when the firm of Meyenberg, Prall & Co. was formed, and the business of silk weaving commenced. The great difficulties attending a novel experiment had been overcome, when the panic of 1873 overtook the house, and broke up the partnership. Soon afterward, Mr. Meyenberg invented an imitation of a bordered lace veil, obtained by printing a white netting with black flocks. The demand for these veils during the following Spring justified a manufacture of 125 to 150 dozen per day. The success of this enterprise required larger facilities, which have been obtained at Paterson, where suitable premises have been engaged, looms and other machinery purchased, and 100 operatives employed.

Atwood and Richmond (Mr. Atwood being a descendant of one of the original Mansfield Silk Co. proprietors) also undertook the manufacture of machine twist at Brooklyn, Conn., in 1866.

In 1869, A. Soleliac & Sons commenced the manufacture of ribbons in West 29th Street, New York, and in 1873 removed to more ample quarters (which their increasing business required) in the Dale Mill, at Paterson. They are among the largest ribbon manufacturers in the country. During the past year, colored dress silks have been a prominent feature in this firm's products.

XV.

Record of Advance since 1869.

THE westward progress of silk manufacture may be inferred at this period from legislative action in California. A law authorizing a bounty for mulberry plantations and the production of cocoons was passed in 1866, but soon afterward repealed. Some years subsequently a bill was introduced in the California Senate "to encourage silk culture and manufacture," but was defeated by a large majority. In 1869, E. de Bossière, a French capitalist, whose efforts at silk culture have been already narrated, started a silk mill in Kansas, at Silkville, Williamsburg P. O., Franklin County; gradually added to his buildings and machinery; and attempted the manufacture from French thrown silk, of velvet ribbons, which have proved of excellent quality. In 1870, the California Silk Manufacturing Co. commenced the manufacture of tram, organzine, fringe silk, sewing-silk and twist, at South San Francisco. Their reported capital was $50,000; while they were desirous of encouraging the production of raw silk in California, they were obliged at first to import their silk from China and Japan. In 1872, the Union Pacific Silk Co. was incorporated at San Francisco, with a capital of $250,000, for silk weaving and the manufacture of broad goods, and had at a recent date a factory with 50 looms in position.

In 1870, the Norwich Loom Company began the manufacture of ribbons at their works in Preston, near Norwich, Conn. They had previously been engaged in the manufacture of suspenders. They changed their style to the "Uncas Ribbon Co.," in July, 1875. W. H. H. K. C. Higgins is their treasurer; E. Oldfield their superintendent.

In 1870, Robert Simon came to the United States, and was engaged by John N. Stearns, then a large manufacturer of gros grain dress silks. In 1871, Mr. Simon passed into the employ of E. P. Moore & Co., of Paterson, who were also

PELGRAM & MEYER
SALESROOM 456 BROOME STREET, NEW YORK.

making dress goods. In 1873, he was engaged by Messrs. Benkard & Hutton to superintend their factory in West Hoboken, N. J. In April, 1875, Robert and Herman Simon started a new mill in the town of Union, N. J., 2½ miles from West Hoboken ferry. They stocked this mill with new machinery, including spinners made by the Danforth Locomotive & Machine Co., of Paterson, N. J.; power-looms by Van Winkle, of the same city; spooling and warping machines imported from Europe; and in addition, looms partly constructed according to peculiar plans furnished by Robert Simon. They now, (1876) have 50 hand-looms and 50 power-looms for making dress silks. Their average production is valued at $350,000 per year.

Streeter and Wood (now Streeter, Merrick & Co.) began the manufacture of machine twist in 1871, at Shelburne Falls, Mass.

The Silk Manufacturing Company of College Point, Flushing, L. I., started the manufacture of tram, organzine and ribbons, in April, 1872. The business has been conducted by Hugo Funke, its former President, for his sole account, since January, 1875, under the firm name of Hugo Funke. In 1872, also, the firm of Pelgram & Meyer established their factory at Paterson, N. J. Their manufacture includes almost every kind of silk fabrics, though ribbons and piece goods are their specialties.

The same year, also, the Central Village Silk Company began operations at Central Village, Conn. In the Summer of 1872, they built a mill 42 x 100 feet, four story and attic, at Scranton, Pa., and were there incorporated in October, 1873, as the Scranton Silk Co. Their specialty from the first has been the manufacture of tram and organzine.

In 1873 the firm of Brainerd, Armstrong & Co. modified the arrangements for the manufacture of their goods by the Nonotuck Silk Company of Florence, Mass., and they have more recently begun making some portion of their own goods at Willimantic, Conn. The firm of Brainerd & Armstrong was formed in 1867, the partners being James P. Brainerd, previously of Williams & Co., silk merchants, 469 Broadway, and Benjamin A. Armstrong, a salesman in the same house.

The admission of L. O. Smith, in 1870, made the present firm of Brainerd, Armstrong & Co. They have salesrooms in New York, Philadelphia and Baltimore.

On the 26th of June, 1869, a meeting of silk manufacturers was held at the rooms of the American Institute. The late William J. Horstmann, of Philadelphia, presided. Resolutions were passed declaring that it was for the interest of the silk manufacturing trade to have the products of the industry well represented at the XXXVIIIth exhibition of the American Institute. An association was formed, on the 2d of July following, to promote the enterprise. Its title was, The National Association of Silk Manufacturers for the Exposition of 1869. The following officers and managers were elected: President, Robert Hamil, of Paterson, N. J.; Vice-President, Frederick Baare, of Schoharie, N. Y.; Treasurer, Albert Tilt, of New York; Secretary, James S. Shapter, of Paterson, N. J.; Managers, William J. Horstmann, Ward Cheney, J. Maidhof, J. Silbermann, L. Kammerer, George B. Skinner, William Strange, John C. Ryle and B. Richardson. At the July meeting a committee was appointed to take measures for obtaining the co-operation of the silk trade.

This was the first organized effort made to unite the silk manufacturers for their common benefit, and it was the germ from which grew the Silk Association of America. The next step leading to that organization was taken by the Silk Industry Association of Paterson, N. J., which re-organized in May, 1872, with the following officers and board: President, Robert Hamil; Vice-President, William Strange; Treasurer, L. R. Stelle; Secretary, J. P. McKay; Managers, Thomas N. Dale, C. Greppo, and B. Salter. That was and still is a local Association; it was founded in 1858, with John Ryle as President, and L. R. Stelle, Secretary.

On the 12th of June, 1872, the Silk Industry Association issued a call to silk manufacturers to form a national organization. Forty-four firms and companies answered the call, and held a meeting in New York City, June 26th, 1872, at which the Silk Association of America was organized. The inception of the undertaking was largely due to the exertions of the late William J. Horstmann, although he did not live to see the Association organized.

The Silk Association of America has for its principal object a hearty union and co-operation of silk manufacturers in all measures and undertakings which affect their common interests. The influence of the silk manufacturers, as a body, has already been largely increased by such unity of purpose and effort. In the various emergencies in which the manufacture is liable almost at any moment to be placed by our legislators, the Association provides a headquarters for counsel, consideration and combined action. There are, of course, many minor matters of general concern to the silk trade in which the Association can render special service. Among its most valuable labors are the preparation of periodical reports on the various branches of the silk trade and manufacture, and the collation of elaborate and careful statistics which throw new light upon the business, and enable operations to be based on an accurate knowledge of supply and demand.

The office of the Association is at 93 Duane Street, New York. The following are the present officers and board: President, F. W. Cheney; Vice-Presidents, Thomas N. Dale, A. B. Strange, and William Ryle; Directors, F. O. Horstmann, B. Richardson, Geo. B. Skinner, Ira Dimock, William Strange, C. Greppo, A. Soleliac, William Skinner, Seth Low, I. A. Hopper, George H. Burritt, L. Bayard Smith, M. M. Belding, D. O'Donohue, A. G. Jennings, Louis Franke, C. Lambert, John T. Walker, J. W. C. Seavey, and Frank Cheney; Treasurer, John N. Stearns; Secretary, Franklin Allen.

The Silk Association of America, in its first annual report, May 14, 1873, announced the production of silk goods by American manufacturers, for the year ending December 31, 1872, as being of the aggregate value of $25,073,201. One hundred and forty-seven establishments reported, and the amount of capital invested was stated at $15,316,414, the number of operatives employed 11,713, and the wages paid them $4,878,054. The home consumption of foreign silk goods had diminished from $34,451,687, in the year ending

December 31, 1871, to $24,214,283 in the year ending December 31, 1873.

In its report presented in May, 1874, the Association announced that there were 156 manufacturing firms in the country, employing 10,651 operatives, and a capital of $15,988,877; their products for the year ending December 31, 1873, (the latter part of the year having been one of financial disaster and panic) were only valued at $19,894,874; forty-two firms were engaged in the manufacture of sewing-silk and twist, and had produced these goods to the value of $6,649,682, or one-third of the whole silk product. The amount of imported silk goods continued to diminish, being almost six million dollars less in the fiscal year ending June 30, 1874, than in the previous year, while the import of raw silk had been steadily increasing until the disastrous year of 1873-4.

The Third Annual Report, presented in May, 1875, represented that there were 180 silk manufacturing firms in the country, in thirteen different States; 167 being in the five States of New York, New Jersey, Pennsylvania, Connecticut and Massachusetts, 3 in California, 3 in Ohio, 2 in Illinois, and one each in New Hampshire, Vermont, Maryland, Missouri and Kansas. The number of operatives employed in the calendar year 1874 was 14,479, viz., 5,134 males and 9,345 females. The amount of wages paid was $4,497,319; the capital invested was reported at $14,708,184, and the product of the year $20,082,482. Of this product the thrown and spun silks amounted to $3,863,325, sewing-silks and machine twist to $5,766,648, dress silks and foulards to $1,900,000, millinery and necktie silks and handkerchiefs to $1,477,477, ribbons to $2,776,836, laces, braids and trimmings to $4,298,196. The imports of raw silk in 1874 were 1,101,681 pounds, and its value $4,504,306; and the value of manufactured silks imported into New York during the calendar year was $23,292,551, nearly $1,100,000 less than the preceding year. For a year of commercial depression the showing was a very fair one. We give elsewhere the statistics of the year 1875, presented at the annual meeting in April, 1876.

XVI.

Methods of Manufacture.—Reeling, Throwing and Dyeing.

THE various processes which silk undergoes in its transformation from the fine and attenuated filaments of the cocoon to the heavy texture of substantial dress silks, or to the wondrous fabrics wrought by the Jacquard loom, involve an enormous amount of labor, the cost of which is chiefly represented in the price of silk goods, the mere cocoons being comparatively inexpensive. The first process is reeling, an art which seems very simple, but which really requires much skill, tact, experience, patience and watchfulness, and on which ingenuity has been lavished. Very numerous have been the inventions of silk reels, by men who did, and not a few by those who did not, appreciate the special mechanical difficulties to be overcome. One of these obstacles is the variable length of silk in the cocoons. No two of the same breed of worms will spin just the same amount; and between cocoons from different breeds, or those spun under different circumstances, the length varies from 300 to 1,300 yards. This variable length necessitates joining the filaments, of which usually from six to ten are reeled together to form a single thread of silk. The cocoons vary not only in length but in fineness; indeed different portions of the same cocoon vary greatly in this respect; and in some of the best reeling the outer third of the cocoon (after the floss is taken off) is reeled by itself, and the inner portions in two separate lots. The reeling must not be too close to the chrysalis, as that portion of the silk is inferior, and not generally of good color. There are also double cocoons, soft cocoons, imperfect cocoons, and those in which from disease the worm has perished, in its not quite completed cocoon. These can never be reeled completely, and often not at all. The water in which the cocoons are placed for reeling must not be too hot, or it partially dissolves the silk; nor too hard, or it renders the gum on the silk too brittle, and makes the silk liable to break. The dupions or double cocoons can only be reeled from boiling hot water, which would greatly injure the good cocoons.

The best method of getting over the difficulties of reeling would seem to be the establishment of filatures or large reeling establishments, in which the reeling can be conducted by steam or water-power, under the management of skilled and competent operators; the proprietors of the filatures purchasing the cocoons at prices regulated by their quality. We make this suggestion with diffidence, for thus far in the history of silk culture in this country no filature has ever been financially successful, nor has the highest price these establishments have been able to pay (and some of them have paid more than they could afford) for cocoons, been sufficient to make the rearing of silk-worms profitable. The question of a filature is, however, one of little present practical importance, as most of the silk imported is already reeled.

And here let us state an interesting fact relative to the reeling of the Chinese silk. In Mr. Lilly's valuable little pamphlet, "The Silk Industry in the United States," already mentioned, he says: 'At the suggestion of Mr. William Atwood, about the year 1840, Mr. Ezra Goodridge, of New York, sent a sample skein of American silk to China, with an order for a few bales of an article to be similar in all respects. In compliance with this order, an invoice came of silk described as 're-reeled Canton.' The skeins were fac-similes of the American sample. They gave great satisfaction; and up to the present time, silk of this character has been the subject of large importation." The attention of Franklin Allen, Secretary of the Silk Association of America, has been especially called to this paragraph. The results of his inquiries may here be briefly stated. Mr. Lilly's statement is undoubtedly true, but it does not cover the whole ground. Mr. Nathan Rixford, already mentioned as a manufacturer of silk machinery, and subsequently of silk, had patented a silk-reel of his own invention, a material improvement on the Piedmont reel, and supplied ten of these reels to Samuel W. Goodridge, of Hartford, Conn., who sent them to China, in 1840 or 1841, by Joseph H. Weed, together with samples of American reeled raw silk, not doubting that the Chinese silk producers would adopt the reels and supply silk reeled with a traverse, like the samples supplied them. A. A. Low, of New York, also in the China trade, sent sixteen of these improved reels to China; but, like Mr. Goodridge, found great difficulty in introducing them, owing to the prejudice of the people. Eventually, however, the desired change in reeling was effected, and the supply of suitably reeled silk thus obtained gave an impetus to its consumption in this country, without which American manufacturers could have made but slow progress. Late in 1853, or early in 1854, John T. Walker sent reels and reelers from Canton to Shanghai; and there had Shanghai silk re-reeled, having previously sent down from Shanghai, a number of bales to be re-reeled at Canton in the same form as the Canton silks were then being reeled. Messrs. Goodridge and Walker received the first lot of re-reeled Shanghai silk sent to New York. At first the re-reeling was well done; but after a time the Chinese became careless about it, and in consequence of imperfect reeling, the re-reeled silk ceased to be exported. Re-reeling of Tsatlees and Hainings was resumed in Shanghai, in 1867, by Ezra R. Goodridge and Co., and has continued to the present day, Frank Goodridge, son of Samuel W. Goodridge, going out to China for the purpose of having the process adopted. The re-reelers have, however, again fallen into their old habits of doing the work carelessly.

It should be remarked that the quality of most of the Chinese raw silk, now brought to this market, is inferior to that of Italy and France, not in the intrinsic character of the filaments themselves so much as in the defectiveness of its reeling. The difference in cost is about two dollars a pound; but the waste and imperfection of the Chinese silk are for some purposes sufficient to make the Italian raw silk the more profitable of the two, even at its higher price. The raw silk, when imported, comes usually in picul bales of one hundred and thirty-three and a third pounds. If these are from China, they are made up in bundles weighing from eight to twenty-five pounds each, protected at the corners by floss or waste. The packages consist of skeins of varying number as they differ in fineness, the Canton silk being of white, golden yellow or straw color, the Tsatlees and Hainings usually white. The Italian silk comes in bales made up of skeins. The Broussa, or "Brutia," (Turkey) silk is a very pure white, and comes in bales.

The silk is taken first to the sorting-room, and the various sizes of thread, or, in other words, the different degrees of fineness, are assorted, each by itself. A parcel of skeins is enclosed in a light cotton bag, and soaked in water at about the temperature of 110° F. for a few hours, for the purpose of softening the gum and facilitating the process of winding. When taken out of the water, these bags are put in an open cylinder, porous on the sides, and set in a machine which is operated by steam power, and causes the cylinder to revolve with great velocity. In five or ten minutes the water is pressed out and the gum sufficiently softened to permit of easy winding. It is then wound first on a spool about 3½ inches in length. If it is Chinese silk, it is cleaned by being passed through the cleaning machine; each thread usually, but not always, passing between two sharp-edged metal plates, which remove any unevenness, leaving the filament smooth, clean and even. The Italian silk does not usually require this cleaning. The silk on the second spool is next passed to a doubling machine, where, if it is intended for tram or organzine, two or more threads are joined together, and drawn upon a third spool. If it is intended for sewing-silk or twist, four, five, six or more are doubled together. The silk in this state is put in the spinning machine, and spun a certain number of turns per inch, the twisting being looser for tram or filling than for warp or organzine. For the latter, two of these threads are doubled and spun upon a fourth spool, the twist being reversed to make the thread stronger. For filling or tram, two threads or more are twisted together somewhat less closely than in or-

SILK REEL MILL.

SILK SPINNING FRAMF.

Exhibited at Philadelphia by the Danforth Locomotive and Machine Company, of Paterson, New Jersey.

ganzine. The number of threads thus joined depends upon the fineness of the raw silk, and also upon the character of the goods to be woven; belt-ribbons, for instance, requiring a coarser shot thread than bonnet-ribbons; and some sashes and silk dress-goods requiring heavier filling than others.

When the silk is thus brought into the condition of thrown silk, tram or organzine, it is usually transferred to a reel and made up into skeins preparatory to being dyed of the desired color.

The processes of winding, cleaning, doubling, twisting, rewinding and reeling the silk, together constitute what is called throwing (from the Saxon *thrawan*, to twist). The manipulator who passes it through these various processes is called a throwster; and the silk thus treated is named according to the various purposes for which it is designed: dumb singles, thrown singles, thrown silk, trams or organzine. If intended for sewing-silk, at this stage called gum silk, it is by most of our manufacturers put upon the stretching machine elsewhere alluded to.

Our American silk manufacturers—especially those in the sewing-silk and twist trade—have long enjoyed the reputation of having improved materially on the European machinery for throwing silks; but the throwing machines built by the Danforth Locomotive & Machine Co. at Paterson, are greatly in advance of any other produced in Europe or America. These machines, of which we give engravings on another page, are adapted to either tram or organzine; they are made either two or three stories high (the third or uppermost tier economizing room, and increasing the capacity of the machine fifty per cent.), and of any length or number of spindles desired. The Company have finished one set 32 and another 37 feet long, for Paterson silk manufacturers. The former set contains 684 spindles. It is claimed that these frames are capable of producing nearly or quite double the amount of work per spindle as compared with the latest style of European frames; while, large as they are, their mechanism is so true and perfect, and runs so evenly and accurately, that they can be managed by two attendants, one on each side. They are so nicely adjusted and evenly balanced that they can be run with ease 7,000 or 8,000 revolutions per minute without the least perceptible wear. The Company sum up the points in which these machines are superior to others, as follows: They are firmer built, giving greater steadiness of spindle, and requiring less labor to keep them in running order; they have a longer drag, which gives the thread a better chance to get the desired complement of twist, thereby overcoming the kink or curl so obnoxious to silk manufacturers; they have also a perfect driving apparatus, easily adjusted, and the most improved collar and step for oiling; they can be made either for friction or positive motion; in the reel mills or reeling machines the spindles can be driven either way without cutting the bands, by simply using a cross or open belt. The very general adoption of these frames by the larger manufacturers, and the constant orders received by the Danforth works, indicate that their claims are fully justified. This Company also build ribbon looms with shuttles for weaving twenty-eight ribbons in each loom.

The adoption of such improved machinery as this, and the other inventions of ingenious manufacturers, have enabled our American silk manufacturers to hold their position in spite of the high price of labor here, by making the machines perform much of the labor which in Europe and the East is performed by hand.

The silk being ready for the dyer, is delivered to him in skeins. He first boils it in soap and water, to free it from any remaining gum, and to give it a more lustrous appearance. When dried it is next put into the dye-vats, and then there is an opportunity for deception either on the part of the dyer or the manufacturer. By the boiling process already mentioned, the silk, if pure, should lose about twenty-four per cent. of its weight, from gum, sugar, waste, &c. If it loses more, the silk has been tampered with or not properly thrown; if less, it must be of remarkably good quality or has not been boiled long enough. A pound of silk delivered to the dyer will thus, after boiling, weigh a fraction over 12 ounces. But by secrets known to his art, the dyer can so fill the interstices of the silk with dye-stuffs as to make it appear more solid, and thicker, and stronger than it naturally would be, although in fact its texture is injured. By thus weighting the silk, as the process is called, he may raise the $12\frac{1}{6}$ ounces to 16, 18, 20, 25, or even to 80 ounces. Many of the foreign dress silks are thus weighted, and while they have the appearance of heavy and valuable silks, their wearers find that they grow thinner rapidly in wearing, and very soon crack or fray from the injury done to the fabric by the dye-stuffs. By general consent, black or dark-colored silk is allowed to be weighted sufficiently to make up partly the loss by boiling. The $12\frac{1}{6}$ ounces may be made up to fourteen or perhaps sixteen without injury. Light colors do not bear so much weighting; most of them, indeed, admit of no addition from the dyes.

When dyed, the silk is wound on spools, a process requiring much skill and care, as it is now in the condition known as *soft silk*. The operatives who perform this work are a separate class known as soft-silk winders. It is now ready, either for sewing-silks, twists, passementerie and dress trimmings or fringes, or to be prepared for weaving in braids, ribbons, laces, sashes, handkerchiefs or broad goods. For each description of goods the processes differ.

For sewing-silk and twist the processes of throwing and dyeing complete the manufacture, except that for these a larger number of threads are twisted together than for tram, organzine or singles, and in twist the twisting is done in the contrary direction from that for sewing-silk. Some of the best sewings and twist are made from Italian raw silk, and the waste on this is so slight that the extra cost of the Italian (about $2.00 per pound) is nearly made up by the difference in the amount of waste. Most of the manufacturers, however, use Chinese silk, and by means of the Atwood & Holland stretching machine are able to make a silk which would otherwise be somewhat rough and knotty, as even and smooth as the best Italian. This machine stretches these uneven strands, while wet, till they become smooth and even, exerting sufficient force, in most instances, to increase slightly the length of the strands. The manufacturers who use the machine say that this amount of stretching does not impair the elasticity of the silk, and that when dry it has a uniform tension. Those who do not use it, contend that it impairs both the elasticity and strength of the goods. Both agree that raw silk of the best qualities (the Italian) does not require much, if any stretching. It is worthy of notice, however, that the greater part of the sewing-silk and twist made in this country is put upon the stretching machines. Mr. Brown, the junior of the firm of L. D. Brown & Son, sewing-silk manufacturers of Middlefown, Conn., has patented a traverse or spreader for the swift or reel used in reeling the soft silk, (that is, silk which has been dyed,) which is said greatly to facilitate the process of reeling and spooling. The Messrs. Brown are also patentees of a weighing and spooling machine, which enables them to put upon each of the large spools just an ounce of silk. Sewing-silk and twist are made of all colors, and the prices at which they can be sold vary with the amount of weighting with dye-stuffs. There is, however, a growing demand for pure silks; some of the trades will use only these, and the manufacturer who is known to weight his silks to any considerable extent, soon finds himself not burdened with a weight of customers. Tests have been invented which enable the purchaser or the conditioner to ascertain exactly how heavily the silk is charged with dye-stuffs. About two-sevenths of the whole product of manufactured silk consists of sewing-silks and twist.

XVII.

Narrow and Broad Goods.—Methods of Weaving.

THE manufacture of laces, braids, and military, upholstery and dress trimmings, is also an important department of the silk manufacture. In a few of these goods, as in cords, some of the tassels, and much of the military and upholstery trimmings, a part of the filling or some of the material is wool or cotton, usually covered with silk; but even in them, the greater part is of pure silk. The manufacturer of dress trimmings, braids, &c., buys the raw silk—usually Canton and Tsatlee—and has it thrown of different degrees of fineness, to suit his various purposes. It is also dyed in the shades of color demanded by the prevailing fashions. It is then distributed to the different departments of the manufactory, where in one place fine cords of cotton are wound with silk by an ingenious machine, and afterwards braided into a cord for trimming; in another the silk is woven into braids of different widths, some very broad, some so narrow and fine that they seem to be only a flat thread. These braids are then crimped by crimping cylinders heated by a gas flame, and subsequently woven into headings, gathered into tassels and fringes, or grouped into masses for the feathery marabout trimming. Part of the silk is made into sewing-silk of varying degrees of fineness (some of it very coarse) for fringe. Part is made into twist or gimp, from which are woven headings for fringe, often of complicated patterns wrought out on the Jacquard loom, but sometimes executed with more labor and greater expenditure of time on the old French and German looms. When the heading is woven, a net-work is attached to it by hand labor, and the fringe, of a great variety of patterns also wrought by hand, is appended to the network. Almost infinite are the varieties of fringes and trimmings thus wrought by hand, because the fashions and patterns change so often that the machinery which would produce those of to-day with greater rapidity than hand labor, is very costly, and in six or eight weeks might be entirely useless; while deft and nimble fingers, impelled by an active and intelligent brain, can adapt themselves at once to the new patterns, and though slower in motion, will in the end do more than the machines. It is the old story of the tortoise and the hare. It is, however, due to the manufacturers to say that, whenever machinery can be made to perform this work, or any part of it, for any considerable period, they are ready to avail themselves of it. Some fringes are woven on looms, and either cut apart in the middle if the fringe is to be short, or divided at the end and so made thicker and heavier, if it is to be long; but the tassel fringes —those having a distinct and bulbous head for each little bunch of fringe—are all wrought by hand; so, too, is the greater part of the marabout trimming, after the braids have been woven and crimped. Much of this trimming is very rich and costly. The larger tassels have a wood foundation, over which the silk is wound or woven, and then perhaps netted by hand, while the braided cord already mentioned is affixed to the tassel to suspend it. Sometimes the braided cord, or a cotton cord covered with silk and doubled and twisted, is used to form the tassel. This is particularly the case with upholstery trimmings. Silk buttons are partly woven and partly wrought by hand, the hand labor forming the greater part, in consequence of the almost infinite variety of the French patterns; for the goddess of fashion yet makes her headquarters in the French capital; her behests, and hers alone, are obeyed all over Christendom. Somewhat more than two-ninths of the whole silk production of the United States is devoted to these small but costly articles.

We come next to the weaving of ribbons and broad goods. There are many varieties of these, each requiring a different method of treatment. Gauze, veiling, and the thinnest silk tissues, form a class by themselves; handkerchiefs, foulards, so-called India silks, and the lighter and thinner ribbons, are also a class by themselves; and so are millinery silks, ties, scarfs, and fancy silks. Figured and embroidered ribbons and silks, brocades, &c., are woven on the improved Jacquard looms; while bonnet, belt and velvet ribbons are woven on gang-looms, weaving from six to forty pieces at the same time. Gros-grain and heavy silks, whether black or colored, are woven on power-looms, and arrangements are now making for the production, by the same means, of the highest grades of dress silks, which in Europe are always woven by hand.

We have not the space, nor is it necessary, to go into a minute description of the various looms in use for silk weaving. The old hand-loom is one of the oldest, simplest, and most widely-used pieces of machinery in the world. It was known in almost its present form to the Egyptians, Phœnicians, Persians, the Aryan tribes who first settled India, and the Chinese, more than 4,000 years ago. There is even reason to believe that it antedates the Flood. The upright posts; the different sets of heddles or harness depending from the cross-beams above, through the loops or eyes of which the threads of the warp are passed; the roller moved by a crank around which the warp is wound, and usually a second roller to receive the woven goods; the shuttle, which with its bobbin or quill carries the thread of the weft or filling; the swinging-bar; the reed which brings each thread home, or in the weaver's phrase, "beats it up," and the treadle which depresses alternately the sets of harness—these are all familiar to our readers. The figure woven depends upon the number of heddles or harness, and the arrangement of the warp; and for particular figures there may be an arrangement of special harness and a variety of shuttles. Checks or plaids may be made by the introduction of shuttles carrying different colored bobbins.

One of the preparations for weaving, whether by the hand or by the power-loom, is making the warp. If the warp is intended for a dress piece to contain five thousand threads, two hundred spools are arranged on steel wires or pins, (on which they revolve as the threads are drawn off), all of which are placed at appropriate distances in an upright frame called a creel. Opposite this, about two or three feet distant, stands the mill, a wooden frame cylinder, about seven feet high, made generally from five to ten yards in circumference. This revolves on pivots inserted above and below, and is turned by a crank at the convenience of the warper, the crank-pulley and the mill-pulley being connected by a rope band. The ends from each spool are taken and pressed through two hundred eyelets forming part of a piece of mechanism called a jack, which serves the double purpose of dividing the threads for a leise, and guiding them on to the cylinder or mill as it revolves.

The jack is affixed to an upright beam, situated between the mill and the creel, traversing from top to bottom and bottom to top, the jack being drawn up by means of a cord attached to the upper pivot and let down by the unwinding of the cord.

For a five-thousand-thread warp, and two hundred threads or spools in the creel, it is evident that twenty-five upward and downward motions of the jack are necessary before the bulk of the warp has received its full quota of threads; a leise, or equal division of the warp, being taken on each arrival of the jack at the upper, or lower part of the mill, as the warper prefers; as by means of this division of threads, a coarse string being introduced, the warp can be drawn on to a loom-roll in a straight, even way, and cleaned or picked by hand. The length of the warp is designated by the number of revolutions of the mill.

When finished, the warp is drawn from the mill and carefully balled on the hand. The ball is then taken to the picking-frame, and drawn on to a roll, and spread out in sections of 30 or 40 inches by means of a comb-like instrument called a hackle. It is next prepared to be drawn on the loom-roll by introducing rods through the warp where the strings were put in. The warp is also put through a reed which is drawn through the warp with the rods while being finally picked and wound on the second or loom-roll, and threaded through the heddle. The number of heddles varies according to the fabric woven, and they are so arranged, as to form, by depressing the treadles and alternately, the shed, through which the shuttle is to be drawn. This is the plan generally used for making organzine warps, though some of the manufacturers have introduced newly adopted labor-saving machinery for this purpose. The warp thus put upon the loom is ready for weaving whether this is performed by the hand or power-loom, and whether the weaving is to be plain, or as satin or velvet, or twilled on one side, or in figures introduced by means of the Jacquard.

Ribbons are usually woven on gang-looms, weaving from seven to twenty-eight pieces at a time. These are generally power-looms. In the practical manufacture of ribbons and broad goods in this country, the hand-loom is very little used. It is too slow in its action to be profitable, and in most descriptions of goods better results can be effected in a tithe of the time by the use of power-looms. In the adaptation of these machines to the varied needs of their several manufactures, several of the leading silk houses have shown great ingenuity and inventive skill. Messrs. Horstmann of Philadelphia have won distinction in this direction. Cheney Brothers, and some of the other large manufacturers, have also made improvements in the adaptation of the power-loom to their special purposes. The problems originally to be solved in the invention of power-looms were: to make the processes of the old hand-loom automatic, exact and rapid; to obtain tenseness in the warp; to effect its gradual unrolling and the rolling up of the woven goods; to drive the shuttle back and forth at the proper time; to beat up the tissue properly; to effect the stopping of the machinery for the substitution of a new filled bobbin when the one in the shuttle was exhausted; to accomplish ten or more times the work of the weaver within a given period. The improvements which have since been added permit the weaving of satins and velvets, and of most goods of regular figure on the power-loom. Various attempts have been made to substitute some other method of carrying the weft or filling for the shuttle. Most of them have failed, but a recent invention known as the Earnshaw Needle Loom, improved by J. H. Greenleaf, has seemed to offer a hope of success. It is in effect an adaptation of the eye-pointed needle and tiny shuttle of the sewing-machine to the loom, in carrying the filling. The so-called needle is an eye-pointed, slender rod, somewhat longer than the width of the goods to be woven. Its eye is threaded with the filling, which is fed to it from a large cop at the right of the loom (see engraving of the loom accompanying on advertising page 5), by a tension something like that of the sewing-machine. The needle rod is driven through the opening in the warp by a variable crank motion, and on the left side interlocks its thread with a fine selvedge thread carried by a small sewing-machine shuttle running in the same direction as the warp, thus producing one selvedge. The needle rod is then retracted and the changing of the warp produces the selvedge on the right edge, as usual in other looms. It is claimed for this loom, that it requires a much narrower opening of the warps, thus avoiding the straining and breaking of them which is a serious difficulty in the use of the shuttle in power-looms; that as the needle rod does not in any case touch the warp, it cannot abrade it, as the shuttle is liable to do; that the needle is fed from the cop continuously (the cop holding if necessary many thousand yards), and thus all stoppages to put in new quills or bobbins into the shuttle, and all danger of overshot places or defective and broken fillings, are avoided. By an ingenious stop-motion, invented by Mr. Greenleaf, the loom stops instantly on the breaking of a single thread. These looms are calculated for greater speed than that of the ordinary power-loom. In weaving ribbons, it is claimed that one girl can attend from six to ten of them, running at the rate of 200 to 250 picks per minute; and can thus weave from 300 to 350 yards of ribbon: while 225 yards is the largest product of the best gang-looms attended by five or six girls. In broad goods the estimated production is 35 yards per day when the power-loom weaves but 25, and the goods should be more free from breaks and flaws. By a very simple modification, the loom can carry two needles, and thus weave goods having the upper and under surface of different colors. The loom is claimed to be well adapted, not only to silk-weaving of all descriptions, but also to making elastic ribbon webs, tapes and braids of all kinds.

NOTTINGHAM LACE WORKS
S.J.COX.N.Y.
PARK AVENUE & HALL St. BROOKLYN.

XVIII.

Silk Laces and Spun Silk.

THE manufacture of silk lace, net, and fancy silk scarfs, has also been introduced into this country, and has attained a considerable magnitude. The manufacture of hair-nets is conducted by several houses, and generally not on a very large scale; but the production of guipure laces, and all the varieties of silk lace, such as is made by machinery at Nottingham, or anywhere else in Europe; of silk lace scarfs, borders and edgings, and to some extent of veils, curtain laces, &c., is in this country attempted by only two or three manufacturers, of whom the chief is A. G. Jennings, of Brooklyn. Mr. Jennings commenced the business of making hair-nets at Jersey City, in 1865 or 1866, and has since undertaken to extend his manufacture so as to include all varieties of machine lace. He removed to Brooklyn and erected the Nottingham Lace Works, at the corner of Park Avenue and Hall Street, in 1871, where he employs a large force, and produces silk laces which greatly surpass the foreign goods in quality, and are sold at a lower price. He is enabled to do this because he conducts all departments of the work on his own premises. At Nottingham, the headquarters of the English lace trade, laces are woven by small manufacturers owning but one or two looms; are then sold to the dyer, who after dyeing them sells to the large jobber, and he in turn to his English and foreign customers. Thus there are three profits to be made on the English goods before they come into the hands of the American importer and jobber. At St. Gall the manufacturing is managed in much the same way. Mr. Jennings buys his silk ready thrown of the throwster; but all the processes of making the patterns for the laces, weaving them on the lace-looms, and introducing his new designs by means of the Jacquard apparatus, dyeing, making up, finishing, and putting up all these goods for the market, is done in his manufactory. Mr. Jennings attempted to make thread lace, but the duty on the very fine threads which it was necessary to import was so heavy that the laces, though of excellent quality, could not be sold at a profit, and he has since confined his attention to silk.

He has been under the necessity of importing his lace-looms from Europe. For some years he was even obliged to send his disk-bobbins, of which he uses over a hundred thousand, to England for repair; but he has now succeeded in obtaining workmen who can repair them successfully. Lace machinery is very costly; single looms cost from $7,000 to $10,000, and the Jacquard attachment which is required for all except those which make only the plainest lace, is a heavy additional expense. The patterns for the figured laces, scarfs, &c., which are each represented by a set of cards of heavy binder's board perforated for each stitch, for the Jacquard, cost from $60 to $100 each.

No description of the lace looms, either with or without the Jacquard apparatus, would be intelligible without abundant drawings, and even with them it could only be comprehended by those who have at least a partial mechanical education. We may say, however, that the warp in these looms is vertical instead of horizontal, and not as close as in the ordinary power-loom, there being a sufficient space for the disk-bobbin and its plate to pass through. The weft, or filling, is fed from a great number of spools at the back and base of the loom (in one case we were told that 2,400 were in use at once), of different degrees of fineness, according to the design to be wrought out. The Jacquard controls the working out of the figure, taking up the necessary number of threads of the warp to accomplish this, and with a skill and delicacy utterly incomprehensible by the novice, completing the most beautiful designs. Mr. Jennings, like other silk manufacturers whom we have named, takes pains to promote the welfare of his numerous employés. A well selected library is furnished for their use. The labor is fairly paid, and not too severe or protracted.

John Marr, at 144 Centre St., New York, is believed to have been the first to attempt lace weaving successfully in this country. We have mentioned his establishment and noted his progress in a previous chapter. He has several lace machines in active operation, as well as the Jacquard attachment.

Our account of the silk manufacture would be incomplete if we failed to notice the great and growing industry in spun silk. This is the utilization of pierced cocoons which cannot be reeled, the floss and waste of silk reeling, the broken threads, &c. A fabric and thread are made from this material of great strength and durability. This is effected by boiling the silk in soap and water, thus freeing it from the gum and impurities. It is then hackled, carded and spun, very much as cotton and linen yarns are; spooled as singles, doubled, twisted and rewound, and receives different treatment according as it is to be used for sewing-silks, filling, or warp. Aside from its employment in sewing-silks, it is now used in warps in making pongees, Japanese silks, poplins, &c.; as filling with organzine warps for an excellent quality of heavy silks, which have all the beauty of the heavy tram and organzine silks, and much more durability than any of them. It is also used largely for both warp and filling of a very endurable but lustreless silk of moderate price, but which, from its serviceableness and substantial appearance, has nearly displaced the best poplins in our markets. These goods are generally known as spun silks. The great reduction in the price of raw and thrown silks, during the year 1875, brought them down to figures which admitted of their use in many cases where heretofore spun silks only could be employed, and hence has diminished to some extent the use of the spun silk. When the price of reeled silk advances again, as it certainly will, the cheaper but more durable product will unquestionably be utilized to a much greater extent. We give elsewhere a table showing the amount of production of spun silks in the different countries of Europe. It is worthy of notice that, in the early days of silk culture and manufacture in Connecticut, the farmers' wives and daughters were accustomed to card and spin the floss and waste, and weave from it, in combination with either wool or flax, a stout, durable stuff, very serviceable, but of not much beauty. Z. Storrs, in the Manual prepared by order of the Secretary of the Treasury, in 1828, estimates that in 1825 these goods were worth, in Mansfield alone, about $14,000.

XIX.

The Jacquard Weaving Attachment.

THE apparatus, known commonly as "the Jacquard loom," is not a loom, but an appendage to one; and can, indeed, be adapted to any loom. It is the invention of Joseph Marie Jacquard, born in Lyons, France, July 7, 1752. He was a weaver by trade, and in the earlier period of his life was exceedingly poor, and assisted his wife in making straw hats. It is said that his first incentive to invention was due to an offer in a newspaper of a reward for an improvement in some kind of machinery. The story is of doubtful authenticity. It is certain that he again followed his trade as a weaver after the disturbances of the French Revolution had subsided, and that a silk manufacturer of Lyons encouraged his inventive talent, and employed him to improve his machinery, with a view to substitute mechanical devices for the labor of the draw-boys in making figured goods. These boys were at that time required to keep a constrained position at their work, which usually ruined their health within a few years. The idea of his invention partially dawned upon Jacquard in 1790; but he did not complete a machine before the close of the century. In 1801 he exhibited his apparatus at the Exposition of National Industry, and obtained a bronze medal.

Soon after this, he contrived an ingenious machine for making nets. Napoleon's police had a sharp eye for smart men, and Jacquard was one day suddenly taken in charge by an officer and sent to Paris. There he was summoned before the ruler of France. Carnot, the Minister of Napoleon, appears to have been the spokesman in the interview. "Are you the man," he said to the inventor, "that has performed the impossible, in making nets, by tying a knot in a taut string?" Jacquard convinced Napoleon of his ability, and was put in charge of the machinery in the *Conservatoíre des Arts et Métiers*. It is currently reported that the loom of Vaucanson, which was among the machines and models under Jacquard's charge, suggested to him some important parts of his own invention. Vaucanson was undoubtedly a man of overflowing ingenuity, as was shown in his automatons. One of these, according to current description, though recent critics throw a doubt over the whole story, was a mechanical duck, which could waddle on a dry surface and swim in water. All its motions were surprisingly natural. It could "quack," eat and drink, and its food was digested by chemical means. As to the loom which Vaucanson invented, however, those who have examined the model are unable to perceive how it could have furnished inspiration to Jacquard. Napoleon gave Jacquard a pension of 1,000 crowns. In 1804 Jacquard returned to Lyons. There he was assailed by a mob of weavers who smashed one of his looms. Two years afterwards the Government bought his invention and made it public property.

The Jacquard apparatus is, as we have said, an appendage to a loom. It is easiest to conceive of it in two parts: (1) A box containing 100 or more wires or needles pointing outward—let us say, toward the left; (2) a hollow, prism-shaped, revolving cylinder, around and on which passes a chain of cards attached to each other by their edges, like a "Jacob's ladder." Let us deal with the box of needles or horizontal wires first. Its position is in the upper part of the loom. The object is to raise the warp threads below, in the order and number required for the passage of the shuttle, according to the pattern. These threads are attached to the lower ends of long, perpendicular wires, arranged in rows. The upper ends of these wires terminate in hooks. In order to make a distinction, let us call these hook-bearing wires, the *vertical* wires. The hooks can catch upon a series of bars; the bars are attached to a frame which is alternately raised and lowered by the proper mechanism. If the bars are all raised at the same time, and every bar while rising carries up its appropriate hook, of course all the warp threads will be elevated; but if some of the hooks are pushed aside—let us say to the right—those hooks will not catch on their respective bars, and their warp threads will not be elevated when the others are. The method of pushing the hooks aside, is this: the shanks of the hooks (*i. e.*, the vertical wires), are passed through loops in horizontal wires. Pushing the latter to the right, evidently would carry the former. The horizontal wires are kept in position in the frame or box, with their points protruding outside of it—say to the left. The other ends (right) of these horizontal wires terminate in spiral springs, which are supported against the inside of the frame or box. It follows that if one of these horizontal wires is pushed to the right, compressing its spring, a certain vertical wire will be so displaced that its hook will fail to catch the bar; but when the force pushing the horizontal wire is withdrawn, the spring will bring back both wires so that the hook can catch the bar, and the corresponding thread of the warp be raised thereby.

To the left of the box of wires is the flat-sided (usually four-sided) revolving cylinder. Each of its sides is pierced with holes corresponding in number and position with the points of the horizontal wires. The cylinder is so placed that each of its sides is brought successively against the points of the wires as it revolves. If the sides of the cylinder were alone opposed to the points, the wires would simply enter the holes, and no effect would be produced; but if some of the holes be stopped, while others are left open, the wires which touch the stopped holes will be driven back and their hooks disengaged, while the wires which enter the holes remain undisturbed, and the warp threads attached to their vertical wires are raised. This stoppage of some of the holes in each face of the revolving cylinder is effected by covering it with a card containing holes corresponding to those in the bar, but fewer in number; so that when the points of the wires come in contact with an unperforated part of the card, they are pushed to the right; but when the points enter the holes of the card, the wires are not moved, and consequently the hooks remain on their bars. By this contrivance the intended pattern is made out. If the pattern be complicated, the number of cards is very considerable. The revolving cylinder presents a new card to the points of the wires at every quarter of a revolution, the holes in the cards being so arranged as to raise in succession those threads which will make out the intended pattern, and it is necessary that there shall be as many cards as there are threads of weft in the pattern.

A portrait of Jacquard, woven in silk by the weavers of Lyons, representing him in his workshop, surrounded by his implements, and planning the construction of the apparatus which bears his name, required 24,000 cards, each card being large enough to receive 1,000 holes. The cards are fastened together in an endless chain, one complete revolution of which makes out the pattern. A picture of the establishment of W. H. Horstmann & Sons, thus woven in silk, required 900 cards; the operation of weaving was performed in fifteen minutes. The Phœnix Silk Manufacturing Co.—B. B. Tilt, President—have three "Centennial looms" in operation at the Exhibition at Philadelphia, which show the Jacquard weaving apparatus. These are called respectively, the 400, 600 and 1000 machine; the figures indicating the highest number of holes that could be punched in a card for each. Their Washington-portrait book-mark requires from 6,000 to 10,000 cards; portraits of Lincoln and Cardinal McCloskey, 4,500 cards each; portraits of the President and Vice-President, 1,500 cards.

In preparing these cards it is necessary first to make out a design, on lined paper, similar to that used for worsted-work patterns; each of the spaces enclosed between the lines represents a thread; and after the pattern is made, the holes for the cards are calculated from it by a simple process, and the holes are punched by a machine provided for the purpose. The Jacquard loom is used for all kinds of figured work on silk goods, except where the figures are small and without curved lines, when the goods can generally be woven on looms of a simpler construction.

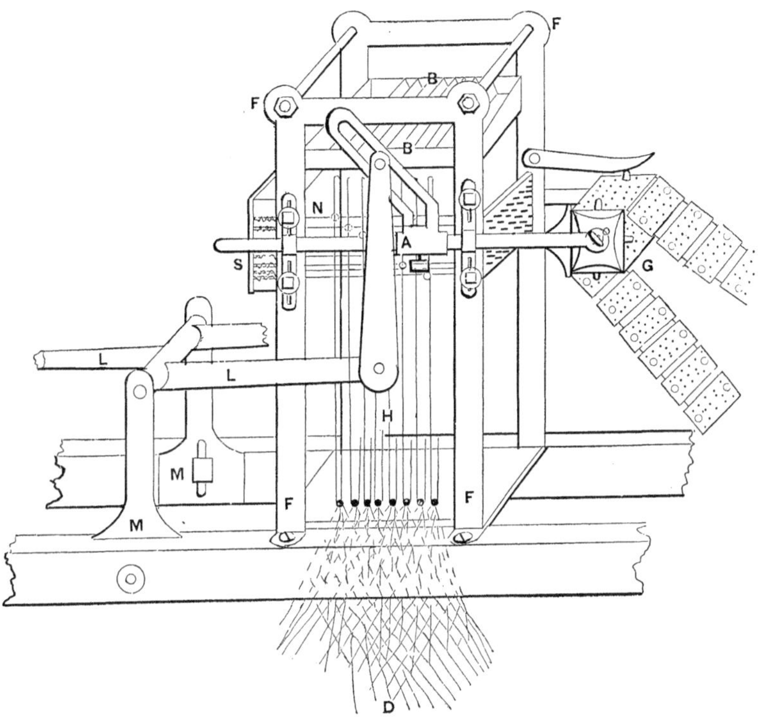

THE JACQUARD MACHINE.

F, rectangular frame, spoken of in the accompanying chapter as a "box," containing the wires of the apparatus. H, vertical wires, at each end terminating in hooks; their upper hooks being capable of catching on the bars, B. Their lower hooks hold the cords, D, which can respectively raise the warp threads. N, the horizontal wires, usually known as "needles," each having a loop through which a vertical wire passes. Spiral springs, S, are shown at one end of each horizontal wire; the other end of each passes through the side of the frame or box, F, and protrudes about half an inch, being pushed out by the spring. G, the flat-faced, revolving cylinder, held by a pin at each end. Each of its faces or sides is pierced with as many holes as there are "needles," N, in the machine. B, the bars or "blades," set within a separate frame (the "blade-frame") which can move up and down in the rectangular frame, F. There is a bar for each upper hook. L, a lever, on bearings M, M; its motion lifts the blade-frame, B, and at the same time, by a cam, A, brings the cylinder, G, to the points of the needles, N. (The drawing happens to be made from the side of the machine opposite to that described in the accompanying chapter; hence, the right hand in that description is the left in the diagram.)

W. H. Horstmann & Sons, of Philadelphia, furnish the above diagram of the Jacquard Machine with which they weave the picture in silk of Independence Hall. Specimens of this piece of weaving form part of their display at the Centennial Exhibition. The design alone involved eleven weeks' labor. The piece requires 1696 cards, and, of course, an equal number of throws of the shuttle, and of threads in the weft; 930 threads are in the warp, and of course there is the same number of bars, of hooks, of needles, and of holes in each face of the cylinder. Werner Itschner & Co., of Philadelphia, exhibit a Jacquard Loom in operation in the Women's Pavilion. Among the patterns woven by his loom is a representation of the Pavilion itself.

XX.

Paterson, the Lyons of America.

NESTLED among the foothills of the Ramapo range, and distant only twenty miles by rail from the Great Metropolis, lies the city of Paterson, which claims the title of "the Lyons of America." Here the tourist going westward by the Erie Railway has his first glimpse of the mountain scenery penetrated by that highway. Here the Passaic river, fed by innumerable rills from loftier heights beyond, plunges suddenly downward in a fall of fifty feet; then tearing its way between perpendicular cliffs that resemble the Palisades of the Hudson, it sinks twenty-two feet further, to the level of the plain. For many years before the Passaic Falls were made to turn the wheels of industry, they served to attract visitors by their picturesque beauty. Thanks to the energy and public spirit of John Ryle, the silk manufacturer, that natural beauty has been measurably preserved in a park, the free use of which he has given to the public.

Proximity to New York, the water-power of the Passaic, the facilities afforded by the Morris & Essex Canal, and at a later date by the Erie Railway—all these were causes which made Paterson a manufacturing town; but the circumstances which centered in it the silk industry were somewhat peculiar, and deserve separate mention. In bringing together the details for a sketch of the origin and growth of the silk manufacture at Paterson, it will be necessary to allude again to some of the facts, and to repeat many of the names already mentioned in this history. Perhaps too much space may thus be given to some of the earlier biographies; but while the mill-owners of the present day do an incomparably larger business, and cover far more ground with their lofty and capacious factories, than did those who first started the silk industry, it must nevertheless be admitted that the pioneers have not yet been surpassed in enterprise, and they deserve credit accordingly.

The Christopher C. that discovered a new world in New Jersey for silk manufacturers, was a son of Christopher Colt of Hartford. The father was President of the Connecticut Silk Manufacturing Co. during its existence, 1835 to 1839: he is described as magnificently furnished with nature's gifts, being exceedingly tall and of commanding presence. Like his brother Samuel Colt, the inventor of the revolving pistol, he was, though in a different way, evidently a man of mark. The senior Colt was enthusiastic on the subject of the silk industry, and his son took to it naturally. Early in 1838, Christopher Colt, Jr., became for a brief period the Agent of the Company over which his father presided. But when the misfortunes which ultimately stopped its looms, began to loom upon the Company, the junior Christopher went to Paterson, N. J.

Samuel Colt had built a large factory in Paterson for making revolvers. He offered the use of the fourth story of this factory to Christopher Colt, Jr., for a silk mill. Here, also, were at hand the power to drive machinery, and many other facilities. So the young Colt came under the roof of the older one; and thus for the first time the silk manufacture was housed in Paterson, N. J. Quite probably some of the other members of the Colt family took an interest in this new enterprise; it was currently reported to have received financial aid from Simeon Draper, of New York. Mr. Draper's firm at that period was Draper & Crumbie; he has since acquired fame as a public-spirited citizen of the Metropolis, and as a member of the firm of Haggerty, Draper & Jones, noted dry-goods auctioneers. A considerable quantity of new machinery was built for the silk mill, and eventually it was started. Its active operations, however, only lasted during three months. It cannot be said that the want of success was due to deficient experience on the part of the Colt family. Perhaps the financial support tapered off. Whatever were the causes, the result was the closing of the mill; its stock, machinery and fixtures, and its good-will, if it had any, awaited a purchaser.

John Ryle, of Macclesfield, England, had in his native town learned the arts of silk manufacture while in the employ of his older brothers, Reuben and William, who had acquired wealth and high position as silk weavers. Reports reached England of the strides that the silk industry was making in America. The *multicaulis* fever was then at its height. Doubtless the glowing hopes of our silk makers were reflected across the Atlantic, and to an English silk-weaver the Western sky was all *couleur du rose.* John Ryle packed his traps and sailed from Liverpool for New York, March 1st, 1839. He had never seen a silk-worm when he reached this country, and he was anxious to see one. A year later many people in this country were anxious never to see a silk-worm again. Mr. Ryle's first step in New York was to make inquiries of Mr. St. John, a tailoring merchant, on Broadway, with whom Samuel Whitmarsh had been in partnership previous to going to Northampton. Following Mr. St. John's directions, Mr. Ryle went to Northampton, but stopped on the way at Hartford long enough to see and talk with Mr. Colt, Senior. The shadows of adversity were even then gathering over the Connecticut Company, and its mills were not in operation. Mr. Ryle was, however, deeply impressed by the advances already made in the processes and machinery, which were described and shown to him by Mr. Colt. At Northampton Mr. Ryle found everything on the grand scale. He recognized there, as at Hartford, the fact that American methods in manufacture were, in many respects, in advance of those of the old country. But on a more careful examination he perceived that many minor economies were neglected, and he felt sure that the mills at Northampton and Florence were not making money on the goods they turned out. He had plenty of opportunity for examination during his stay, for his duties were light. The actual fact was that the manufacturing there, at that period, was carried on for a mere show. The works were overrun with visitors, and the appearance of an active business in manufacturing silk filled their minds with notions of the wealth to be derived from silk culture. In short, the mills were kept running in order to increase the sale of mulberry trees. The most important thing for himself which Mr. Ryle did in Northampton was to make the acquaintance of G. W. Murray.

During the great depression which followed the collapse of the *multicaulis* bubble, Mr. Ryle visited several silk factories in his search for employment. Months elapsed. One day, to his great joy, he met Mr. Murray on the street in New York. In the long talk over the fortunes of the silk business that ensued, Mr. Ryle suggested that when things were at their lowest, then was the time to buy; and that he had heard that the silk mill at Paterson was for sale. The upshot was that after taking Mr. Ryle's judgment in the matter, Mr. Murray bought Colt's machinery as it stood in the fourth story of the pistol factory, for $3,200. He put Mr. Ryle in charge under a contract for three years' employ. That was the foundation of successful silk manufacture in Paterson, which was then a village of 7,000 inhabitants.

At the expiration of the three-year contract, a partnership was formed, the firm being Murray & Ryle. Three years later, in 1846, Mr. Ryle was assisted by his brothers in England, to buy out Mr. Murray's interest. Up to this period Mr. Ryle had not attempted weaving broad goods, but as soon as he became sole owner of the establishment he proceeded to carry out this darling idea. He set a few looms at work and produced several pieces of dress silk of a thousand yards' length. In 1847 he still further expanded his facilities by purchasing the building that contained his machinery. To complete his knowledge of silk manufacture, he went to Europe in 1850, and visited the principal factories of France and Italy.

For nearly twelve years from its foundation, the silk mill of Mr. Ryle had no rival in Paterson. His first competitor in the business—John C. Benson, a cotton manufacturer—then built a small silk mill on Bridge Street. For three years afterward that was the only competitor. A fair specimen of the capacity of Mr. Ryle's establishment, at this period, was the manufacture of the large flag which waved over the Crystal Palace during the Exhibition usually called "the World's Fair," at New York, in 1852. About this time, he purchased the romantic heights bordering Passaic Falls. He conceived the idea of making this charming spot a public park, free to all comers—a breathing-place where the working-people of Paterson could come and enjoy themselves. To this end, in the following years, he expended large sums of money in adorning the place with bridges and other structures, and laying out suitable walks and drives. Popularity came with prosperity, and the citizens of Paterson made him their mayor. In 1854 he built the Murray Mill, covering 15,000 square feet with a two-story building, which was then one of the largest, and perhaps most thoroughly equipped of the silk factories in America. His oldest brother, who had retired from business in Macclesfield, came over to see him. Mr. Ryle, of course, took his visitor to the Park, showed him the improvements, pointed out the manufacturing establishments, the growing city, the fertile plain below. Then calling his attention to a hill where he proposed building a mansion, he urged his brother to bring his family from England and settle there. To clinch matters, John Ryle offered to build the new home and present it to his brother. The reply was short and decisive:

"John, I would not come here to live if you would give me the whole State of New Jersey!"

The reply may serve to contrast English conservatism with American enterprise. Nearly all of the men who have since 1860 made Paterson the centre of the silk industry, came there from other localities, and most of them came "to live." The few who preceded that date were, however, exceptions to one or the other of these generalizations.

Taken in the order of their starting in Paterson, the first of the great rivals with whom Mr. Ryle's establishment had afterwards to compete, started business on a small scale in 1854, as the firm of Hamil & Booth. They began as throwsters, having been brought up to the trade. At first they had only twenty operatives. This firm felt their way slowly and cautiously to success, only increasing their facilities and enlarging their operations as circumstances strictly warranted. For fourteen or fifteen years they continued to be exclusively throwsters. We shall have further occasion to speak of the products of their establishment, the Passaic Silk Works, at a later period. Stelle & Walthall, in 1856, were the next to invade the domain. L. R. Stelle had been the editor of a newspaper, and was perhaps a convert to the many "articles" he had read upon the silk industry. In 1858, his name figures as the Secretary of the Silk Industry Association; John Ryle was its President. The Association was not intended to carry on business; its chief object was simply to hold meetings for the interchange of views. There are few records of its activity until it was reorganized in 1872. The firms of Stelle & Walthall and L. R. Stelle & Sons have always confined themselves to the business of "throwing" silks. The removal of this establishment to Sauquoit, near Utica, N. Y., has been referred to in a previous chapter. The next of silk manufacturers to try the capacities of Paterson, was C. L. Bottum, of Mansfield, Conn. His stay was brief. A change of partnership induced him, after a short experience of New Jersey, to return to Connecticut. Meanwhile John Ryle's business had largely expanded. He was employing in 1857-8 from 400 to 500 operatives, and his manufacture consumed 2,000 pounds of raw silk per week—an amount of business at that time unprecedented in the history of a silk mill in America. Again, in 1859-60, he attempted to produce dress silks; but the prospect of war checked this enterprise, since a period of depression in affairs preceded the outbreak of hostilities.

Certain important facts in the history of Paterson's silk industry should here be noted. (1) The weaving of dress silks was not successful as a business during the whole period prior to the Tariff Act of 1861, though the broad goods occasionally made were quite satisfactory in appearance, texture and quality. (2) Under the low tariff there was no competition in silk manufacture at Paterson for nearly twelve years;

and when, under the tariff, competition did begin, it was very limited in character and extent. (3) Under the tariff of 1861, as we shall proceed to show, Paterson became the centre of a great silk industry, in which many prominent concerns engaged, and large amounts of capital were invested. The competition became exceedingly active and strenuous. The manufacture included a wide variety of goods, some of which had never been made in this country before; and the weaving of broad goods and fancy silks was fairly established.

These facts are the more remarkable when we consider the circumstances. Paterson had been favored from the first with abundant water-power, proximity to a great commercial port, and excellent facilities for transportation. As to the first of these elements of attractiveness, it may be admitted that great power is not required for a silk mill, and that steam is almost as economical as water for driving light machinery. But water itself, in large quantities, and of fair purity, is absolutely required in the processes of silk manufacture, especially in cleansing the silk by repeated washings to bring out its natural lustre. Paterson could from the first supply pure water abundantly. More important than anything else, however, was cheap labor. Without this, the other advantages would have been of small account. Paterson had at an early period drawn together a laboring population. The men were employed in machine-shops and on heavy work. Their wives and children needed employment; and although this was afforded by the cotton mills, the operatives objected to it as being too confining and hard. The silk mill afforded a welcome relief. Its work called for care and dexterity instead of severe and protracted effort; and was cleanly and wholesome. The girls and young women of Paterson thought it an honor, or at all events an evidence of respectability, to be employed in the silk mill. As a consequence, Paterson offered that greatest desideratum of the silk-maker, cheap labor. Yet under a low tariff, few manufacturers came thither. Under that of 1861, they not only came; they crowded in. By their own competition they raised the price of labor, and moreover, its price was also raised by the factitious values of the war. Nevertheless, they still drop in (a few did in 1875-6) and settle at Paterson; and bringing with them capital and experience, help to keep its inhabitants busy and make it a prosperous city.

The first of the great drops before a thunder-shower was the Phœnix Silk Manufacturing Company. Brief details of the career of its President, B. B. Tilt, have been given on previous pages. It may here be mentioned that the Phœnix Manufacturing Company was, previous to the war, a large corporation, owning the Phœnix Mill, and engaged in cotton manufacture. The war cut off the supply of cotton. Mr. Tilt, after having become a prominent stockholder, re-organized the concern, and changed its business to silk manufacture. The new Company rapidly rose to importance. Ultimately its Jacquard weaving obtained greater prominence than that of any other establishment in Paterson; the general range of its manufacture including fancy silks, handkerchiefs, gentlemen's scarfs, etc. Of late, however, it has been overtaken by misfortune; and in March, 1876, temporarily succumbed.

The year 1864 was signalized by the formation of the Dale Manufacturing Company, and the commencement of building the Dale Silk Mills,—a vast structure, which cost a half million of dollars. Thomas N. Dale, the President of this Company, has been closely identified with all the later progressive movements in Paterson that have for their object the welfare of the operatives. He has a fine library in the mill, with deadened walls, so that the noise of the surrounding machinery cannot penetrate. Here too are paintings by members of his family, and a fine mineral collection, gathered by his eldest son, T. Nelson Dale, Jr., who now superintends the practical details of manufacture. The senior Mr. Dale is First Vice-President of the Silk Association of America. There has been hardly any limit to the variety of silk manufacture which Mr. Dale's Company has undertaken.

In 1864, also, the firm of J. H. Booth & Co. began manufacturing tram and organzine, at Paterson. Three new concerns were established there in 1866; Dunlop & Malcom building a mill for making machine-twist and sewing-silk, and

The Dale Silk Mill, Paterson, New Jersey.

Dye Works of Weidmann & Greppo, Paterson, N. J.

John D. Cutter hiring premises for the same purpose, over the machine shops of the Grant Locomotive Works. The same year also Mr. Greppo started his dyeing establishment at Paterson. It is not intended to repeat here the details elsewhere given in this history, and hence, in many instances, there can be given nothing more than date and name. It should be mentioned, however, with regard to the dyeing business, that Mr. O'Neal was the first to open a dye-house at Paterson, at which goods were received on commission. He had been carrying on this business in New York City, and moved to Paterson, to meet the wants of his largest customers. Most of the silk mills, prior to this date, performed their dyeing on their own premises, and several of them still continue to.

The next year (1867) another of the large silk manufacturers entered upon the field; the firm of Dexter, Lambert & Co. transferred their enterprise from Boston to Paterson, and built a large mill to accommodate their business, which began with ladies' dress trimmings and ribbons, and has since been developed in all sorts of fancy silks, Jacquard weaving, handkerchiefs, etc. In the year following, Wm. Strange & Co. left Williamsburg, N. Y., and started a ribbon factory at Paterson. They are now running the Greppo Mill and the Velvet Mill. They have always done their own "throwing." Ribbons of all kinds (and of excellent quality) have from the first been their specialty; but of late they too have been making fancy goods, silk handkerchiefs, etc. They employ 700 operatives. Mr. Strange is Vice-President of the Paterson Board of Trade, and enjoys deserved popularity as an active citizen of Paterson. In the Silk Association of America, Mr. Strange is Chairman of the Committees on Statistics and Revenue Laws; in this capacity rendering valuable service to the Association and to the silk manufacture in general.

Paterson attracted Frederick Baare in 1871, from Schoharie, N. Y., where he had a very successful mill, weaving all kinds of broad silks, ribbons and galloons. His establishment at Paterson is the Baare Silk Manufacturing Company. His personal earnestness and energy have already procured for him a marked influence in his new locality. Mr. Hamil (of the firm of Hamil & Booth), in the same year (1871), bought another mill which had previously been used for making cotton goods. This is known as the Hamil Mill, and it considerably enlarged the firm's facilities for silk manufacture. The Silk Industry Association of Paterson, N. J., was reorganized in the following year, with Robert Hamil, President, and J. P. McKay, Secretary. The other officers and board have been named in a previous chapter. Mr. McKay is a manufacturer of dress, plain and fancy silks. Benjamin Salter, one of the Managers, was at that time in partnership with John D. Cutter, making buttonhole twist. Pelgram & Meyer's factory was established at Paterson at this time. They began with ribbon manufacture, but more recently advanced to broad silk and Jacquard weaving, and also do their own "throwing."

A. Soleliac & Sons, of New York City, selected Paterson, in 1873, as the best place for establishing a ribbon manufacture. They occupy the second floor and part of the third in the Dale Mill. Gros-grain and colored dress silks have more recently been woven by this concern. Mr. Soleliac is an importer of many years' standing; has been connected with silk manufacture in Lyons, France; conducted a ribbon-weaving establishment in New York for four years before his removal to Paterson; and is well informed respecting foreign goods. He is a valuable member of the Revenue Laws Committee in the Silk Association of America.

But this chapter is already too long, and the more recent arrivals in Paterson can scarcely have room for more than the mention of their names; and quite probably some may unintentionally be omitted. Among the larger recent establishments are the braiding works and throwing mill of Louis Franke, where ladies' dress trimmings—very fine goods—are made. Morlot & Stettheimer began as dyers, but are now also engaged in ribbon weaving. S. M. Meyenberg makes a specialty of hair nets; Stephen Lum, of ribbons; Grimshaw Brothers, of millinery and tie silks; Joseph Fletcher, of twilled silks; C. B. Auer & Co., millinery and ties; the Day Manufacturing Co., fancy silks. The Manhattan Loom Co., organ-

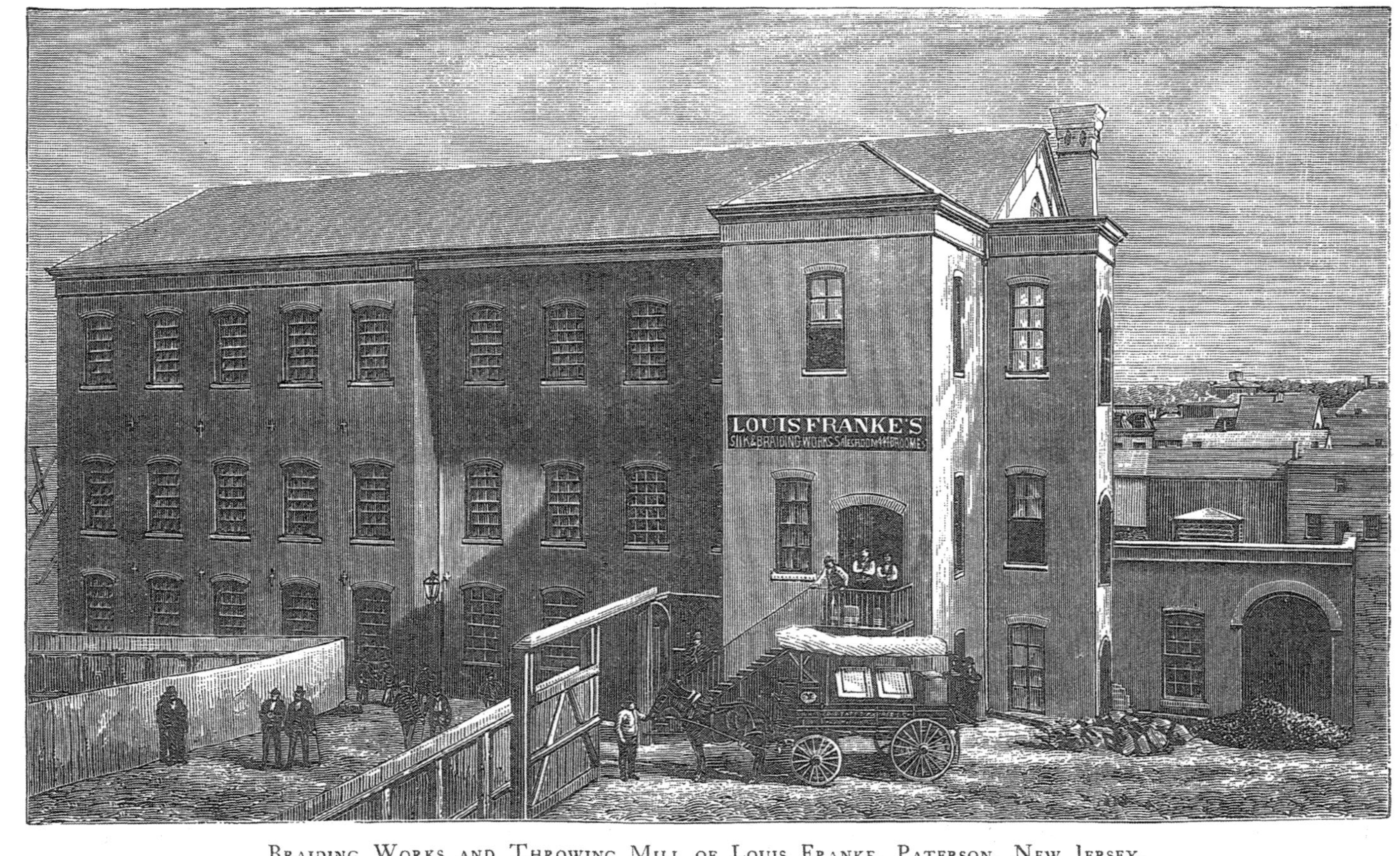

Braiding Works and Throwing Mill of Louis Franke, Paterson, New Jersey.

ized by John Burns & Co. of New York, make ribbons and fancy silks; P. & I. Bannagan are throwsters, but they also make tie silks and handkerchiefs. J. Jackson Scott and See & Shean, with Morlot & Stettheimer and Weidmann & Greppo already mentioned, complete the list of dyers, there being four in all. A much longer list of manufacturers could be made by including the numerous instances in and around Paterson, where a so-called master-weaver who has previously been a journeyman weaver, has two or three looms in his house. Within the past year the number of this class of weavers has been largely increased by immigration from France and England. They bring their looms with them.

Noteworthy changes in the whole character of the silk industry have taken place since Paterson became its centre. Among these are the profitable manufacture of broad goods by firms after repeated trials, the earlier efforts having been unfortunate; the successes of John Ryle & Sons in 1872, and Hamil & Booth in 1873 after unavailing efforts in 1868–70, may be cited. Similar facts could probably be assumed with correctness as to nearly all the others who have been mentioned as manufacturing dress goods. The increase of the number of firms engaged in weaving silk is partly owing to the demands of fashion, and partly to the circumstance that the concerns that once confined themselves to the throwster's business, have nearly all been obliged to begin weaving or retire from silk manufacture; a result following upon the practice adopted by the weavers of doing their own throwing. Hamil & Booth offer a conspicuous example of a throwster's firm undertaking weaving from this cause. The last-named firm sell their own goods: but many of the manufacturers of Paterson have yielded to the persuasion of the foreign importing houses in New York, and consign their goods for sale, making the New York houses their sole agents. Weaving, as distinguished from the other branches, is characteristic of the industry in New Jersey, as sewing-silk and machine-twist are of the manufacture in New England; and only two concerns,—those of John Dunlop and John D. Cutter—continue in Paterson to make a specialty of sewings and twist.

The following are the statistics of the silk industry in Paterson at the close of the year 1875, as compiled from the records of the Silk Association of America:

Classes of goods and manufature: Gum silks, tram, organzine, fringe silks, sewing-silks, machine-twist, dyeing, weaving, ribbons, dress and fancy silks, scarfs, handkerchiefs, veils and veiling, ladies' dress trimmings, braids and bindings, upholstery trimmings, &c.

Number of firms and corporations engaged in the silk manufacture. - - - - - - - - - -	32
Dyeing establishments, in addition to private dye-houses of manufacturers (this number was reduced to 4 in 1876), -	5
Number of operatives, - - - - - - -	nearly 8,000
Proportion of female operatives, - - - - -	two-thirds.
Proportion of operatives under 16 years of age, - -	one-fourth.
Amount of wages paid during the year, - - - -	$2,664,993
Amount of capital employed and invested in mills, machinery, and manufacturing - - - - - - -	$5,926,804
Number of throwing-spindles, - - - - - - -	74,323
Number of power-looms, - - - - - -	730
Number of hand looms, - - - - - - - -	563
Number of braiding spindles, - - - - -	23,445
Number of pounds of silk dyed, - - - - -	550,000

XXI.

Awards to Silk Exhibitors.

THE Silk Manufacture has, at frequent intervals, called forth expressions of approval and awards of merit to exhibitors at the more important public displays of American industry. The following is an incomplete list of these awards, etc., at some of the more prominent exhibitions:

1830: M. d'Homergue exhibited at the Fair of the Franklin Institute, Philadelphia, two banners, each 12 feet long and 6 feet wide, made of Pennsylvania silk; and a few other woven articles.

1841, '42 and '43: William H. Jones, of North Manchester, Conn., received premiums and medals from the American Institute, of New York, and the Hartford County Agricultural Fair, for sewing silk of fine lustre, wound on a reel of his own invention, from cocoons which he had raised. The specimen of sewing-silk exhibited in 1842 by A. B. and W. H. Jones, of Manchester, Conn., at the Fair of the American Institute, was considered the best, and received the first premium.

1841: Awards by the American Institute of New York:

John McRae, New York; manufactured silk, (shawls, cord and braid)—best; silver medal.

B. S. Yates, New York; silk handkerchiefs, silk for dresses, cords and tassels; silver medal.

Mathias Price, Newark, N. J.; floss silk, cleansed silk, and spun silk hose; diploma.

1842: Awards by the American Institute of New York:

Edmund Golding, Mansfield Centre, Conn.; specimen of sewing-silk; second premium.

Auburn State Prison; specimens of sewing silk, twist, etc., made entirely of American silk; worthy of notice.

John Ryle, Paterson, N. J.; specimens of ball twist, sewing-silk and floss, of good manufacture; entitled to a premium.

William B. Frink; specimens of sewing-silk, made entirely by a hand-wheel; worthy of notice.

State Prison, Mount Pleasant, N. Y.; 36 yards black silk—well made; entitled to a premium.

John McRae, New York; cords, gimps and bindings—brought to great perfection; silver medal previously awarded; diploma.

Wakefield Mills, Germantown, Penn.; silk shirts and drawers, made of imported silk; deserving of notice.

Peter Gruet, Orange, N. J.; specimens of bonnet wire—best exhibited; deserving a premium.

1843: Awards by the American Institute of New York:

Northampton Association of Education and Industry; raw silk; diploma. Sewing-silk—second best; diploma.

William Hayden, New York; silk dyeing; diploma.

New England Silk Company, Dedham, Mass.; black and colored sewing-silk—best; silver medal.

Haskell & Hayden, Windsor Locks, Conn.; spool sewing-silk, colored—superior; a gold medal previously awarded; diploma.

John W. Gill, Mount Pleasant, O.; silk goods—the greatest variety; gold medal.

Timothy Smith, Amherst, Mass.; a piece of plain, drab silk—"the best piece of silk in the fair"; silver medal.

Murray & Ryle, Paterson, N. J.; ladies' and gentlemen's cravats and twilled silk handkerchiefs; gold medal.

John Denmead, New York; silk gimps, wire and coat bindings; silver medal.

Mrs. Mary Beach, Newark, N. J.; a pair of white silk hose; diploma.

1845: Awards by the American Institute of New York:

John W. Gill, Mount Pleasant, Ohio; silk goods—best; $50 and the Van Schaick medal.*

William Hayden, New York; sewing-silk—best; superior dyeing; silver medal.

Miss Gertrude Rapp, Economy, Penn.; white silk pocket handkerchiefs—best; silver medal.

Jeffrey Hutchinson, Riverhead, L. I.; sewing-silk, of very pure color; second premium.

A. L. Jones, Manchester, Conn.; sewing-silks; diploma.

Miss Ann Lecraft Manny, Beaufort, N. C.; heavy sewing-silk; diploma.

S. & S. Halstead, New York; silk coat-cord—superior; diploma.

---

*Myndert Van Schaick, a merchant of New York, on the 16th of July, 1844, addressed a letter to the American Institute, in which he dwelt upon the advantages to be derived from the silk industry, and in order to promote it, agreed to give the Institute $100 a year for ten years, to be distributed in annual premiums for the best piece of silk stuff manufactured of native silk in each year.

1846: Awards by the American Institute of New York:

COMBIER DESCHAUX, New York; silk dyeing—best; silver medal.

WILLIAM HAYDEN, New York, silk dyeing—second best; diploma.

Mrs. CAROLINE SWARTZ, New York; silk dyeing; diploma.

MURRAY & RYLE, Paterson, N. J.; colored sewing-silk and silk twist—best, and silk handkerchiefs; gold medal.

VALENTINE & SOWERBY, Northampton, Mass.; sewing-silk—second best; silver medal.

HASKELL & HAYDEN, Windsor Locks, Conn.; spool silk; silver medal.

JOHN FOX, Wheeling, Va.; manufactured silk; silver medal.

JOHN W. GILL, Wheeling, Va.; black satin, black striped velvet and grey lavender twilled handkerchiefs; silver medal.

PETER GRUET, Orange, N. J.; silk wire—best; silver medal.

J. S. PIERCE, Burlington, Vt.; silk vest patterns; diploma.

HARTFORD KNITTING Co., New York; silk knit shirts; silver medal.

G. W. SHARP, New York; printing on silk handkerchiefs; diploma.

1847: Awards by the American Institute of New York:

Mrs. JOHN S. PIERCE, Burlington, Vt.; piece of silk for dresses, (60 yards in length,)—best; Van Schaick premium, $50, and bronze medal.

J. W. GILL, Wheeling, Va.; piece of black silk; Van Schaick premium, $30, and a bronze medal.

JOHN FOX, Sen., Wheeling, Va.; silk velvet; Van Schaick premium, $20, and bronze medal.

JAMES MILWARD, New York; satin—best; silver medal.

CHARLES BANFIELD, Wheeling, Va.; satin—second best; diploma.

COURT & DESCHAUX, New York; silk dyeing—best; silver medal.

W. FISHER, HEYDEN & Co., New York; silk dyeing—second best; diploma.

NORTHAMPTON SILK Co.; sewing-silk—best; Van Schaick premium, $10, and bronze medal.

NATHAN RIXFORD, Mansfield, Conn.; sewing-silk—second best; silver medal.

1848: Awards by the American Institute of New York:

S. O. LOOMIS, Windsor, Conn.; sewing-silk—best; silver medal.

ATWOOD & RUSS, Mansfield, Conn.; sewing-silk—second best; diploma.

THOMAS RYLE, Paterson, N. J.; sewing-silk on spools; diploma.

NEW YORK DYEING AND PRINTING ESTABLISHMENT, New York; silk twist—best; silver medal.

COURT & DESCHAUX, New York; silk dyeing—best; silver medal.

Miss HARRIET SUMMY, Lancaster County, Penn.; sewing-silk, superior; diploma.

JAMES MILLWARD, New York; piece of satin; (silver medal having before been awarded,) diploma.

1849: Awards by the American Institute of New York:

J. W. GILL, Wheeling, Va.; piece of silk, 27 inches wide and 60 yards in length—best; Van Schaick premium, $60, and bronze medal.

J. W. GILL, Wheeling, Va.; silk for handkerchiefs, 25 yards in length—best; Van Schaick premium, $20, and bronze medal.

JAMES MILLWARD, New York; pieces of satin; silver medal.

JOHN FOX, Sen., Wheeling, Va.; plaid silk velvets—best; Van Schaick premium, $10, and bronze medal.

JULIUS HOVEY, Mansfield, Conn.; sewing-silk, 12 lbs.—best; silver medal.

TURNER & GURLEY, New York, sewing-silk—superior; silver medal.

CLEVELAND & Co., New York, colored and spooled silk; diploma.

C. B. HATCH, New York; oiled silk; diploma.

C. COURT, New York; silk dyeing (silver medal having been before awarded); diploma.

HERMAN SCHWIETERING, New York; silk button coverings; diploma.

1850: Awards by the American Institute of New York:

WILMER, CANNELL & Co., Philadelphia; printed silk handerchiefs—best; silver medal.

CRABTREE & WILKINSON, Staten Island; printed silk handkerchiefs—second best; diploma.

R. RENNIE, Lodi, N. J.; printed foulard silk; silver medal.

JAMES MILLWARD, New York; silk shawls; gold medal.

E. R. GURLEY, Mansfield, Conn.; silk twist; silver medal.

CHENEY BROS., Manchester, Conn.; E. H. Arnold, Agent, 34 Beaver Street, N. Y.; sewing-silk; diploma.

DUNCAN MCFARLANE, New York; 14 pieces of silk ribbon; Van Schaick premium, $10, and bronze medal.

1851: Awards by the American Institute of New York:

F. S. DUMONT, Paterson, N. J,; silk plush—best; silver medal.

HASKELL & HAYDEN, Windsor Locks, Conn.; sewing-silk—best; silver medal.

T. EULER, 59 Robinson Street, New York; specimen of watering on silk; silver medal.

1852: Awards by the American Institute of New York:

JOHN RYLE, Paterson, N. J.; sewing-silk—best; silver medal.

JOHN RYLE, Paterson, N. J.; printed silk handkerchiefs—best; silver medal.

SHEPHERD & HOWE, New York; printed silk handkerchief, second premium; diploma.

NEWPORT SILK MANUFACTURING Co., Newport, Ky.; superior silk vestings; silver medal.

1852: Award by Franklin Institute, Philadelphia:

WM. H. HORSTMANN & SONS, Philadelphia; fancy taffeta bonnet ribbons; gold medal, highest reward of Institute, in consideration of extraordinary merit.

1853: Awards by the American Institute of New York:

J. NEWSTAEDTER, New York; silk brocade; gold medal.

E. J. JENKINS, New York; printing on pongee handkerchiefs; diploma.

1855: Awards by the American Institute of New York:

C. W. CROSLEY, New York; upholstery, cords and tassels; silver medal.

NEWPORT SILK FACTORY, Newport, Ky.; silk fabrics; silver medal.

BAY STATE MILLS, Lawrence, Mass.; richly embroidered silk shawls; silver medal.

M. HEMINWAY & SON, Watertown, Conn.; sewing-silk on spool, and embroidery silk—best; silver medal.

EXCELSIOR SILK AND TWIST Co., Mansfield Centre, Conn.; silk twist for machine use, and colored sewing-silk—best; silver medal.

1856: Awards by the American Institute, of New York:

M. HEMINWAY & SON, Watertown, Conn.; best sewing-silk—(a silver medal having been before awarded); diploma.

CLEVELAND & Co., New York; sewing-silk—second best; bronze medal.

1857: Awards by the American Institute, of New York:

M. HEMINWAY & SONS, Watertown, Conn.; sewing-silks, tailors' twist and sewings on spools, sewing machine twist, embroidery, and knitting silk; large silver medal.

1863: Awards by the American Institute, of New York:

M. HEMINWAY & SONS, Watertown, Conn.; sewing-silk (a silver medal having been before awarded); diploma.

JOHN TURNER, Norwich, Conn.; fishing lines, satin finish, fancy twines and machine-made picture cord; bronze medal.

1867: Awards by the American Institute, of New York:

CHENEY BROS., Hartford, Conn.; silk goods—best; medal and diploma.

DUNCAN MACFARLANE, New York; silk shawl—second best; medal and diploma.

J. H. & G. HOLLAND, Willimantic, Conn.; sewing-machine twist—third best; medal and diploma

1869: Awards by the American Institute of New York:

NONOTUCK SILK CO., Florence, Mass.; bleached and colored sewing-silk, machine twist and sewing in the gum—best; medal and diploma.

EXCELSIOR MANUFACTURING COMPANY, New York; sewing-silk in the skein and on spools, and machine-twist—best; medal and diploma.

P. G. GIVERNAUD, Hoboken, N. J.; plain black and colored silk dress goods—best; medal and diploma.

CHENEY BROS., Hartford, Conn.; fancy striped silk, and silk and worsted poplins—best; medal and diploma.

DALE MANUFACTURING CO., Paterson, N. J.; silk serges, scarfs and braids—best; medal and diploma.

WM. H. HORSTMANN & SONS, Philadelphia; silk, silk and cotton trimmings, fringes, tassels and navy belts—best; medal and diploma.

HAMIL & BOOTH, Paterson, N. J.; organzines twisted in the gum. machine-twist and embroidery silks—best; medal and diploma.

ONEIDA COMMUNTY, Oneida, N. Y.; ribbons and machine-twist—best; medal and diploma.

GEORGE COMINGS, New York; mohair and silk tassels and silk trimmings—best; medal and diploma.

BERNSTEIN & MACK, New York; silk chenille—second best; medal and diploma.

JAMES S. SHAPTER, Paterson, N. J.; silk serges, black satin, cotton filling, dress silks, reps, etc.—second best; medal and diploma.

FREDERICK BAARE, Schoharie, N. Y.; silk and wool poplins—second best; medal and diploma.

W. G. WATSON & SON, Paterson, N. J.; black and colored sewing-silk, machine-twist, etc., canton in gum, black and colored—second best; medal and diploma.

WERNER ITSCHNER & CO., Philadelphia; fancy striped silk ribbons and black silk cravat—second best; medal and diploma.

CANTRELL & CHAPIN, Cresskill, N. J.; machine twist—second best; medal and diploma.

NOTTINGHAM MANUFACTURING COMPANY, A. G. Jennings, Agent, New York; silk webbings, crochet, webbing, silks, hand nets, silk lace and silk buttons—second best; medal and diploma.

O. W. CROSBY, New York; silk fringes—second best; medal and diploma.

1870: Awards by the American Institute of New York:

HEMINWAY & SONS' SILK CO., New York; sewing-silk and twist; first premium.

CHENEY BROTHERS, Hartford, Conn.; silk goods; first premium.

BACHMANN BROS., New York; silk dyers' goods; first premium.

NOTTINGHAM LACE WORKS, New York; silk lace hair nets; honorable mention.

1870 and 1872: Awards of the Cincinnati Industrial Exposition:

BELDING BROTHERS & Co., Rockville, Conn.; sewing-silks; prize medal.

1872, '74 and '75: St. Louis Exhibition:

BELDING BROTHERS & Co.; same as above.

1873: Awards by the American Institute of New York:

SINGER MANUFACTURING Co., New York; machine twist; diploma.

BRAINERD, ARMSTRONG & Co., New York; machine twist and sewing-silk; diploma.

JOHN N. STEARNS & Co., New York; silks; bronze medal.

NONOTUCK SILK Co., Florence, Mass.; machine twist and sewing-silk; bronze medal.

PHŒNIX SILK MANUFACTURING Co., Paterson, N. J.; fancy silk goods—best, and ribbons; silver medal.

CHENEY BROTHERS, Hartford, Conn.; silk—best samples; silver medal.

A. G. JENNINGS, New York; lace and silk goods—best; silver medal.

JOSEPH NEUMANN, San Francisco, Cal.; silk cocoons, raw silk and flags—best; silver medal.

ONEIDA COMMUNITY, Oneida, N. Y.; machine for measuring and testing spool silk—best; silver medal.

1874: Maryland Institute for the Promotion of the Mechanic Arts:

BELDING BROTHERS & Co., Rockville, Conn.; sewing-machine twist; prize medal.

1874: Franklin Institute of the State of Pennsylvania

BELDING BROTHERS & Co.; same as above.

AUB, HACKENBURG & Co., Philadelphia; machine-twist and sewing-silk; prize medal.

XXII.

The Present and the Future.

THE Centennial year of our national existence finds us, even in a time of financial depression, manufacturing not less than one-half of all the silk goods used in our country, and furnishing them to our people at a price, if the quality of the goods be taken into consideration, below that which ruled when the silks of England, France and Italy were admitted into our ports nearly free of duty. The processes already invented, and in practice, enable us to produce better fabrics than have been offered here before. In this case at least, the imposition of the duty of 60 per cent. has not enhanced the price of goods. Nor, on the other hand, has the high rate of duty so far diminished importation as to reduce the Government's revenue. The duties collected on manufactured silk goods in the whole period from 1843 to 1875, amounted to over $275,000,000; but $150,000,000—more than half of it—was paid within the last ten years. The fact becomes even plainer if the average annual revenue under different tariffs be considered. Thus from 1843 to 1856, with a duty of 30 and 25 per cent., the average annual revenue was about five million dollars; from 1857 to 1864, with duties ranging from 24 to 40 per cent., the average was about five and a half millions; but from 1865 to 1875, with a duty of 60 and 50 per cent., the average revenue rose to fourteen and a half million dollars. Meanwhile, vigorous competition, both at home and abroad, has greatly cheapened domestic production, and substituted in many of the processes machine-labor for hand-labor; the result being a great improvement in American goods as well as a marked reduction of their prices.

This great advantage has been gained also, in the very field where Great Britain has almost completely failed. With an established manufacture of great extent, reaching back nearly two centuries; with highly skilled workmen, abundant capital, and a nearer market than we have in which to purchase her raw material, (as from climatic causes the silk culture had been a failure,) she was obliged to abandon her manufactures of silk, except in the production of spun silk, hosiery, silk laces, and some descriptions of ribbons, as soon as the silks of France and Italy were admitted duty free. Twenty years ago, our supply of dress silks, ribbons, silk laces, shawls, &c., was drawn in about equal quantities from England and France. To-day, beyond a few fancy goods (like silk lace, hosiery, ribbons, and mixed goods of silk and linen, silk and cotton, and silk and wool, mainly of spun silk), we buy no silks from Great Britain. The duties on manufactured silks which were abrogated by the Cobden treaty, were not very heavy, few of them exceeding thirty per cent.; but they were sufficient to prevent the ruinous competition which resulted in the substantial overthrow of the business throughout Great Britain, the closing of the mills at Macclesfield and Manchester, and the beggaring of the owners and thousands and tens of thousands of skilled and worthy workmen. To-day the spindles of some of these mills, purchased at a mere nominal price, are running in American silk mills.

This great failure of the silk manufacture in Great Britain should teach a lesson, perhaps more than one. Our manufacturers are working under a tariff of 60 per centum ad valorem on most silk goods. This duty does not enhance the price of silk goods; for, as we have already said, dress silks, ribbons and sewing-silks were never so low as now, from the strong competition at home; but it does keep off to some extent, the crushing rivalry of foreign manufacturers, who would be willing to make great sacrifices for a time in order to break down American manufacturers, in the hope of gaining ere long a complete monopoly of the trade. If the sudden onset upon British manufacturers ruined them, with their large capital and established trade, how should our manufacturers fare if similarly exposed—who have not yet arrived at adolescence in this manufacture; whose capital is comparatively limited, and who labor under the disadvantage of having to procure their raw material from other countries, and of paying higher wages than are paid in England or on the Continent?

There is, happily, no immediate danger of any serious effort to reduce the duties on manufactured silks. It is fortunate that silk goods are a luxury; a luxury which will better bear a portion of the burden of taxation when a country finds a large revenue a necessity, than the necessaries of life; so that while our government has so much interest to pay on its bonds, the duty on silks, which furnishes a considerable part of the revenue, is not likely to be diminished seriously. But it is needful to prepare steadily and skillfully for the changes in the tariff that may be expected, when the reduction of the national debt shall diminish the amount of revenue required.

Every improvement in machinery, or in processes of manufacture, which will facilitate the production of better goods, or of the same qualities at less cost (for we believe it is pretty generally admitted that our goods are now, in many departments of manufacture, superior to those imported), should be encouraged and adopted. All methods of reeling or throwing silk, which accomplish by automatic machinery what has hitherto been accomplished by hand-labor, should be studied, and if found promising in good results, should at once be tested in actual operation. There is yet room for great improvement in the weaving of plain goods, and some of the new looms recently brought forward, when perfected may be found to be a great advance on those now generally in use.

Hitherto the outlook has not been favorable for the production of the best grades of heavy dress silks; the stock has been too costly, the labor too expensive, and the weaving too slow. But a review of what has been already achieved, may give new courage for the future. By some process, perhaps even now discovered, the cost of the stock may be reduced; the labor of a rapid automatic power-loom, no whit more wonderful than the improved Jacquard, may be substituted for the long hours of toil which the most skillful weavers of Lyons now expend upon the best grades of silks. Our manufacturers have achieved a great and wonderful success in their dress silks, made wholly or in part from spun silk. It is but one step further to a greater triumph, in competing with the best products of the Lyons looms. As yet, too, the higher grades of velvets, especially in broad goods, have not been made here to any great extent.

There is no immediate prospect of a great or speedy revival of silk culture; but in each State where the climate and circumstances are favorable to the rearing of silk-worms, a filature, conducted by skilled reelers and moved by steam or water-power, which should buy all good cocoons offered, might be started to advantage. These filatures would gradually serve to renew the interest in silk culture, and provide for its eventual increase. They would not prove directly profitable, but they might supply the lack of silk in bad years, and would help our manufacturers in maintaining their position, in spite of all assaults.

These are but a few of the many points in which there is encouragement to go forward and aspire to a yet higher position in the manufacture. Our visions of the coming time are not so rose-colored as those of our fathers in 1835–40. No one expects to see in the present generation, every citizen of the great Republic sitting under the shade of his own *multicaulis* trees, or gathering the leaves with utmost diligence, to supply the ravenous appetites of the million of worms in his own cocoonery; or busying himself with the vain endeavor to make all his cocoons—peanut, sulphur, mammoth and white—reel alike. Nor does any one believe, that in our time, every farmer will go to his work in silk attire, or that every milk-maid will attend to her duties, in a brocaded silk with a trail two yards in length.

But there is room to hope that, before the dawn of the twentieth century, we shall be exporting instead of importing silk goods; that the moderate-priced but durable spun silks will claim their place as the most economical of dresses for our American women while engaged in their every-day duties; and that the display of laces, ribbons, silks and velvets, greeting the eye of the visitor to the Grand Exposition which in this country shall welcome the beginning of a new century of the Christian Era, will greatly surpass the products of European looms.

The reader of this history can scarcely fail to notice the general similarity of the experiences that have been narrated. As the alternating periods of adversity and prosperity sweep with storm or sunshine across the whole field of silk industry, the story of one individual becomes the history of all. Bound thus together by community of experience as well as of interest, the silk manufacturers of America also share a common hope that is the basis of all their endeavors—the hope that the products of their textile art may meet the ordinary needs as well as the highest tastes of their countrymen and countrywomen.

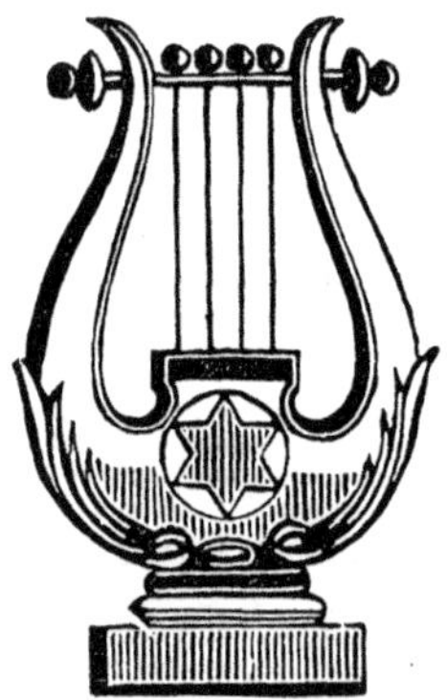

APPENDIX.

SILK DYEING.

For many reasons it may appear that a brief notice of the progress made in the art of dyeing silk in America, should have constituted one of the chapters of the foregoing history. It has been found, however, most convenient in the present edition, to present the facts in an appendix; more especially as they include the mention of several enterprises that have been already described.

The art of dyeing silk, as now practiced, requires more actual skill and knowledge of applied chemistry than the dyeing of cotton or woolen goods. The secrets of the art are more carefully guarded in Europe than in America; but here as well as there they have been handed down in families or firms as a heritage of value. The progress of modern science has to some extent interfered with this exclusiveness, by introducing simultaneously, new methods and new dyes. The pathways which are opened by science, sooner or later become free to all who may choose to enter.

During the period when, in many parts of the United States, the nurture and care of the silk-worm, and the production of silk, constituted a household industry, the dyeing of the silk thus obtained, was embraced among the processes carried on in the household. A good wife was expected in a general way to understand something of the dyer's art; its application to silk yarns presented few new difficulties. The same kinds of dyes and dyestuffs were used that had given tint to homespun garments or to half worn dresses a new lease of service. The chief dyes were the yellow and red oak, chestnut, butternut, logwood, Brazil wood, redwood, nutgalls, madder, indigo, annatto, and sometimes, though rarely, small quantities of cochineal. The mordants most in use were alum, copperas (sulphate of iron), bluestone (sulphate of copper), and occasionally, muriate of tin. Recipes for dyeing make a separate department in the volumes of that period which describe the household arts; and appear also in the treatises on silk culture, such as the report of Secretary Rush, the essays of Dr. Pascalis and J. D'Homergue, and the manuals of Cobb, Kenrick, Vernon, Comstock, and Smith.

In Mansfield, Conn., between 1829 and 1838, a woman who had developed peculiar skill in dyeing, monopolized the business furnished by the silk manufacturers in the neighborhood. The chief complaint against American sewing-silk was that its dye was inferior to the Italian; and a prejudice in favor of the foreign sewing-silk, based chiefly on supposed superiority of color, survived long after the American silks surpassed all others in lustre, brilliance and permanence of hue, as they unquestionably did in strength of material. The prejudice has not wholly died out at the present day, being yet unjustly applied to some descriptions of dress goods, though long ago at an end in respect to sewing-silk.

When, in August, 1838, Edward Vallentine and Lewis Leigh came to this country and started the business of silk dyeing, at Gurleyville, Conn., they had both these obstacles to meet: a woman had the local trade, and a high reputation as a dyer; and at best it was not popularly believed that American sewing-silk could be the equal, especially in color, of the Italian. With foreign black sewing-silks, the contest at that period seemed almost hopeless; but in the lighter colors the field was more promising. Mr. Vallentine brought with him his own experience as a silk dyer at Spitalfields, England, where he had succeeded to the business of his father, a Huguenot, descended from a family exiled by the persecutions which followed the revocation of the Edict of Nantes. The younger Vallentine well understood his trade and was ambitious in the use of brilliant colors; he was also remarkably successful in making a permanent black dye. These efforts were ably seconded by Mr. Leigh; he is living at the present day, and is still spoken of as a "master of the craft." Northampton, in 1839, under the prodigal management of Samuel Whitmarsh, seemed to be fast becoming the focus of the silk industry, and thither Mr. Vallentine removed. The products of the mills at Florence and at South Manchester were sent to his dye-house; and in 1844 he was joined by Wm. Skinner, who had been a dyer in England. The amount of dyeing required about this period by the Nonotuck Silk Co., was possibly 50 pounds of silk per week; by Cheney Brothers, perhaps twice that quantity. Each of these concerns at last resolved to do its own dyeing. The Nonotuck Silk Co. bargained with Mr. Vallentine to have its own dyer, Mr. Atkins, taught the art; applying the threat, in case of refusal, of bringing out from England another dyer to supplant Mr. Vallentine. Ward Cheney followed up this entering wedge, and himself spent some months in Northampton, acquiring "all the secrets of the art" from Mr. Vallentine for the sum of three hundred dollars. In Mr. Cheney's case Mr. Vallentine afterwards occasionally boasted that he kept some of his knowledge in reserve; but at all events, the Cheney Brothers never appeared conscious of the deficiency. The subsequent withdrawal of these two largest customers, probably brought about Mr. Vallentine's failure in business in 1848. He died in 1851. Several of these incidents concerning Messrs. Vallentine

& Leigh are among the valuable contributions to the early history of the silk industry in Connecticut, which first appeared in the pamphlet of A. T. Lilly, referred to in previous pages.

William Skinner, as has been elsewhere mentioned, began manufacturing at Northampton, at the date of Mr. Vallentine's failure in 1848. The relics of the dyeing business at that time fell into Mr. Skinner's hands; he prolonged it for six years in a dye-house adjoining the silk mill built by Capt. J. Conant, between Northampton and Florence. The removal of Mr. Skinner to the vicinity of Haydensville in 1854, closes his record of business as a dyer of silks on commission.

The larger manufacturing concerns have, in general, found it to their interest to carry on their dyeing within their own walls; the smaller ones, in the majority of instances, send their goods to the larger ones to be dyed. But, where a number of small and large concerns have congregated, as, for instance, at Paterson, N. J., the opportunity for making a separate business of the dyeing of silks on commission, has been again developed. Its beginnings in Paterson have been sketched already in this history, and the names of the four dyeing establishments in that city (the chief of which is that of Weidmann & Greppo), have been given. There are about the same number in and near Philadelphia, the Quaker City Dye & Print Works of Rudolph Klauder & Co. being the most important; the others are Charles Morel & Sons, T. Jones & Son, and M. C. Cuttle. In New York City, James Heidenrick has an extensive dye-house; and there are dye-works on Staten Island of established reputation in handling silks as well as woolens.

The art of dyeing has undergone a notable change since the discovery of the aniline colors. These were promptly accepted by Fashion, the arbitress of the dyer, and each new hue has compelled him to make some change in his processes, until at the present day the older colors and methods are, with few exceptions, unknown in the dye-house. France took the lead in the discovery and use of most of these modern colors, but the science and ingenuity of Americans have not proved wanting in the altered circumstances, and it is now admitted abroad as well as at home that the color obtained by our silk dyers is, in purity, delicacy and permanence, generally equal and in many instances superior to the foreign production.

A further advantage has been obtained from the fact that the trick of weighting silks by introducing heavy chemicals in the dye, has been carried to a far more injurious extent in Europe than here. If we may trust a recent writer in a French journal, we must admit that France has surpassed all other countries in achieving this bad eminence. The percentage of added material with black silks, is stated, in the publication referred to, as amounting to 100, 200, and even 300 per cent. The salts used to effect this increase, are compounds with iron, tin, and the alkalies as bases—

mostly astringent salts, but among them are the cyanides, all of which are prompt and deadly poisons. The weight and apparent lustre of the fabric are preserved, and there is a semblance of silk with a good "body" that attracts purchasers. Very brief wear reveals the deception. The cohesiveness, the real strength of fibre, and the elasticity are largely reduced. As an evidence of the change, the goods have become highly combustible; but when burned they fail to give the usual odor of animal matter by which burnt silk is readily recognized when tested for comparison with vegetable fabrics. A few years ago there were two or three instances of spontaneous combustion among goods of this class, stored in Paris. The portions yet unburned were found, on an official investigation, to be changed to a kind of tinder. American manufacturers justly pride themselves on having discountenanced this species of fraud: pure dye silks are with them the rule; weighted goods, the rare exception.

Erratum.

On page 107, line 33, for "bar," read *cylinder*.

In connection with the History of Silk Industry, it has been thought desirable to present also, the last Annual Report of the Silk Association of America; the one giving a picture of the past, more or less remote, the other, of the active, living present. The Report contains a variety of interesting information not elsewhere attainable. It includes reviews of the silk trade and manufacture for the past year, written by men actually engaged in the respective branches of business which they describe; these are of unquestionable value to the trade, and are not wanting in interest to the general public that consumes silk goods. Elaborate statistics, covering the whole range of silk production are also appended, which will prove of service to all who study the movements of commerce, the advances of industry, or the relations of capital and labor.

Secretary's Office, 93 Duane Street, New York.
June, 1876.

FOURTH

ANNUAL REPORT

OF

THE SILK ASSOCIATION

OF AMERICA.

WEDNESDAY, APRIL 26TH, 1876.

COMMITTEE ON STATISTICS.

WM. STRANGE, Paterson, N. J.
WM. RYLE, New York.
GEO. B. SKINNER & Co., Yonkers, N. Y.
SEAVEY, FOSTER & BOWMAN, Canton, Mass.
CHENEY BROTHERS, South Manchester, Conn.
HAMIL & BOOTH, Paterson, N. J.
A. SOLELIAC & SONS, Paterson, N. J.
WEIDMANN & GREPPO, Paterson, N. J.
WM. H. HORSTMANN & SONS, Philadel'a, Pa.
FRANKLIN ALLEN, *Secretary*.

NESBITT & CO., PRINTERS, N. Y.

THE

SILK ASSOCIATION OF AMERICA.

BOARD OF GOVERNMENT 1876—77.

President.

FRANK W. CHENEY, - - - - Hartford, Conn.

Vice-Presidents.

THOMAS N. DALE, - - - - Paterson, N. J.
A. B. STRANGE, - - - - - New York.
WILLIAM RYLE, - - - - New York.

Directors.

F. O. HORSTMANN, - - - - Philadelphia.
B. RICHARDSON, - - - New York.
GEORGE B. SKINNER, - - - - New York and Yonkers.
IRA DIMOCK, - - - - - Florence, Mass.
WILLIAM STRANGE, - - - - Paterson, N. J.
C. GREPPO, - - - - - Paterson, N. J.
A. SOLELIAC, - - - - - New York.
WILLIAM SKINNER, - - - - Holyoke, Mass.
SETH LOW, - - - - - - New York.
I. A. HOPPER, - - - - - Newark, N. J.
GEO. H. BURRITT, - - - - New York.
L. BAYARD SMITH, - - - - New York.
MILO M. BELDING, - - - - Rockville, Conn.
D. O'DONOGHUE, - - - - New York.
A. G. JENNINGS, - - - - - Brooklyn, N. Y.
LOUIS FRANKE, - - - - New York.
C. LAMBERT, - - - - - Paterson, N. J.
JOHN T. WALKER, - - - - New York.
J. W. C. SEAVEY, - - - - - Canton, Mass.
FRANK CHENEY, - - - - South Manchester, Conn.

Treasurer.

JOHN N. STEARNS, - - - - New York.

Secretary.

FRANKLIN ALLEN, - - - - 93 Duane Street, N. Y.

COMMITTEES OF THE ASSOCIATION.

1876.

Silk Conditioning.

WILLIAM STRANGE,
WILLIAM RYLE,
GEORGE B. SKINNER,
B. RICHARDSON,
JOHN N. STEARNS,
SETH LOW.

Adulterations of Asiatic Silks.

B. RICHARDSON,
F. W. CHENEY,
JOHN N. STEARNS,
SETH LOW,
IRA DIMOCK.

Revenue Laws.

WILLIAM STRANGE,
F. O. HORSTMANN,
B. RICHARDSON,
A. SOLELIAC,
SETH LOW,
ROBERT HAMIL, *Honorary.*

Annual Dinner.

THOMAS N. DALE,
P. RICHARDSON,
JOHN D. CUTTER,
F. O. HORSTMANN,
The SECRETARY.

Statistics.

WILLIAM STRANGE,
WILLIAM RYLE,
GEO. B. SKINNER & CO.,
SEAVEY, FOSTER & BOWMAN
CHENEY BROTHERS,
HAMIL & BOOTH,
A. SOLELIAC & SONS,
WEIDMANN & GREPPO,
WM H. HORSTMANN & SONS
The SECRETARY

Finance.

A. B. STRANGE,
GEO. B. SKINNER,
SETH LOW

CATALOGUE OF

MEMBERS AND SUBSCRIBERS.

THE SILK ASSOCIATION OF AMERICA.

1876.

Aub, Hackenburg & Co.,	20 North 3d St., Philadelphia, Pa.
C. A. Auffmordt & Co.,	10 Greene St., New York.
David A. Barnes,	Paterson, N. J.
A. Begoden,	12 Old Slip, New York.
Belding Bros. & Co.,	Rockville, Conn.
Bernstein & Mack,	479 Broadway, New York.
C. L. Bottum & Co.,	Willimantic, Conn.
Brainerd, Armstrong & Co.,	469 Broadway, New York.
Geo. H. Burritt,	32 Burling Slip, "
Cary & Co.,	90 Pine St., "
S. W. Clapp,	7 Mercer St., "
John Caswell & Co.,	87 Front St., "
O. S. Chaffee & Son,	Mansfield Centre, Conn.
C. Chaffonjon,	Hudson City, N. J.
F. W. Cheney,	Hartford, Conn.
Frank Cheney,	South Manchester, "
Samuel Coit,	Hartford, "
A. A. & H. E. Conant,	Willimantic, "
Wm. H. Copcutt & Co.,	350 Canal St., New York.
J. D. Cutter,	92 Church St., "
Thos. N. Dale,	Paterson. N. J.
Ira Dimock,	Florence, Mass.
D. O'Donoghue,	48 Howard St., New York.
A. B. Fenner, Treas. Scranton Silk Co.,	Central Village, Conn.
Wm. H. Fogg,	32 Burling Slip, New York.
Louis Franke,	489 Broadway, "
Hugo Funke,	343 Canal St., "
A. H. Gibbes, Agent Swire Bros.,	68 Wall St., "
J. C. Graham,	525 Cherry St., Philadelphia, Pa.

C. Greppo, - - - - - - - 400 Broadway, New York.
J. H. Hayden, - - - - - - - Windsor Locks, Conn.
Thos. F. Hayes, - - - - - 77 University Place, New York.
E. L. Hedden, of Wetmore, Cryder & Co., 74 South St., "
Jacob Heinemann, - - - - - - 28 Howard St., "
Hensel, Colladay & Co., - - 22 North 4th St., Philadelphia, Pa.
E. Holdsworth, - - - - - - - Shanghai, China.
B. Hooley & Son, - - - 226 Market St., Philadelphia, Pa.
I. A. Hopper, Pres't Singer Mf'g Co., Union Sq. and 16th St., New York.
Wm. H. Horstmann & Sons, - Fifth and Cherry Sts., Philadelphia, Pa.
F. O. Horstmann, - - - - " " " " "
F. S. Hovey, - - - - - 248 Chestnut St., " "
Wm. Iles, - - - - - - - - Yonkers, New York.
Werner Itschner, - - - - - 233 Chestnut St., Philadelphia, Pa.
A. G. Jennings, - - - - - - 428 Broome St., New York.
Rowland Johnson, - - - - - 54 Beaver St., "
Alexander King & Co., - - - - 52 White St., "
Rudolph Klauder, - cor. Howard & Oxford Sts., Philadelphia, Pa.
Tobias Kohn, - - - - - - - - - Hartford, Conn.
C. Lambert - - - - - - 10 Greene St., New York.
A. A. Low & Bros., - - - - 31 Burling Slip, "
Seth Low, - - - - - - - " " "
McFarlane Bros., - - - - - - Mansfield Centre, Conn.
S. M. Meyenberg, - - - - - 40 Lispenard St., New York.
Wm. F. Milton & Co., - - - - - 71 South St., "
Nonotuck Silk Co., - - - - - - - Florence, Mass.
Oneida Community, - - - - - - - Oneida, N. Y.
Pelgram & Meyer, - - - - - 456 Broome St., New York.
J. C. Phillips & Co., - - - - - 130 Water St., "
Phœnix Silk Manufacturing Co., - - - - - Paterson, N. J.
B. Richardson, - - - - - - - 5 Mercer St., New York.
F. G. Richardson, - - - - - - - " " "
R. Rossmässler, - - - 319 to 323 Garden St., Philadelphia, Pa.
John Ryle, - - - - - - - - - Paterson, N. J.
Reuben Ryle & Co., - - - - - 19 Mercer St., New York.
Wm. Ryle, - - - - - - - 297 Broadway, "
Seavey, Foster & Bowman, - - - - - - - Canton, Mass.
J. Silbermann & Co., - - - - - 21 Mercer St., New York.
Geo. B. Skinner, - - - - - 59 Walker St., "
Wm. Skinner, - - - - - - - - - Holyoke, Mass.

Chas. F. Simes, - - - - - 48 Howard St., New York.
Herman Simon, - - - - - - - Town of Union, N. J.
L. Bayard Smith, - - - - 77 William St., New York.
H. Erskine Smith, - - - - " " "
A. Soleliac & Sons, - - - - - 92 Grand St., "
A. B. Strange, - - - - - - 455 Broome St., "
Wm. Strange, - - - - - - - - Paterson, N. J.
John N. Stearns, - - - - - 43 Mercer St., New York.
L. R. Stelle, - - - - - - Sauquoit, near Utica, N. Y.
Geo. W. Talbot (Olyphant & Co., of China), 104 Wall St., New York.
Albert Tilt, - - - - - - 477 Broome St., "
Vogel, Hagedorn & Co., - - Hong Kong & Shanghai, China.
John T. Walker, - - - - - 81 Pine St., New York.
Warner & Lathrop, - - - - - - Northampton, Mass.
Jacob Weidmann, - - - - - - - Paterson, N. J.
Wood, Payson & Colgate, - - - - 64 Pine St., New York.

HONORARY MEMBERS.

Robert Hamil, President Silk Industry Association,
of Paterson, N. J., - - - 57 Walker St., New York.
T. Tomita, Vice-Consul of the Empire of Japan, 7 Warren St., "

PREAMBLE AND BY-LAWS

OF THE

SILK ASSOCIATION OF AMERICA,

IN FORCE APRIL, 1876.

WHEREAS, the Silk interest constitutes an important branch of National Industry, largely involving the labor and capital of the country; and, whereas, its future growth and permanent success require greater co-operation on the part of those engaged in it, than has heretofore existed;

Therefore, for the purpose of promoting the advancement and prosperity of this interest more effectually, by the increase of information, by the interchange of ideas, by harmonious action, and by all other appropriate means, we, the subscribers, agree to associate ourselves together, under the name of The Silk Association of America, and be governed by such rules and by-laws as the Association may, from time to time, adopt.

BY-LAWS.

ARTICLE I.

CONDITION OF MEMBERSHIP.

SECTION 1.—Any person being a principal or partner of a firm or officer of a corporation engaged in the Silk Industry of the United States, or any person holding power of attorney of a member, may become a member of this Association.

Persons not residing in the United States engaged in pursuits in any wise connected with the Silk trade of America, may become members of this Association.

SEC. 2.—No person shall be eligible for membership who is not proposed for election by some actual member, by written notice to the President or Secretary; and no person shall be admitted if five or more negatives are given against him.

SEC. 3.—The Government, at any duly organized meeting, may elect corresponding and honorary members, by the unanimous vote of the members present; such corresponding or honorary members shall be entitled to all the privileges of regular members, except the right to vote or hold office.

Sec. 4.—Each person admitted as a member of the Association, except corresponding or honorary members, shall pay to the Secretary the sum of twenty-five dollars as an admission fee, which shall be in full for the year in which he is elected, and thereafter he shall pay annually, while he shall remain a member, the sum of twenty-five dollars.

Sec. 5.—Upon the refusal or failure by any member to pay his just dues and subscriptions, his name shall be presented to the Government, and upon their vote, shall be struck from the list of members.

Sec. 6.—Any member can withdraw from the Association after fulfilling all his obligations to it, by giving written notice of such intention to the Secretary.

ARTICLE II.

CLASSIFICATION OF MEMBERS.

Sec. 1.—The members of the Association may be classified by the Secretary in five several divisions, according to the branch of the silk business in which they are respectively engaged, which divisions shall be as follows:

Division A....Importers, dealers and brokers in raw silk.
" B....Throwsters of and dealers in gum silk.
" C....Manufacturers of sewing silks and twist.
" D....Weavers and Dyers.
" E....Manufacturers of fringe, braid, trimmings, &c.

The divisions may be separately organized by the selection of a chairman by each, with such other officers and committees as may be desired, and shall occupy the rooms of the Association for their meetings, under arrangement with the Government; and through their chairman, may report to, or communicate with the Association at its general meetings upon any matter relating to their special branches.

Sec. 2.—Members engaged in several branches of the silk business may be registered under each.

ARTICLE III.

OFFICERS AND THEIR ELECTION.

Sec. 1.—The officers of the Association shall consist of a President, three Vice-Presidents, a Treasurer, not less than twelve and not more than twenty Directors, who together shall constitute the Government of the Association, and five of whom shall form a quorum for the transaction of business.

Sec. 2.—The Government shall have power to manage the affairs of the Association; to hold meetings at such times and places as they may think proper; to appoint committees on particular subjects from the members of the Government, or from other members of the Association, with full power to act on such committees as though members of the Government; to audit bills, and appropriate the funds of the Association; to print and circulate documents, and publish articles in the newspapers; to carry on correspondence and otherwise communicate with other Associations interested in the development of the Silk Industry; to employ agents, and to devise and carry into execution such other measures as they may deem proper and expedient to promote the object of the Association.

SEC. 3.—After the first choice, all the officers of the Association shall be annually elected by ballot at the annual meeting, at such place as the Government may appoint, a majority of the members present being necessary to constitute an election, and such officers shall continue in office for the term of one year, or until their successors are elected and qualified to take their places.

SEC. 4.—The Government of the Association shall choose a Secretary and fix his salary; and may fill any vacancies occurring in their body, by death, declination to serve, resignation, or any other cause, after the annual election, at any regular or special meeting at which a quorum shall be present.

ARTICLE IV.

DUTIES OF OFFICERS.

SEC. 1.—It shall be the duty of the President, or, in his absence, of one of the Vice-Presidents, in order of seniority, to preside at all meetings of the Association and of the Government; and the President or one of the Vice-Presidents shall audit and sign the annual accounts of the Treasurer.

SEC. 2.—The Treasurer shall keep an account of all moneys received and expended for the use of the Association, and shall make disbursements only upon vouchers approved, in writing, by the Secretary and any member of the Government. When his term of office expires, he shall deliver over to his successor all books, moneys and other property; or in absence of the Treasurer elect, to the President.

SEC. 3.—It shall be the duty of the Secretary, who shall not be engaged in any branch of the Silk Industry, to give notice of, and attend all meetings of the Association and its several divisions, and to keep a record of their doings; to conduct all correspondence, and to carry into execution all orders, votes and resolves, not otherwise committed; to keep a list of the members of the Association; to collect the fees, annual dues and subscriptions, and pay them over to the Treasurer; to notify officers and members of the Association of their election; to notify members of their appointment on committees; to furnish the chairman of each committee with a copy of the vote under which the committee is appointed, and at his request give notice of the meetings of the committee; to prepare, under direction of the Government, an annual report of the transactions and condition of the Association; and generally to devote his best efforts to forwarding the business and advancing the interests of the Association.

ARTICLE V.

MEETINGS OF THE ASSOCIATION.

SEC. 1.—The regular meetings of this Association shall be held at such place as the Government may appoint, upon the second Wednesday of February, May, August, and November, and notice of such meetings, signed by the Secretary, shall be mailed to the address of each member, at least ten days before the time appointed for the meeting.

SEC. 2.—The meeting in May shall be the Annual Meeting, for the election of officers, and receiving the report of the Government.

Provided, that in the year 1876 the annual meeting for the election of officers to serve in the year ensuing and for receiving the report of the Board of Government, may be held on the last Wednesday of April, at such place as the Board of Government may appoint instead and in lieu of the second Wednesday of May as provided for in sections 1 and 2 of article V of the by-laws: the said change being deemed advisable in consequence of the said second Wednesday of May, 1876, having been designated by the United States Centennial Commission for the opening and inauguration services of the International Exhibition at Philadelphia.

Sec. 3.—Special meetings may be called by the Government, or upon the written application to the Secretary, of ten members, not in the Government; notice thereof to be given in the same manner as for the Regular Meetings.

Sec 4.—It shall require ten members present at any meeting to form a quorum; and, in case of there not being a quorum, the meeting may be adjourned by the presiding officer.

ARTICLE VI.

The order of business shall be as follows:

1.—Calling of the Roll.
2.—Reading of the Minutes.
3.—Election of Officers or New Members.
4.—Reports of Officers.
5.—Reports of Committees.
6.—Receiving Communications.
7.—Unfinished Business.
8.—New Business.

ARTICLE VII.

Sec. 1.—These By-Laws may be amended or repealed by a vote of two-thirds of the members present at any duly organized meeting of the Association; provided notice of such proposed change shall have been presented, in writing, at a previous meeting.

FOURTH ANNUAL MEETING OF THE ASSOCIATION.

APRIL 26th, 1876.

The fourth annual meeting of the Silk Association of America was held at its office, No. 93 Duane Street, New York, on the 26th of April, 1876, at 2 P. M.; the members present representing the raw silk importing interest, and silk manufactures established in Massachusetts, Connecticut, New Jersey and New York.

Mr. William Ryle, 3d Vice-President, occupied the chair.

The minutes of the last meeting, held February 25th, were read and approved.

The election of officers for the ensuing year was, on motion, deferred until after the reading of the Annual Reports.

The Annual Reports of the Treasurer, Secretary and the Committee on Statistics were then presented, and, on motion, were accepted.

On motion, a Committee on Nominations was ordered to report the names of suitable officers for the Association. Messrs. John N. Stearns, S. W. Clapp, and Wm. Strange were thereupon appointed a Committee on Nominations, and upon their request that a representative of the raw silk importing interest be added to the Committee, Mr. Seth Low was so appointed by the Chair. The Committee reported as candidates for election, the gentlemen elsewhere named under the head of "Board of Government, 1876-77."

The said candidates were unanimously elected officers of the Association for the ensuing year.

On the call of committees,

Mr. William Strange, Chairman of the Silk Conditioning Committee, reported in favor of making an earnest effort at this time to establish a Silk Conditioning Bureau, under the control of a committee to be appointed by the Association, that should act as an advisory Board to the chemists, Messrs

Bourgougnon and Doremus. He reported that the conditioning apparatus provided by these chemists at their own expense had recently been inspected by the committee; that samples from bales of silk conditioned at Lyons had been conditioned by them, and the returns found to agree substantially with the conditioning papers of the Lyons establishment; and that the only element of success lacking is a general assent to the project.

On motion the report of the Committee was accepted, the Committee was continued, and Mr. Seth Low was elected an additional member of the Silk Conditioning Committee of the Association.

On the call for new business, a member inquired whether a rule could be adopted by the trade which would settle the amount of tare in weight of raw silk to be allowed the purchaser by the seller. The question of the jurisdiction of the Association on the subject was discussed, as well as the subject itself; and it was agreed that while the Association is not clothed with power to enforce a rule regulating purchase and sale which shall be binding upon the trade, the custom of the trade has usually been found to give satisfaction, viz: to allow one per cent. tare on re-reeled Tsatlees; that in general the customary manner of putting up silks is implied: that when an extraordinary amount of paper, string, etc., is found in the package, the buyer usually asks and receives a proportionate allowance; and that a departure from the customary manner of packing silk is not binding upon either party for a fixed rate of allowance, but is a matter for individual agreement and settlement between the buyer and seller.

On motion, it was

Resolved, That the Annual Dinner of the Association this year be given at such time and place as the Board of Government of the Association may appoint.

The Secretary referred to the need existing for the utmost economy in expenditures in carrying on the work of the Association, and desired it to be generally understood that he would personally co-operate to the best of his ability in limiting the expenses to the lowest point rendered necessary by the dullness of trade at the present time; and he asked for the appointment of a Committee to supervise the expenditures of the Association. The opinion was generally held that the revenues of the Association have reached a point which make the appointment of a Finance Committee desirable, and on motion it was

Resolved, That this meeting favors the appointment of a Finance Committee of the Association, and that the matter be referred to the Board of Government for appropriate action.

On motion, the meeting adjourned.

FRANKLIN ALLEN,
Secretary.

SECRETARY'S REPORT.

In conformity with the by-laws of the Association, the Secretary has the honor to submit the following report, prepared under direction of its Board of Government, and presenting a review for the past year of the transactions and condition of The Silk Association of America.

The year 1875 was the most prosperous that the silk industry in America has ever experienced, if considered in respect to the quantity of raw material consumed, and the amount of labor employed in silk manufacture. True, the margin of profits of employers was small, relatively to the amount of business done, as compared with some previous years; but it is an encouraging fact, that during a period of general depression in other branches of industry, the silk manufacturers were not only enabled to furnish employment to as many operators as usual, but to give steady work and fair wages to a considerable additional number. Specially has this increase taken place in Paterson, New Jersey, where in the past year, the manufacture of broad goods was greatly extended, and the production of ribbons, handkerchiefs, fancy silks for trimmings, ties, &c., was more than double that of 1874.

A marked feature of the increased activity in the silk trade at Paterson during the past year, has been the immigration of a number of so-called master silk-weavers from France and England. These men individually own several looms, which in many instances they have brought with them. They carry on the weaving at their homes, one or more rooms being fitted up for this purpose. As business increases, they employ so-called journeymen weavers, who in turn will become master weavers and loom owners, and thus build up a valuable though independent auxiliary to the great factories. We learn that this movement meets with the approval and support of the employers, and undoubtedly in time those who approve themselves to the good opinion of the manufacturers will be helped in the purchase of machines, and the way be opened for better understanding and more cordial relations between employers and employed, to the manifest advantage of both.

The import of raw silk in 1875 to supply our manufactures was 50 per cent. larger than in 1874, and 38,807 lbs. in excess of 1871, which, previous to 1875, was the largest year.

The following table shows the quantity imported since the year 1868:

1868	600,035	pounds.
1869	695,353	"
1870	738,381	"
1871	1,291,675	"
1872	1,244,193	"
1873	831,728	"
1874	806,774	"
1875	1,330,482	"

An unmistakable "sign of the times" is the fact that foreign commission houses in this city are now seeking consignments of American silks.

Reviews of the different branches of manufacture, supplemented by valuable suggestions and observations, will be found herein presented by representative houses in the several departments of trade. In the following tables there is compiled a summary of the returns that have been received in response to the requests of the Committee on Statistics:—

VALUE OF PRODUCTS, CLASSIFIED BY ARTICLES, MANUFACTURED IN THE YEAR ENDING DECEMBER 31, 1875.

Article		Pounds	Value.
Tram,	lbs.	461,518	$2,976,501
Organzine,	"	230,606	1,819,000
Spun Silk,	"	150,000	850,000
Fringe "	"	42,327	243,489
Floss "	"	6,861	42,568
Sewing Silk	"	85,211	885,079
Machine Twist,	"	459,259	5,535,754
Dress Goods			1,412,500
Millinery and Tie Silks			2,544,191
Women's Scarfs			104,523
Men's "			30,000
Handkerchiefs			905,115
Foulards			450,000
Ribbons			4,815,485
Laces			164,000
Coach Laces			35,652
Veils and Veiling			65,264
Silk Hose			6,000
Braids and Bindings			383,100
Military Trimmings			33,000
Upholstery "			459,613
Ladies' Dress "			3,397,237
Total Products 1875,		1,435,782 lbs.	$27,158,071

	Pounds.	Value.	
Reeled Silk consumed	1,285,782	$11,502,391	
Spun " "	150,000	850,000	
Total Silk Threads	1,435,782	12,352,391	12,352,391
Consumed in sewings & twist	544,470	6,420,833	
do in weaving	891,312	$5,931,558	$14,805,680

GENERAL STATISTICAL VIEW OF THE SILK INDUSTRY IN AMERICA,

FOR THE YEAR ENDING DECEMBER 31ST, 1875.

STATES.	No. of firms and Manufacturing Corporations.	KIND OF ARTICLES MANUFACTURED.	NO. OF OPERATIVES EMPLOYED.					WAGES PAID.	Value Capital Invested and Employed.	Total Value of Production.
			MALES.		FEMALES.		TOTAL.			
			Over 16 Years	Under 16 Years	Over 16 Years	Under 16 Years				
New Jersey....	57	Gum silks, tram, organzine, fringe silks, sewing silks, machine-twist, dyeing, weaving, ribbons, dress and fancy silks, scarfs, handkerchiefs, veils and veiling, ladies' dress trimmings, braids, and bindings, upholstery trimmings, etc......	2349	748	3902	1382	8381	$2,969,993	$5,926,804	$10,930,035
New York....	76	Gum silks, tram, organzine, fringe silks, sewing silks, machine-twist, dyeing, weaving, ribbons, dress and fancy silks, handkerchiefs, ladies' dress trimmings, guipure laces, upholstery trimmings, etc..........................	920	209	1792	671	3592	1,497,563	3,703,983	5,735,069
Connecticut....	24	Gum silks, tram, organzine, spun silks, fringe silks, floss silks, sewing silks, machine twist, dyeing, weaving, ribbons, dress and fancy silks, handkerchiefs, foulards, braids and bindings, etc.	830	183	1374	476	2863	925,367	4,570,449	5,430,692
Massachusetts...	12	Gum silks, tram, organzine, sewing silks, machine-twist, dyeing, weaving, ribbons, ladies' dress trimmings, upholstery trimmings, etc....	241	114	791	252	1398	374,381	1,506,290	2,748,431
Pennsylvania....	24	Gum silks, tram, organzine, fringe silks, floss silks, sewing silks, machine twist, dyeing, weaving, ribbons, braids and bindings, ladies' dress trimmings, upholstery trimmings, military trimmings, etc	330	112	738	248	1428	486,107	1,706,632	1,857,494
California......	4	Tram, machine-twist, dyeing, ladies' dress trimmings and upholstery trimmings.........	34	14	53	28	129	37,710	277,000	141,000
Ohio.........	5	Ladies' dress trimmings and upholstery trimmings	8	5	25	14	52	24,550	49,500	75,000
Illinois	3	Ladies' dress trimmings and upholstery trimmings	6	5	21	14	46	21,917	41,200	65,000
Kentucky......	2	Ladies' dress trimmings and upholstery trimmings	6	3	21	11	41	20,330	31,200	50,000
New Hampshire.	1	Sewing silks, machine-twist and dyeing	2	6	..	12	20	4,980	27,000	44,000
Maryland	1	Ladies' dress trimmings.....................	6	4	10	6	26	14,325	26,200	35,000
Missouri.......	1	Ladies' dress trimmings and upholstery trimmings	4	2	5	3	14	6,595	11,700	15,000
Tennessee	1	Ladies' dress trimmings and upholstery trimmings	4	2	5	3	14	6,595	11,700	15,000
Vermont.......	1	Machine-twist and dyeing	1	2	..	5	8	1,380	14,200	15,000
Kansas	1	Ladies' dress trimmings	2	..	2	1	5	463	10,000	1,350
Exhibit for 1875.	213		4743	1409	8739	3126	18017	$6,392,256	$17,012,858	$27,158,071

THROWN AND SPUN SILKS.

DIVISION B.—THE SILK INDUSTRY OF AMERICA. STATISTICS FOR THE YEAR ENDING DECEMBER 31, 1875.

STATES.	No. Firms and Manufacturing Corporations.	Machinery.		No. of Operatives Employed.					Wages Paid.	Capital Invested.	Amount and Value of Production.						
		Horse Power.	No. of Throwing Spindles.	Males. Over 16 years.	Males. Under 16 years.	Females. Over 16 years.	Females. Under 16 years.	Total.			Number of lbs.	Tram.	Organzine.	Spun Silk.	Fringe Silk.	Floss Silk.	Total.
New Jersey..	20	550	78,552	392	373	1,742	540	3,047	$867,315	$2,149.500	509,785	$2,177,712	$1,315,400	$.......	$64,000	$.......	$3,557,112
Connecticut..	4	300	21,979	326	64	200	115	705	250,365	1,780.000	184,938	130,000	80,000	850,000	7,062	22,000	1,089,062
New York...	4	175	28,026	128	74	375	204	781	189,775	650,752	98,168	434,495	180,856	....	49,500	....	664,851
Pennsylvania.	5	82	14,781	74	48	242	125	489	71,850	305,000	76,961	196,606	114,500	....	113,643	20,568	445,317
Massachusetts	1	30	7,500	16	33	55	10	114	27,064	50,000	20,060	22,988	128,244	....	9,284	....	160,516
California....	1	10	200	2	2	7	3	14	2,400	16,000	1,400	14,700	... .	....	....	....	14,700
Exh. for 1875.	35	1147	151,038	938	594	2,621	997	5,150	$1,408,769	$4,951,252	891,312	$2,976,501	$1,819,000	$850,000	$243,489	$42,568	$5,931,558

SEWING SILKS AND TWIST.

DIVISION C.—THE SILK INDUSTRY OF AMERICA.—STATISTICS FOR THE YEAR ENDING DECEMBER 31ST, 1875.

STATES.	No. of Firms and Manufacturing Corporations.	MACHINERY.		NO. OF OPERATIVES EMPLOYED.					WAGES PAID.	CAPITAL INVESTED.	AMOUNT AND VALUE OF PRODUCTION.			
		Horse Power.	No. of Throwing Spindles.	MALES.		FEMALES.		TOTAL.			No. of lbs.	Sewings.	Twist.	Total.
				Over 16 years.	Under 16 years.	Over 16 years	Under 16 years.							
Massachusetts...	8	225	14,150	167	72	706	230	1,175	$291,623	$1,358,290	204,447	$581,119	$1,908,796	$2,489,915
Connecticut....	17	200	12,896	166	79	698	251	1,194	309,334	1,184,223	202,546	157,410	2,125,120	2 282,530
New Jersey....	8	98	6,271	45	20	197	60	322	102,400	504,288	67,280	39,000	813,425	852,425
New York. ...	5	58	3,848	40	15	177	57	289	79,016	347,630	46,815	38,786	488,149	526,935
Pennsylvania....	2	30	2,166	21	8	50	10	89	19,400	121,460	12,482	57,764	93,464	151,228
California......	1	20	1,046	6	8	26	14	54	9,600	64,000	5,600	....	58,800	58,800
New Hampshire.	1	8	500	....	6	....	12	18	4,200	25,000	3,900	11,000	33,000	44,000
Vermont......	1	4	288	....	2	....	5	7	1,100	13,000	1,400	....	15,000	15,000
Exhibit for 1875.	43	643	41,165	445	210	1,854	639	3,148	$816,673	$3,617,891	544,470	$885,079	$5,535,754	$6,420,833

BROAD GOODS AND RIBBONS.

DIVISION D.—THE SILK INDUSTRY OF AMERICA. STATISTICS FOR THE YEAR ENDING DECEMBER 31ST, 1875.

STATES.	No. Firms & Man'f'g Corp'ns.	Machinery.					No. Operatives Employed.					Wages Paid	Capital Invested.	Value of Production.							
		Horse Power.	Broad Goods.		Ribbons.		Males.		Females.		Total.			Dress Silks.	Millinery & Tie Silks.	Ladies' Scarfs.	Gent's' Scarfs.	Handkerchiefs.	Foulards.	Ribbons.	Total.
			Power Looms.	Hand Looms.	Power Looms.	Average No. of Shuttles.	Over 16 years.	Under 16 years.	Over 16 years.	Under 16 years.											
New Jersey..	28	230	805	698	400	4710	1594	330	1816	700	4440	$1,750,410	$2,593,016	$777,500	$1,945,431	$104,523	$30,000	$580,115	$.......	$2,625,165	$6,062,734
Connecticut..	3	71	250	24	160	1860	228	30	448	90	796	270,098	1,141,226	625,000	200,000	....	....	125,000	450,000	486,000	1,886,000
New York..	13	100	302	197	200	3022	390	17	440	152	999	429,500	923,201	10,000	398,760	....	....	200,000	....	1,338,357	1,947,117
Pennsylvania.	2	30	71	56	60	952	50	5	100	42	197	71,000	340,172	....	....	....	....	....	....	330,463	330,463
Massachusetts	1	...	....	3	...	.....	4	3	6	4	17	5,200	12,000	....	....	....	....	....	....	18,000	18,000
California....	1	...	....	27	...	.....	18	...	....	...	18	4,400	160,000	....	....	....	....	....	....	17,500	17,500
Exh. for 1875	48	431	1428	1005	820	10544	2284	385	2810	988	6467	$2,530.608	$5,169,615	$1,412,500	$2,544,191	$104,523	$30,000	$905,115	$450,000	$4,815,485	$10,261,814

DYEING.

DIVISION D.—THE SILK INDUSTRY OF AMERICA. STATISTICS FOR THE YEAR ENDING DECEMBER 31, 1875.

STATES.	No. of Firms.	No. of Men Employed.	Wages Paid.	Capital invested in Dye-houses and Fixtures.	Original No. of lbs. Silk Dyed.
New Jersey	13	276	$137,433	$190,000	611,525
Connecticut	9	98	68,570	135,000	395,484
Massachusetts	6	38	25,334	33,000	208,447
New York	10	57	35,272	54,400	159,815
Pennsylvania	3	17	8,915	25,000	35,661
California	2	3	2,250	7,000	9,000
New Hampshire	1	2	780	2,000	3,900
Ohio	1	2	750	1,500	3,000
Illinois	1	1	563	1,200	2,250
Kentucky	1	1	500	1,200	2,000
Maryland	1	1	425	1,200	1,700
Vermont	1	1	280	1,200	1,400
Missouri	1	1	150	1,200	800
Tennessee	1	1	150	1,200	800
Exhibit for 1875	51	499	$281,372	$455,100	1,435,782

LACE, BRAIDS AND TRIMMINGS.

DIVISION E. THE SILK INDUSTRY OF AMERICA. STATISTICS FOR THE YEAR ENDING DECEMBER 31ST, 1875.

STATES.	No. of Firms and Manufacturing Corporations.	Machinery.						No. of Operatives Employed.					Wages Paid.	Capital Invested.	Value of Production.								
		Power Looms.	Hand Looms.	Braiding Spindles.	Chenille Spindles.	Cord Spinning Wheels.	Lace Machines.	Males. Over 16 years.	Males. Under 16 Years.	Females. Over 16 Years.	Females. Under 16 Years.	Total.			Laces.	Coach Laces.	Veils and Veilings.	Silk Hose.	Braids and Bindings.	Military Trimmings.	Upholstery Trimmings.	Ladies' Dress Trimmings.	Total
New York....	60	244	426	3,620	94	180	50	305	103	800	258	1466	$764,000	$1,728,000	$164,000	$......	$7,500	$6,000	$12,000	$......	$150,000	$2,256,666	$2,596,166
Pennsylvania..	14	124	202	4,700	46	68	..	168	51	346	71	636	314,942	915,000	......	15,652	......	......	18,000	33,000	184,613	679,221	930,486
New Jersey...	7	53	41	23,445	35	17	..	42	25	147	82	296	112,435	490,000	......	......	57,764	......	200,000	......	40,000	160,000	457,764
Connecticut...	3	..	6	12,053	..	..	..	12	10	28	20	70	27,000	330,000	......	20,000	......	......	153,100	......	......	......	173,100
Massachusetts..	4	10	30	600	4	8	..	16	6	24	8	54	25,160	53,000	......	......	......	......	......	......	10,000	70,000	80,000
Ohio	5	..	40	200	5	20	..	6	5	25	14	50	23,800	48,000	......	......	......	......	......	......	15,000	60,000	75,000
Illinois........	3	9	20	270	3	9	..	5	5	21	14	45	21,354	40,000	......	......	......	......	......	......	20,000	45,000	65,000
California.....	2	..	8	150	3	6	..	5	4	20	11	40	19,060	30,000	......	......	......	......	......	......	15,000	35,000	50,000
Kentucky.....	2	..	15	180	2	6	..	5	3	21	11	40	19,830	30,000	......	......	......	......	......	......	15,000	35,000	50,000
Maryland......	1	..	8	400	2	4	..	5	4	10	6	25	13,900	25,000	......	......	......	......	......	......	......	35,000	35,000
Missouri	1	..	4	....	1	2	..	3	2	5	3	13	6,445	10,500	......	......	......	......	......	......	5,000	10,000	15,000
Tennessee.....	1	..	4	....	1	2	..	3	2	5	3	13	6,445	10,500	......	......	......	......	......	......	5,000	10,000	15,000
Kansas	1	..	5	....	..	..	..	2	..	2	1	5	463	10,000	......	......	......	......	......	......	......	1,350	1,350
Exhibit for 1875	104	440	809	45,618	196	322	50	577	220	1454	502	2753	$1,354,834	$3,720,000	$164,000	$35,652	$65,264	$6,000	$383,100	$33,000	$459,613	$3,397,237	$4,543,866

RESUMÉ OF STATISTICAL TABLES FOR YEAR ENDING DECEMBER 31st, 1875.

DIVISIONS B, C, D AND E,—THE SILK INDUSTRY OF AMERICA.

Divisions.	Kind of Articles Manufactured.	No. of Operatives Employed.					Wages Paid.	Value Capital Invested and Employed.	Total Value of Products.
		Males.		Females.		Total.			
		Over 16 Years.	Under 16 Years.	Over 16 Years.	Under 16 Years.				
B	Thrown and spun silks	938	594	2,621	997	5,150	$1,408,769	$4,951,252	$5,931,558
C	Sewings and machine twist ...	445	210	1,854	639	3,148	816,673	3,617,891	6,420,833
D	Broad goods and ribbons	2,284	385	2,810	988	6,467	2,530,608	5,169,615	10,261,814
D	Dyeing	499	......	......	......	499	281,372	455,100	....
E	Laces, braids and trimmings..	577	220	1,454	502	2,753	1,354,834	3,720,000	4,543,866
	Exhibit for 1875..........	4,743	1,409	8,739	3,126	18,017	$6,392,256	$17,913,858	$27,158,071

NUMBER OF FIRMS IN SILK BUSINESS, April 26th, 1876.

The Silk interest in America is scheduled in the Directory of the Association as follows, some changes having taken place since the last Annual Report:

Division.			Number Firms.
A.—	Comprising	Importers, Dealers and Brokers in Raw Silk	25
B.—	"	Throwsters of, and Dealers in Gum Silk	41
C.—	"	Manufacturers Sewing Silk and Twist	43
D.—	"	Weavers and Dyers	65
E.—	"	Manufacturers Fringes, Braids, Ladies' Dress Trimmings, Upholstery Goods, &c.	105
		Total	279

Of these, 120 reside in New York State,
" 67 " New Jersey,
" 28 " Pennsylvania,
" 27 " Connecticut,
" 15 " Massachusetts,
" 6 " California,
" 5 " Ohio,
" 3 " Illinois,

Of these, 2 reside in Kentucky,
" 1 resides in Vermont,
" 1 " New Hampshire,
" 1 " Maryland,
" 1 " Missouri,
" 1 " Tennessee,
" 1 " Kansas.

	N. Y.	N. J.	Pa.	Conn.	Mass.	Cal.	Ohio	Ill.	Ky.	N. H.	Vt.	Md.	Miss.	Tenn.	Kan.	Total.
A	23	..	1	..	..	1	..	..	..	..	..	..	..	..	..	25
B.	9	20	5	4	2	1	..	..	..	..	..	..	..	..	..	41
C.	5	8	2	17	8	1	..	..	..	1	1	..	..	..	..	43
D.	23	32	5	3	1	1	..	..	..	..	..	..	..	..	..	65
E.	60	7	15	3	4	2	5	3	2	..	..	1	1	1	1	105
	120	67	28	27	15	6	5	3	2	1	1	1	1	1	1	279

Manufacturers engaged in several branches of the silk business are registered under each.

RAW SILK.

Season of 1875–1876.

[Presented by Mr. WILLIAM RYLE.]

The season of 1875–6 has been an eventful one in the history of the silk trade. Production and consumption of the raw material have both been on the increase, and prices have been such as to offer much encouragement. The production of raw silk in China has been greater than during the preceding year. This is accounted for by a very large increase in the Canton districts, which has more than counterbalanced the slight falling off at Shanghae.

Shanghae silks have been fully up to the average in quality, but some of the lower grades of re-reels—more especially Tsatlee sorts—have been very dirty, and most abominably adulterated, as much as 21 per cent. of adulteration having been detected in one lot. The older and best-known chops of re-reeled Haineen have fully maintained their character, both as to quality and freedom from adulteration. Would that the same could be said of best R. R. Tsatlees! A note-worthy—because characteristic—instance of Chinese deception occurred during the past season in this description of silk. A manufacturing firm, desirous of obtaining a supply of one chop of silk, so as to insure uniformity in their goods, placed an order at the commencement of the season with a prominent re-reeler for 100 bales of raw silk, deliverable in shipments of twenty bales per month. The price contracted for was a liberal one on the part of the manufacturer, and one that would have been remunerative to the reeler, had he furnished pure silk, as stipulated in the order. The opportunity to cheat was too much for Mongolian virtue to resist, and the deliveries were made with the following results: The first shipment was as near as possible to the sample, and contained five per cent. of foreign matter. Every subsequent shipment was more and more impure, until the last arrived with twelve and a half per cent. adulteration, thus proving the perpetration of a systematic fraud.

One would suppose that the loss of business arising from such deceitful practice would induce more faithful fulfilment of contracts; but experience proves that all considerations are inoperative to make the Chinaman honest in his dealings with the foreigner.

Canton sorts have been fully up to the standard of the best years as to quality; but would have been more acceptable to the trade had half the crop been reeled in coarse sizes.

Japan, although increasing her export nearly thirty per cent., has contributed but a nominal quantity to our market, and is the only country from which we draw a supply that has reduced its dealings with us during the past year. After so much complaint has been made in past years, it is very gratifying to report that the small quantity received this season from Japan has been of good quality, and some of it particularly well adapted to the requirements of our trade. In winding, the silk proved equal to any from Europe; and was so uniform as not to vary more than 4 deniers in 2 threads organzine. Silk of this quality, at a reasonable price, would soon obtain currency in our markets, and could be used in almost any size from 14 to 24 deniers. Sizes from 18 to 24 deniers should, however, be afforded at a price that will compete with coarse re-reeled Cumchucks and Tsatlees.

European Silks.—The crop of silk in Europe during the past season was less than its predecessor, the total production of cocoons showing a falling off of ten per cent., and of raw silk of about twenty per cent. The silk was reeled as well as usual, but was not equal to some previous crops in the properties which manufacturers so highly prize, and which have especially characterized the productions of Northern Italy.

Bengal, Brutia and Persian silks, not being used here, do not require extended report.

It is a noteworthy feature that the diversion of silk from England to the countries of continental Europe has increased to such extent that London is no longer the chief recipient of China silk. During this season Marseilles has carried off the palm, the exports from Shanghae to France having increased about 2,000, while to England they show a falling off of nearly 7,000 bales. From Hong Kong we find an increase of less than 1,000 bales to London, while France shows a gain of 3,400. From either Asiatic port France has received more silk than England, the excess from Shanghae being about 25, and from Hong Kong nearly 40 per cent. Switzerland and Italy also came in for an increased business, having imported from Shanghae more than double their receipts of the previous season.

Before closing this paper, it is perhaps well to recur to the subject of the adulteration of Shanghae silks. We have, without avail, written so much upon this topic, and endeavored to bring so many considerations and influences to bear upon the Chinese, both through the press and the action of the Chamber of Commerce, at Shanghae, to induce them to discontinue these dishonest practices, that it behooves us to look around for some other means. It would perhaps be well to consider the advisability of seeking a supply of re-reels from other countries, by obtaining, if possible, a reconsideration of the ruling of the Treasury Department, dated March 28, 1866, which imposes a duty of 35 per cent. upon silk re-reeled in all countries other than those of its production. The removal of this restriction would open new avenues of supply of re-reeled Chinas from England or continental Europe, where labor is so much cheaper than here. It would also enable our manufacturers to avail themselves of the low sales frequently made in the London market of raw silks. These, if re-reeled, could here be used advantageously; but in the original reels they are entirely unsuited to our wants.

During the past two years, Bengal silks have sold at notably low prices in England; but being in the original reel, they were unsuited to our operatives, and therefore could not be used here. They were, however, manufactured into goods in Europe and sent to our market to compete with our manufacturers, whose goods were made from a more costly material. Had we been able to have such raw silks re-reeled in Europe, and import them free of duty, American manufacturers could have defied this competition, and found lucrative employment for hundreds of looms which have either been unprofitable to their owners or condemned to positive idleness, on account of being debarred from the use of these cheap silks by this Treasury regulation.

ASIATIC RAW SILK EXPORTS.

Tabular statement of the export of raw silk from the various ports of China and Japan, for the seasons of 1874–75 and 1875–76.

SHANGHAE SILK.

Shipments from Commencement of the Season to March 30th.

		Bales.		Bales.
1875–76, to	England	25,596	1874–75	32,331
"	France	30,179	"	28,734
"	America	6,460	"	3,911
"	Switzerland and Italy	3,356	"	1,744
"	Hong Kong and Bombay	1,457	"	2,150
		67,048		68,870

CANTONS.

Shipments from Commencement of the Season to March 29th.

		Bales.		Bales.
1875–76, to	England	5,516	1874–75	4,994
"	France	7,469	"	3,320
"	America	2,747	"	2,401
"	India	5,216	"	5,500
		20,948		16,215

JAPANS.

Shipments from Commencement of the Season to April 7th.

		Bales.		Bales.
1875–76, to	England	4,337	1874–75	5,214
"	France	7,142	"	6,246
"	America	88	"	115
"	Other countries	234	"	366
		11,801		11,941

THROWN SILKS.

[Presented by Messrs. Geo. B. Skinner & Co.]

Reviewing the business of 1875, this branch of industry appears to have been very moderately, if at all, remunerative. As was stated in last year's report on Thrown Silks, the Spring season opened with a fair prospect for an early brisk trade in nearly all grades, with a market mostly bare of the staple articles. Being thus encouraged to greater confidence than in many previous months, all the manufacturers of these goods increased their production. The demand soon fell away, having been largely based upon a forced effort to start the season's business; and was followed by a return to the languid condition that had preceded it. The market then and for some time afterward presented features chiefly advantageous to the buyer; the demand being slow and fluctuating. Lower prices were demanded and concessions obtained during an earnest competition on the part of sellers. At no time was a disposition shown to place orders in advance; business was down on the "hand to mouth" principle; lower prices marked each successive purchase, until, as before stated, this branch of trade became almost unremunerative.

Although the cost of labor and all other expenses in throwing silk have risen forty to fifty per cent., the prices obtained for the goods have ranged fully five per cent. lower than at any time during the last twenty years. This statement applies to the whole class of silks used by the manufacturers of Trimmings and Passementerie.

Tsatlee and Haineen Tram and Organzine, as supplied for ribbons and piece goods, demand something more than passing notice; the adulterations of the raw silks should command the serious consideration of the Association, in the interest alike of the throwster and of the general public. The reports from the manufacturers of Ribbons and Fancy Silk goods will doubtless indicate a year of prosperity, as a fairly active demand for Thrown Silks has resulted from their needs. The throwster might have shared in this prosperity, but for his losses by adulteration. We believe that this dishonest practice with raw silk is more destructive to the growth and prosperity of the whole silk trade than would be an immediate reduction of the tariff on the manufactured goods. The latter alternative would indeed be an advantage, as an open warfare is less perilous than an encounter with a concealed foe.

It has become impossible to obtain in the American market a pure R. R. Tsatlee raw silk. Importers admit the fact, and acknowledge their inability to correct the evil. Raw silk is bought on the supposition that it contains a certain percentage of adulteration. Close inspection shows that this percentage constantly varies in amount. The throwster might be expected so to adjust his scale of prices as to allow for the adulteration; but this proves impracticable, since the prices of raw silks are quoted by importers and brokers freely to all comers, and the manufacturer is ready to believe that the throwster requires too wide a margin for his share of the work. With the quoted price of the raw silk in his hands, the manufacturer holds the throwster at his mercy; on the latter the whole loss of adulteration falls, and in it he sinks his profits. On the other hand, the thrown silk is subjected to rigorous tests—some of them very unfair—and even to the chemical analysis of experts, as to possible dampness or impurity.

English importers do not so fully admit as do Americans, an inability to check the adulteration or to furnish pure silk. It may be mentioned that only the re-reeled silk is adulterated, while it is evident that all grades might thus be treated if there were a market for them after being tampered with. It is possible that the Asiatics are aware that the London importers have their silks tested at a conditioning house, and are also aware that the Americans do not; and hence take advantage of our deficiency. The proclamation of Taotai, though conceived with the best of intentions, has entirely failed in curing the evil; the check upon it must be brought about in a natural way, through the trade; perhaps by means of the agents and representatives of our importers in China.

If they were clearly instructed to reject adulterated silk, the object might be readily accomplished. The method of testing is simple, easy, and requires but little room or machinery. There is no more reason for accepting adulterated silk than for taking counterfeit or base metal in trade. At present the buyers of R. R. Tsatlee raw silk need to test separately every shipment and each purchase, to learn the real cost of their goods. To relieve them from such anxiety, the Association can do much, but the importers still more. Some light may be thrown on the subject by the "Report on Raw Silk." With the continuance of the fraudulent system, a decline of the smaller interests in the silk industry is threatened. This may result in a concentration of capital and business sufficient to warrant direct importations; these alone offer at present a sure means of obtaining pure silk.

SPUN SILK.

[Presented by Messrs. CHENEY BROTHERS.]

The general depression in business during the past year has not affected so severely the demand for the cheaper grades of silk, which are now among the necessaries of civilized life, as that for the more expensive kinds, which belong to the luxuries, only within reach of a limited class of consumers.

Since spun silk comprises all yarns produced by carding, combing and spinning silks which cannot be reeled into the shape known as raw silk, the fabrics made of them are growing in favor for all purposes in which weight and durability are of more importance than the high lustre, obtained at higher cost, in reeled silk goods. The low price of raw silk and the competition of throwsters, have reduced the cost of thrown silks to a point which they have not touched for many years, and make them available for many purposes for which spun silks have heretofore been almost exclusively employed. But cheapness and good wearing qualities are more sought for in hard times, and spun yarns have entered into consumption quite as largely as in years more generally prosperous. The yarns, themselves, it is true, have as yet but a very limited outlet on the open market, in this country, and the spinners are compelled to become weavers as well, and to complete their processes and turn out finished woven fabrics. This places great restrictions on the rapid development of silk spinning, and almost confines the production of yarns to the manufacturer's capacity to weave them. No doubt, before long, the same subdivision of labor will take place here that is found in the old countries, where a high state of perfection is attained in the different branches of manufacture by having for each the specialty of establishments devoted exclusively to it. Here a manufacturer has to take raw materials, and, with but little outside aid, put them through all stages till they are ready for market, and then follow them till they are sold, in almost a retail way. This state of things necessitates the combination of many trades in one establishment, and it is impossible to secure the proper attention to details, on which success depends, without an extensive business organization and large outlay of capital.

The use of what were formerly considered waste materials is now attracting great attention, and late discoveries in the arts and sciences have changed the estimate once placed on them, so that some of them are now looked upon as articles of primary rather than of secondary importance. In estimating how much has been accomplished in the manufacture of spun silk, it must be kept in mind that this branch of industry utilizes a vast amount of raw material, which could not be used in the old ways as reeled silk, but which is now put into a shape in which, for many purposes, it is of nearly equal value. For this mainly is the manufacture now entitled to an honorable place among the productive industries of the world.

SEWING SILKS AND MACHINE TWIST.

[Presented by Messrs. SEAVEY, FOSTER & BOWMAN.]

Having been selected to report upon sewing silk and machine twist, we have now to offer the following sketch of some features of the business; not undertaking a complete history of it, however appropriate such a narrative might be at the beginning of the nation's second century of existence.

Comparing the aggregate value of the sewing silk and machine twist manufactured in the year 1874 (as given in the last annual report of this Association), with that of any other class of silk goods of American production, it will be found very nearly double in amount. Comparing also the amount stated as manufactured in the year 1875 with that of the two or three previous years, a very large increase is apparent in this branch of the silk industry. We feel it to be a cause for congratulation that this increase has not been due to any sudden freak of fortune, or change of fashion, which is likely to pass away even more suddenly than it came, leaving manufacturers to sell their goods below cost, or let their machinery stand idle. It has been caused by the natural growth and development of manufactures, in connection with the general use of sewing-machines in the manufacture of boots and shoes and clothing, and in the household economy of nearly every home in the land. It is also due to the skill and energy of American manufacturers in producing goods of such quality and at such prices as entirely to prevent the importation of machine twists into our markets, and very nearly stop that of sewing silks—an endeavor that would have been entirely successful, were it not for the old prejudice which yet remains in a few minds against silks of American manufacture. That in reality our domestic silks are much better and cheaper than imported goods, is illustrated by the fact that quite large quantities of American machine twists and sewing silks annually find a market in the British North American Provinces. Yet there they are compelled to pay a duty of 15 per cent. in gold, and the seller must come into competition with large English manufacturers who have held the trade for many years with little fear that Yankee enterprise would ever be a match for their vast resources of wealth and experience. We think that this branch of the silk industry has attained to a standard of excellence in this country equal to that of any other nation, and that the coming Centennial Exhibition will witness a display in this department never excelled. Nothing but adverse legislation, or some mistaken policy on the part of manufacturers themselves, can prevent it from having a prosperous future.

This branch of trade has, it is true, suffered in common with almost every other from the depressed condition of business, and from the active competition of those engaged in it, thus reducing the margin of profit to a narrow limit, and demoralizing prices to such an extent as to cause some solicitude among manufacturers for the future prosperity of the business. Yet we trust that some action may be taken to establish proper standards of lengths and sizes, to which all engaged in the business may conform; and then by concerted and harmonious action, protect the public as well as themselves.

PLAIN AND FANCY BROAD SILKS.

[Presented by Messrs. HAMIL & BOOTH.]

The year 1875 has been a prosperous one for the silk manufacture, and the broad silk weavers have been favored with a good demand for their goods.

They have added largely to the number of looms employed, and have also made goods not before attempted in this country. While the older manufacturers have increased their capacity to produce, several new firms have been organized, and manufacturers not heretofore engaged in weaving have turned their attention in that direction. With the increase in looms, greater competition and enlarged experience, we have had the usual result of lower prices; but the knowledge gained in the last five years should be sufficient to enable the trade to make goods at such prices as the market can pay. The home manufacturer, notwithstanding the tariff, has many difficulties to meet; he is confined entirely to our own market, where every buyer wishes to buy the same article at the same time. If he has wise foresight, or a lucky inspiration, so that he gets his goods started a little ahead of the demand, he is successful; but if he changes his machinery and organization after the demand begins, he has always the possibility of a heavy loss, from a sudden change in the demand, or an over-production of the article, because all the manufacturers make the same thing. The importance of making a greater variety of fabrics, and those most stable in demand, must impress itself on our manufacturers. It is evident that a uniform and stable trade is more profitable, at a smaller percentage, than one which requires constant changes in styles and organization. The last year was satisfactory in the fancy silk trade, and goods for ties, scarfs, millinery, trimmings, etc., were in demand till late in the year. In October, and the remaining months, by an unexpected stagnation, large quantities of goods which had been made were not called for; on these goods large concessions had to be made, and prices lower than cost accepted. This dullness has continued to the present time, and unless a change occurs, our report for 1876 cannot be so favorable. Silk handkerchiefs were called for late in the Summer at satisfactory prices, but a falling off in the demand, and an apparent over-production, started somewhat of a panic among the holders and manufacturers, which brought prices down below cost.

Styles and quality of goods produced show a steady improvement, and our designs are artistic and more favorably received in this market than the imported.

The manufacture of the finer qualities of dress goods is gradually increasing, and promises to be successful, so that we may expect to produce goods to rival those of the celebrated European makers. The Centennial Exhibition, soon to open, will undoubtedly astonish the country in the display of home productions in silk goods; and the quantity of goods, the quality and designs, and the perfection of manufacture and coloring, will be surprising to most of the visitors.

RIBBONS.

[Presented by MR. WM. STRANGE.]

It seems to me a subject for congratulation and pride, not only to those directly interested, but also to the community at large, that, while nearly all the various industries of the country have been forced into inactivity and distress since the panic of 1873, during the past year our branch has formed, in many respects, an exception to the general rule.

Since the date of our last annual report, and until October, 1875, the ribbon trade found occupation for its factories, steady employment for a largely increased number of operatives, and an outlet for a much greater amount of home production than in any former year; and although the demand has been for specialties, which had to be manufactured, (thus precluding, in a great measure, sales from stocks accumulated during the preceding seasons of unprofitable speculation) the result, if not satisfactory in a pecuniary point of view, has been gratifying, inasmuch as it has prevented a further accumulation, and furnished the means of comfort and sustenance to 8,000 operatives in Paterson alone, where, had it not been for the more thriving state of our industry, great distress must inevitably have prevailed among the poorer operatives, many of whom, having been deprived of employment, were dependent upon the wages earned by their children in the silk mills for the support of their families. Nearly $2,500,000 has been paid to the operatives of Paterson by their employers, for labor performed during the past year. Our foundries, machine shops, wood turners and box makers have, in a great measure, been kept busily employed with orders from our factories, and this has furnished an additional outlet for the distribution of capital and employment of labor. I say, therefore, that the bare accomplishment of such results is of itself sufficient cause for thankfulness on our part; but when, in addition thereto, we can assert, with verity, that all this has been effected by means of capital drawn from the wealthy, who could afford to pay for luxuries, and without the imposition of direct or indirect taxation to the amount of one dollar upon the less fortunate classes, so many of whom have received benefit therefrom, I think our claims for appreciation from the people of America are fully sustained.

Apologizing for this slight digression from the matter under consideration, I will now return to the main subject.

As previously intimated, the expectations of improvement in the ribbon trade, which were foreshadowed in our last report, have been fulfilled.

Early in the month of March, 1875, a growing demand for light and medium blues, pink, lavender, lilacs, écru, paille, seal brown, drab, cerise and scarlet, in widths varying from Nos. 4 to 12, and 7 and 8 inch sashes, began to be manifest, and continued through the month of April.

In May, sales increased with higher prices, adding cream to the shades in demand, and Nos. 20 and 30 to the widths in vogue.

The prevailing colors in June were cardinal, seal brown, and light blues; during this month the demand for Nos. 20 and 30 fell off perceptibly, and Nos. 7, 9 and 12 became the fashionable widths.

In July the sales were comparatively small, but satisfactory, considering the advanced state of the season; marine blue was added to the shades previously in demand, the widths remaining the same as in the preceding month.

August and September gave promise of bright prospects for the Fall trade; new shades in myrtle, green, prune, marine, and seal brown, were put upon the market, and found a ready sale at sustained prices; but a material decline became perceptible in October, when 7 and 8 inch sashes, which had until then, been in brisk demand, became unsaleable, even at reduced figures; and from thenceforth, up to the first of February 1876, general stagnation prevailed.

In February and until the middle of March the manufacturers who needed an outlet for accumulated stock attempted to compete among themselves. This as a natural consequence had the effect of reducing prices and inciting speculation on the part of buyers. Increased sales at a great sacrifice to the producer were thus effected; but a diminished demand, want of confidence in the maintenance of prices, and the forcing of goods upon a market already amply supplied, soon produced the inevitable results—creating a demoralization in the trade, which from present prospects, bids fair to continue for some time to come.

But the past, and not the future, is my theme; and, on behalf of our branch of the silk industry, I am pleased to be able to report an increase of at least fifty per cent. in production and consumption over any previous year, with a corresponding decline in imports, which have been reduced from one-half to a little over one-third of the requirements of our home market.

This is one of the most satisfactory features which I have to present for your consideration as an indication of real development. As a mark of progress in perfection of fabrics, I would mention that, in view of a prospective demand for fancy or *jacquard* work, most of our manufacturers have prepared themselves to meet the requirements of changing fashion, and are even now successfully competing, both in quality and price, with that class of foreign production. Although these rapid advances have been in a measure due to the protection which the American people have granted us in a high tariff, still it must not be surmised that the country has not reaped a proportionate share of the benefits which have been bestowed; for it must be borne in mind that while the home manufacturers are speedily and surely assuming a position which will in the future defy foreign competition, the people on the other hand, as consumers of our productions, by fostering a home competition, are just as indisputably reaping benefit, through a cheaper market under the high protective tariff of 60 per cent., than in 1862, '3 and '4, when the duty was only 40 per cent.; thus showing that the burden is not borne by the people, as many suppose.

A retrospect of the past year's transactions in our branch of the industry although, as shown, comparatively satisfactory in the aggregate, reveals, nevertheless, many stumbling blocks which we have had to overcome; not the least of these have been undervaluation of imports; imperfect reeling and adulteration of China raws; and decline of value in, and loss of interest on, accumulations of stock from previous disastrous seasons, the last-named evil having been a serious impediment to our still greater progress.

Little do the working classes realize, when clamoring for higher wages at the first indication of returning prosperity, to what extent they have been indebted for employment in bad times, to the losses voluntarily incurred by the manufacturers, in order to keep them together so as to be ready to start when prices revive. They do not recognize the laws of trade, when brought to bear upon their labor; but seem to be impressed with the idea that their employers are in duty bound to accede to their demands, however unjust. In the endeavor by means of strikes and combinations, to force employers into acquiescence, workmen meet with varying success; but the practice is suicidal to both parties, for if the manufacturer is deprived of an opportunity to recover from the losses which his sacrifices have entailed, he must eventually succumb to the force of circumstances, and the working class must lose an opportunity for labor.

In conclusion, allow me to remark that, although the stability of the ribbon manufacture is undoubted, its immediate future as an important branch of American industry, is a matter for serious consideration; and it behooves each and every person engaged in it to act with extreme caution. Demand and supply must, as ever, regulate our operations. An overstocked market, unproductive capital, labor strikes, and unfair competition, are fraught with evils which only our combined efforts and sound judgment can avert. Let us, then, discard all petty jealousies and selfish purposes in this supreme moment of peril; for in union we will find strength which may enable us to overcome and conquer all our difficulties, and consolidate our position against foreign competition.

THE TRIMMING TRADE.

[Presented by Messrs. Wm. H. Horstmann & Sons.]

Laces, braids, and dress trimmings form an important component of the silk industry of this country, and well deserve a separate sketch, in view of the advances that have been made in this branch of the manufacture, and the number of persons interested in it or dependent upon it for support. Nearly a quarter of a century ago the Committee on Exhibition of the Franklin Institute found occasion in their report to express their pleased surprise that the productions of American looms would bear full comparison with those of Lyons or St. Etienne. After referring to the fact that this commendation could be justly applied not only as to brilliancy of color and weight of material, but also in respect to evenness of manufacture, the Committee say, "*This introduces a new era in American industry.*"

The prophecy has been fulfilled. It was suggested in that report that fostering this branch of industry might help to distribute at home, the millions of dollars then going abroad for a species of merchandise that is required only by taste and fashion. The tables of imports show that this result has been achieved. The statistics of the silk industry show it yet more conclusively. The 2,753 operatives—of whom more than three-fifths were women—employed in this country in 1875 in making laces, braids and trimmings, are living witnesses to the fact.

Results like these are not achieved by accident. Money alone will not produce them. Governments may foster but cannot force them; they must come from steady, patient, hopeful, honest effort—the whole-souled endeavor to produce good work. The details of the experience of the firms and manufacturing corporations—nearly one hundred—that have engaged in this branch of the business, need not be given here. It would be a varied record, in which the periods of struggle and adversity are longer than those of ease and affluence; but the lesson is everywhere the same—perseverance in well-doing brings its reward.

Even the past year, though one of peculiar hardship in many branches of business, has not been in this department wanting in pleasant features. The dress trimming trade has, in general, been quite satisfactory. The home manufacturers supply the demand, so that now there are very few colored dress and cloak trimmings imported. The variety of patterns for sale at the trimming stores is so great that ladies find no difficulty in perfectly matching the colors of their dresses. While thus meeting all the requirements of taste, the American fringes and trimmings are in general of the best material. Being made of pure silk, they will usually outlast the garment they ornament. They contrast in this respect with imported goods of similar appearance, but made from inferior silk and hence apt to fade by exposure, or wear out and fall off. Greater care in the processes by which they are made has also contributed to the notable superiority of American trimmings. The use of fringes for trimming dresses has given great encouragement to our manufacturers. These fringes are made of silk thread and of silk tape; they are wide, and are used in such profusion that the fronts of dresses are literally covered with them: except, however, as to the higher priced silk fringes, there has been, probably, less business done in them this year than last.

In very fine goods, such as fringes and marabout trimming, much progress has been made. The manufacturers who have made these a specialty deserve marked credit for the taste and ingenuity which their new styles display. They have been rewarded by an appreciation on the part of the public, silk marabout being very largely worn; it is made in a variety of styles, and is composed of silk loops and silk tape arranged to be worn as braids, though much more elaborate. On the whole, the result in this department speaks well for our domestic manufacture in a year when no importations of dress trimmings have proved profitable. The domestic silk and worsted fringes, as well as those which are all worsted, have counterbalanced by their ready sale any falling off in silk fringes. Mixtures of silk with silk crimped braids have produced styles much in demand, and although higher in price than the imported articles, have proved more saleable, being preferred on account of superior crimping and better quality.

The demand for guipure laces has somewhat fallen off during the past year, the preference of style being more in favor of écru laces. A considerable trade has been created in supplying the home demand for lace scarfs and neckties for ladies' wear.

In narrow textile fabrics such as star and embroidery braids, chenilles, bindings, cords, &c., the trade has been as good as in average years, and there is no special progress to report.

For upholsterers', shade and blind, and undertakers' trimmings, there has been the usual demand, though resulting in smaller profits to the manufacturer. The result of low prices in these goods has been to induce the manufacture—apparently—of the poorest articles that will sell at all. This is, of course, a grave and unfortunate mistake, since the goods must fail to give satisfaction and hence will lose their market. The production of the best possible goods, even though at the closest margin of profit, proves far more remunerative than any other plan, since it holds the fashion longer and the market permanently.

There has been only a very limited demand for carriage laces and trimmings; but this is a branch of the business that must revive with the return of a general prosperity.

U. S. CUSTOMS TARIFF.

We consider it a favorable circumstance to the manufacturing interests of the country that the free trade party in the National Congress decided to present, at this first session, their measure for a general reduction of import duties, rather than defer it till the long session next winter. This course —because of the unlikelihood of the bill obtaining the assent of the Senate even should it pass the House—insures for the measure an amount of deliberation, inquiry, and thoughtful discussion which tariff alterations in former years in this country have, in most instances, unfortunately failed to obtain.

The delicately adjusted relations of the present tariff, with regard to the National revenues, to foreign commerce and to internal development, have been the work of years to attain—years of diligent inquiry into the principles which ought to govern an American system in this respect, and of exhausting labor on the part of those who have sought to shape the policy of their country in conformity to those underlying principles.

The opinion is entertained by many that its several parts are not adjusted with the desired nicety to cause all interests alike to share in the burdens of taxation; but the questions involved in readjustment are of the highest order of importance, and require that sufficient time be given for a thorough investigation of the subject before any action shall be taken. The evils of hasty legislation have seldom been more strikingly illustrated than in the history of changes in the tariff.

But haste is not the only danger to which tariff legislation is exposed. Congressmen err more frequently through a want of knowledge of the practical bearings of their work than from any deliberate intent. They are mostly lawyers by profession, and their notions of the interests of trade are not derived from personal and intimate knowledge of the underlying facts. Ignorance has been called the parent of vice; it has, more frequently than malice, given birth to vicious laws.

The approaching Centennial Exhibition will afford our legislators, as well as the rest of our countrymen, an opportunity of seeing for themselves just what the tariff laws have accomplished for this country in respect to manufactures.

As regards the silk duties, while they are confessedly a tax on luxuries for the support of Government, we point with satisfaction to the fact that the prices of silk goods in our markets are lower to-day than they have been for fifteen years; lower, even, than they were under a tariff of 24 to 30 per cent. before the war. Competition among home manufacturers, aided by a full supply of raw Asiatic silks, has largely brought about this state of things. It supplies a conclusive answer to those who have alleged that a sixty per cent. duty on silk would make the prices of silks higher than if, by a low rate of duty, the control of the market were surrendered to the foreign manufacturer. In point of fact, the consumer of silk goods in America has been largely benefitted, both as to quality of goods and in the price at which he can obtain them, by the protective policy. The present price of raw silk being now equivalent to that which prevailed prior to the increase of duties, we are enabled to meet, with the test of actual experience, those who have charged the American silk manufacturer with adding the rate of duty to the asking price abroad for similar goods. In the words of one of our own manufacturers, as expressed at our last meeting, "Consumers can ask for no better *free trade* than plenty of home competition." Considered merely from the point of view of revenue, it is difficult to imagine how the proposed reduction of tariff would sufficiently affect the cost of importation to increase the quantity imported. The silk market is now so overstocked with goods, both foreign and domestic, that foreign silks are seeking purchasers at prices little above the rate of duty which the Government is supposed to have received from them.

CUSTOMS REVENUE AT NEW YORK.

Since our last report an important change has taken place in the Custom House management at this port. Appraiser Darling having resigned, the Hon. Stephen R. French has been appointed to fill the vacancy. Mr. French is an ex-member of Congress, as well as a business man of many years' experience, and has filled positions of trust and responsibility. He commences his career under more favorable auspices than most of his predecessors have done, Mr. Darling having succeeded in introducing many administrative reforms in the Appraiser's Department of this port, especially during the past year, while seeking to make his department a model of efficiency in carrying out the revenue laws.

The new regulations of the Secretary of the Treasury, for the control of the Inspectors of the Port of New York, have been in operation for some months. The effect of these regulations has been practically to diminish smuggling by passengers on steamship lines. What was once an every-day event has become a story of the past. People do not buy abroad expensive silk dresses for themselves and friends with the hope of evading duties. The officers have become more careful, and few passengers will take the chances of escaping detection. Probably the best evidence of this change is shown by the conduct of men who formerly sought the duty of examining baggage. Instead of being a favorite pursuit, it is regarded as onerous and burdensome. This is a good sign. No more trunks filled with silks now arrive weekly, as in the old time when regular officers regularly met and "passed" the so-called baggage without fear of consequences. Already the principal dry goods merchants on Broadway have experienced a decided improvement in their sales of the classes of goods that used to be brought to this port as passengers' baggage. The following observation, made by one who has full opportunity for knowing the facts, covers the point. He says: "Without doubt *genteel smuggling* has ceased during the past year." Collector Arthur has weeded out many incompetent and unfaithful officers, and is still striving to render more competent the force that is intrusted with the serious duty of inspecting merchandise imported from foreign shores. The Government has not taken proper measures to assist the Collector in this important work. A deduction has been made in the scanty wages of these men, and the anomaly is presented of an employer expecting increased faithfulness while reducing the pay of employés. Under the present rate of three dollars and sixty cents per day, recently reduced from four dollars, discharging officers think they cannot live without accepting fees and presents, although the practice is expressly forbidden by the law. This is a very unfortunate condition of affairs, as we all know how great are the temptations surrounding officers entrusted with the enforcement of the revenue laws.

In a district of over sixty miles, where these men are compelled, at their own expense, to visit ships and discharge cargoes, often purchasing their meals while so employed, it is unwise and unjust on the part of the Government to confine them to inadequate salaries, while exposing them to the temptation of the gratuities which shipowners and importers are ever ready to offer. No one who has personal knowledge of the qualities required in the men placed in charge of ships and steamers constantly arriving from foreign countries, will doubt the wisdom and fairness of properly remunerating this very important body of officials. On a steamship-wharf, by means of steam-power, hundreds of tons of valuable merchandise are landed in the space of twenty-four hours—the officers remaining on duty constantly day and night until the vessel is discharged. Now, if the intelligent observer will notice how closely the regulations must be carried out to avoid confusion and fraud, and how many cargoes are daily landed without loss to the Government or the merchant, it will be readily seen that judgment and ability of no common order must be the qualifications of the men selected to perform the most arduous of all duties connected with the collection of the revenue. Recognizing the fact that these officers cannot support families on their limited pay, heads of departments have winked at a practice "more honored in the breach than in the observance." It is that of steamship companies allowing certain fees to officers detailed to discharge a ship. Strictly, and in law, this is all wrong, and the practice has been from time to time forbidden; but so long as men are inadequately paid, they appear to consider it fair to escape starvation by accepting presents.

In our previous report we spoke of the difficulty of detection and prevention of smuggling under the present system. Although great improvements have been made, perfect success is far distant. So long as passengers are landed at many different wharves badly lighted and but poorly protected from the weather, just so long will the law be carelessly carried out. There are numerous instances where officers are sent at night-fall to steamer wharves to examine baggage of passengers very anxious to get home. The steamship companies having no interest in the collection of revenue for the Treasury of the Government, do not half light the immense sheds where trunks and boxes are scattered promiscuously. Often boxes of monstrous size are brought from Europe by passengers who claim to have used household effects while residing abroad. These cases the officer cannot properly inspect on the wharf. Even under the best circumstances, and with the assistance of experienced men to unpack, the labor would be extremely difficult; but on a crowded wharf, with a *single cooper* to assist the officer, who is frequently cold or hungry or desirous of getting away from unpleasant surroundings, the proper enforcement of the customs regulation is next to impossible. Should the Government provide a suitable place for the landing of passengers and the storing and examination of baggage, many thousands of dollars now lost would be collected annually. Without reflecting on the heads of departments who have long recognized the crying evil, or on the Secretary of the Treasury who has no means at his disposal to erect a barge office at the Battery where baggage can be brought and thoroughly examined by officers detailed specially for this service, the matter is worthy of notice by Congress at this time, since that body alone has the power to make appropriation for the erection of suitable buildings. This change has often been recommended; it was never more needed than at present.

Special agents from Washington, unacquainted with the practical workings of the revenue law, may find fault with individual officers and complain of the demoralization recognized by all intelligent members of the outside force of the Custom House. *It is not to be rectified by fault-finding, but must be met squarely and reformed fairly.* Weighers' assistants have the handling of many millions of goods during the year; and the unscrupulous importer knows well how poor their pay and how uncertain their compensation. Of course temptations surround these men. They should be placed above the necessity of accepting presents.

So with the force employed in the inspection of goods on the docks. When we think of the opportunities for dishonest gains which are offered to these men, it is surprising that the Government is defrauded so little. The remedy is to give them a fair compensation in proportion to the duties performed. As it is now, the District Officer, who simply reports the arrival of vessels, is paid as much as the men who discharge cargoes. This is evidently unfair, and leads to much ill-feeling and consequent neglect of duty. In practical execution of the revenue laws, no posts are more responsible than those of the officers who discharge vessels. The men should be selected for this most important duty only with regard to capacity and character, and not with reference to party service. So long as party-claims influence the selection of men to fill places in the civil service of the country, just so long will the revenues fail to be collected, and the burden of taxation be carried by the honest and truthful merchant.

The business men of the country must continue to recommend reforms in the administration of the Government. Politicians must not control, since already the burdens of taxation are heavily felt by the citizens. Statesmen are needed to rule the country, who will alter the laws only to suit the necessities of our ever-growing Republic. The time is at hand when these reforms must be initiated, and none have a better right to advise and recommend them than the merchants of our great commercial metropolis.

Nor need the frequent exposures of the present day lead hasty observers to despair of the virtue of the Republic. We are not, as a nation, more corrupt than formerly; we are, in fact, more honest. The evidence of honesty is to be found in the vigor with which the work of unearthing fraud and breaking up systems of corruption has been prosecuted. Time was when the doctrine "to the victors belong the spoils" was subscribed to by both political parties; now each is striving to prove itself foremost in the work of reform. It is one of the best signs of the centennial year that politicians are basing their calculations and framing their plans with a view to putting forward men of acknowledged integrity; and that none who have been tainted with the suspicion of corruption, or have even winked at it among their subordinates, have the slightest prospect of the suffrages of the people.

CHARTER OF THE ASSOCIATION.

The suggestion offered at the last Annual Meeting to incorporate the Association, has resulted in its formal organization, under the general law of the State of New York. In accordance with the provisions of the Statute, five citizens of this State, members of the Association, filed a certificate of incorporation on April 11th, 1876, and the Silk Association of America has now acquired a legal, and, we may hope, a permanent status.

Following is a statement of the general laws under which the Association is incorporated.

CHAPTER EIGHTEEN, TITLE SEVEN OF THE REVISED STATUTES.

SOCIETY—HOW FORMED—CERTIFICATE OF NAME AND BUSINESS OF SOCIETY.

SEC. 1. Any five or more persons of full age, citizens of the United States, a majority of whom shall be citizens of this State, who shall desire to associate themselves together for literary, scientific purposes, &c., may make and acknowledge a certificate in writing in which shall be stated the title of the Society, its business and objects, the number of trustees, directors or managers for the first year of its existence; which certificate shall be approved in writing by a Justice of the Supreme Court of the District where the principal office of the society shall be located,

WHEN TO BECOME A BODY CORPORATE AND POLITIC.

SEC. 2. Upon filing such certificate the persons who shall have signed and acknowledged the same, and their associates and successors, shall thereupon be a body politic and corporate, shall be capable of sueing and being sued, may have a common seal, shall alter the same at pleasure, shall be capable of receiving, purchasing and holding real estate for the purposes of their incorporation, and *for no other purpose*, to an amount not exceeding Fifty Thousand Dollars in value, and personal property for like purposes to an amount not exceeding Seventy-five Thousand Dollars in value; but the clear annual income of such real and personal estate shall not exceed the sum of Ten Thousand Dollars per annum. To make laws for the management of its affairs. To elect and appoint the officers and agents of the society for the management of its business, and to allow them a suitable compensation.

ELECTION OF TRUSTEES.

SEC. 3. The Society may annually elect from its members its trustees, directors or managers, at such time and place as are specified by its by-laws, who shall have the management of the affairs of the society, a majority of whom shall be a quorum for the transaction of business, if not otherwise provided by the by-laws, *except* that no purchase, sale or lease of real estate shall be made, unless two-thirds of the whole number are present at the meeting at which it is ordered.

VACANCIES.

When any vacancy shall happen among such trustees, directors or managers, such vacancy shall be filled in such manner as shall be provided by the by-laws of such society.

PROVISION IN CASE NO ELECTION IS MADE.

SEC. 4. In case it shall at any time happen that an election shall not be made on the day designated by the by-laws, it shall be lawful to hold an election on any other day in such manner as shall be directed by the by-laws of such society,

RESTRICTION.

SEC. 5. The provisions of this Act shall not extend or apply to any association or individuals who shall in the certificate filed use a name or style the same as that of any previously existing incorporated society in this State.

REAL OR PERSONAL PROPERTY MAY BE HELD.

SEC. 6. Any corporation formed under this Act shall be capable of taking, holding or receiving any property, real or personal, by virtue of any devise or bequest, contained in any last will of any person whomsoever, the clear annual income of which shall not exceed the sum of ten thousand dollars.

PROVISO.

Provided no person leaving a wife, or child, or parent, shall devise to such corporation more than one fourth of his or her estate, after the payment of his or her debts, such devise shall be valid to the extent of one fourth; and no such devise shall be valid in any will, which shall not have been made and executed at least two months before the death of the testator.

LIABILITY OF TRUSTEES.

SEC. 7. The trustees of any corporation organized under the provisions of this Act, present at any meeting authorizing the contraction of any debt, and acquiescing in the passage of any resolution or order authorizing the same, shall be jointly and severally liable for any such debt, provided a suit for the collection of the same shall be brought within one year after the debt shall become due and payable.

SOCIETY TO BE SUBJECT TO VISITATION BY JUSTICES OF THE SUPREME COURT.

SEC. 8. Shall be subject to visitation and inspection of books and vouchers by Justices of the Supreme Court, or by persons who shall be appointed by the Supreme Court for that purpose.

CERTIFICATES TO BE FILED IN THE MONTH OF DECEMBER IN EACH YEAR.

It shall be the duty of the Trustees, or a majority of them, in the month of December in each year, to make and file in the County Clerk's office, where the original certificate is filed, a certificate under their hands, stating the names of the Trustees and officers of such corporation, with an inventory of the property, effects, and liabilities thereof, with an affidavit of the truth of such certificate and inventory, and also an affidavit that such corporation has not been engaged directly or indirectly in any other business than such as is set forth in the original certificate on file.

GENERAL POWERS.

SEC. 9. Every corporation formed under the provisions of this Act shall possess the powers, and be subject to the provisions and restrictions contained in the third title of the eighteenth chapter of the first part of the Revised Statutes.

RIGHT TO REPEAL.

SEC. 10. The Legislature may at any time amend, annul, or repeal any incorporation formed or created under this Act.

PRIVILEGES.

SEC. 11. Trustees, Directors, or Stockholders of such corporation, may, by conforming to the 1st Section of this Act, re-incorporate themselves, or continue their existing corporate powers for the period limited by the Act, and all property and effects of such existing corporation shall vest in, and belong to, the corporation so re-incorporated or continued.

SUPREME COURT TO HAVE POWER TO MAKE ORDERS FOR MORTGAGING REAL ESTATE.

SEC. 12. The Supreme Court shall have power in case it shall deem it proper on application of corporation to make order for the mortgaging of any real estate belonging to the corporation, etc.

By the death of our President, Ward Cheney, which occurred on the 22d of March, the Association has lost a warm friend and earnest supporter. The following resolutions, adopted by the members at a meeting held on the day succeeding his death, are expressive of the feelings evoked by this event. It has also touched the chord of feeling in a wider circle of human hearts. Rarely, indeed, does it happen that a private citizen not prominent in the walks of literature, science, or art, wins so largely from his fellow-men the tribute of a warm personal regard, ripening on closer acquaintance into esteem and love. There is a certain amount of admiration, not always unmixed with envy, that is usually accorded to mere pecuniary success; and within limited degrees the world is apt to honor the favorites of fortune. But the affection with which his friends regarded Ward Cheney was of a different nature; it was based upon what he was, not what he had. He labored for others' welfare as well as for his own; and as he loved others, was himself beloved.

Mr. Cheney's connection with the Association began with its organization in June, 1872, when he became its first Vice-President. On the retirement of our first President, Mr. John Ryle, in May, 1873, Mr. Cheney was elected in his place, and was re-elected to the Presidency in 1874 and 1875. Your Secretary has lost much more than a respected chief—a dear and warm-hearted friend. The sense of security was attached to all enterprises with which Ward Cheney's name was identified. He gave an incentive and stimulus to higher aims and better development in the work of the Association, and his connection brought the assurance that what of advancement had been gained could not be lost. He was ever in sympathy with plans to give our Association a permanent character. The silk trade of America has indeed sustained a heavy loss in the decease of so eminent a representative.

The resolutions were as follows:

Whereas, In the ordering of Providence our dear friend and most worthy President, Ward Cheney, has been taken from us; and

Whereas, Mr. Cheney was a man of unspotted reputation, true and just in all his dealings, kind and genial in all his intercourse, ripe and mature in his judgment, and in every way well deserving and well befitting the proud position he occupied in the silk trade and in this Association; therefore be it

Resolved, That we unfeignedly mourn the loss of Ward Cheney, and deeply sympathize with his family in their great bereavement; that we hold up for imitation his character, his integrity and his enterprise; that we are proud of his name and will keep his memory green whilst the silk trade shall last; that as a mark of affectionate respect a committee of this Association shall be delegated to attend the funeral of Mr. Cheney; and that a copy of this preamble and resolution be engrossed and framed for presentation as a memento to Mr. Cheney's family.

The following members represented the Association in the funeral services at South Manchester.

THOMAS N. DALE, 1st Vice-President.

GEO. B. SKINNER,	J. H. HAYDEN,
B. RICHARDSON,	IRA DIMOCK,
JOHN T. WALKER,	TOBIAS KOHN,
ROWLAND JOHNSON,	FRANKLIN ALLEN, Secretary.
T. TOMITA, Vice-Consul of Japan, at New York.	

FINANCES.

The revenues of the Association have not been as great in the past year as in the year preceding. In most other departments of industry, and especially our own, reduced revenue has been accompanied by a demand for a more economical administration. The sources of receipts and the items of disbursements are as follows:

FOURTH ANNUAL VOLUNTARY SUBSCRIPTIONS.

Cheney Bros., - - - - - -	$800 00
Wm. H. Horstmann & Sons, - - - -	400 00
Nonotuck Silk Co., - - - - -	300 00
William Ryle, - - - - , -	300 00
Wm. Strange & Co., - - - - -	300 00
Jno. N. Stearns & Co., - - - - -	300 00
A. A. Low & Bros. - - - - -	300 00
Belding Bros. & Co., - - - - -	200 00
Dexter, Lambert & Co., - - - -	200 00
Wm. H. Fogg & Co., - - - -	200 00
B. B. Tilt & Son, - - - - -	180 00
Dale Manufacturing Co., - - - -	150 00
A. Soleliac & Son - - - - -	100 00
The Singer Manufacturing Co., - - -	100 00
Werner Itschner & Co., - - - -	100 00
Jno. T. Walker, - - - - - -	100 00
J. Silbermann & Co., - - - - -	100 00
Wood, Payson & Colgate, - - - -	100 00
Wm. H. Smith & Son, - - - -	100 00
Tetsnoske Tomita, Vice-Consul of Japan at N. Y.,	100 00
Cary & Co., - - - - - - -	75 00
A. G. Jennings, - - - - - -	75 00
Aub, Hackenburg & Co., - - - -	50 00
Louis Franke, - - - - - -	50 00
S. M. Meyenberg, - - - - - -	50 00
	$4,730 00
Annual dues of members, $25.00 each, -	1,450 00
11 Initiation fees, new members, $25.00 each, -	275 00
Sundry receipts, - - - - -	52 29

Making the total sum for the year, - -		$6,507 29
Which added to the balance on hand at the last annual meeting, say -		2,429 59
presents a total of - - - - -		$8,936 88

less $450.00 in suspense account, voluntary subscriptions remaining unpaid to the Treasurer at this date.

To the debit of the account we have $7,422.25 of disbursements classified under the following heads:

Office Rent, - - - - - -		$350 00
" Furniture, - - - - - -		126 85
Newspaper Subscription Account,		
Subscriptions and Purchases, -	$145 69	
Society of Arts, London, - -	12 04	157 73
Library Expenses, Sundry Books, - -		71 65
Stationery and Printing, - - - -		1,471 04
Postage and Expressage, - - - - -		367 44
Telegram Account, - - - -		13 92
Coal and Gas Bills, - - - - - -		28 24
Incidental Expenses, - - - - -		113 34
Office Expenses, - - - - - -		65 16
Petty Cash Expenses, - - - - -		75 42
Traveling Expenses, Secretary, - - -		82 70
Raw Silk Manifests, New York and San Francisco,		222 76
Office Clerks, - - - - - -		1,276 00
Franklin Allen, Secretary, - - - -		3,000 00
		$7,422 25

leaving a balance in the hands of the Treasurer at date, of $1,064.63. [N. B. The balance on hand at the last annual meeting was $2,429.59].

AMENDMENT TO BY-LAWS.

On the 25th of February, the following amendment to the By-laws of the Association was adopted, notice of the proposed change having been presented in writing at the meeting of February 9th:

Provided, that in the year 1876 the annual meeting for the election of officers to serve in the year ensuing and for receiving the report of the

Board of Government may be held on the last Wednesday of April, at such place as the Board of Government may appoint, instead and in lieu of the second Wednesday of May as provided for in sections 1 and 2 of article V of the by-laws: the said change being deemed advisable in consequence of the said second Wednesday of May, 1876, having been designated by the United States Centennial Commission for the opening and inauguration services of the International Exhibition at Philadelphia.

PREPARATIONS FOR THE CENTENNIAL.

The question as to the best action of the Association in reference to having the silk industry fully represented at the Centennial Exhibition, was referred by the Board of Government to a Committee selected therefor. The Committee reported that after due effort had been made in calling the attention of manufacturers to the subject, the projected plan of effort on the part of the Association had not been encouraged. The Committee therefore recommended that the matter be left to individual effort and enterprise. A circular was sent to each silk manufacturer and maker of silk machinery, stating the foregoing facts and suggesting the steps needful to insure a good display, as well as urging the importance of promptness in making them. The matter being thus relegated to individual manufacturers, a considerable number of prominent firms have undertaken the work with spirit, and there will be, as a result, a creditable display made of the advances of the silk industry.

In last year's report the hope was expressed that a descriptive pamphlet might be prepared for circulation at Philadelphia, giving an account of the origin, growth and success of the silk industry in this country. It was proposed to make this pamphlet of a popular character, and to have it sold at a nominal price to the visitors at the Exhibition. The sum of money necessary for the preparation of the pamphlet was subscribed by the manufacturers; permission for its sale during the Exhibition was obtained from Director General Goshorn; and the writing of the pamphlet was entrusted to a gentleman well versed in the subject, and of repute in literature. The "History of Silk Industry in America," thus prepared, will prove entertaining in itself, while it must serve to enlighten the public upon the advances that have been made by American skill, ingenuity, and persevering effort.

Respectfully submitted,

FRANKLIN ALLEN,

New York, April 26, 1876. Secretary.

Dr. THE SILK ASSOCIATION OF AMERICA in account with JOHN N. STEARNS, Treasurer. **Cr.**

1875.			
May	27	To Cash paid Secretary on accounts rendered	$400 00
June	21	" "	300 00
July	10	" "	416 46
July	24	" "	150 00
Aug.	5	" "	432 15
Aug.	31	" "	200 00
Sept.	3	" "	127 80
Sept.	3	" "	400 00
Oct.	2	" "	573 82
Oct.	22	" "	750 00
Oct.	22	" "	150 00
Nov.	10	" "	158 17
Nov.	19	" "	250 00
Nov.	27	" "	300 00
Dec.	18	" "	200 00
Dec.	29	" "	125 00
1876.			
Jan.	17	" "	175 00
Jan.	27	" "	200 00
Feb.	5	" "	302 27
Feb.	11	" "	375 00
March	9	" "	150 00
March	15	" "	200 00
April	6	" "	500 00
April	19	" "	300 00
April	24	" "	163 52
April	26	" "	50 76
		To balance to new Account	1,064 63
			$8,414 58

1875.			
May	12	By Balance in hands Treasurer	$2,363 09
		" Annual Dinner Acc't	7 29
		" A. A. Low & Bros., Cable Tel. Acct.	39 20
		" 2 Initiation Fees, 1874–75	50 00
		" 9 " 1875–76	225 00
		" 1 Annual Dues, 1874–75	25 00
		" 57 " 1875–76	1,425 00
		" Subscriptions to Deficiency Fund IV	4,280 00
			$8,414 58
1876.			
April	26	By Balance from old Acc't	$1,064 63

Outstanding Items,

Annual Dues unpaid........ $200 00
Subscriptions unpaid....... 450 00

E. & O. E.
New York, April 26, 1876.
JOHN N. STEARNS, *Treasurer.*

SETH LOW,
ALBERT TILT, } *Auditors.*

Imports, Re-Exports and net dutiable Imports of Raw Silk, with rates of duty and estimated amount of duty from 1823 to 1842 inclusive.

Fiscal Years ended Sept. 30.		Imports of Raw Silk Dutiable.	Re-Exports of Raw Silk	Net Imports.	Rate of Duty.	Amount of Duty (Estimated)
1823		$4,673	....	$4,673	15%	$701
1824		1,254	....	1,254	"	188
1825		8,090	....	8,090	"	1,214
1826		192,496	....	192,496	"	28,874
1827		135,230	....	135,230	"	20,285
1828		608,738	$560,129	48,609	"	7,291
1829		101,796	35,967	65,829	"	9,874
1830		119,074	108,975	10,099	"	1,515
1831		134,376	88,557	*45,819	"	....
1832		48,938	48,800	138	12½%	17
1833		135,348	66,456	68,892	"	8,612
1834		139,256	78,706	*60,550	"	....
1835		10,715	4,114	6,601	"	825
1836		37,507	....	37,507	"	4,688
1837		211,694	118,434	93,260	"	11,657
1838		79,251	29,938	*49,313	"	....
1839		39,258	4,682	34,576	"	4,322
1840		234,235	200,239	33,996	"	4,250
1841		254,102	227,113	26,989	"	3,374
1842		33,002	420	32,582	20%	6,516

* Via Cape of Good Hope.

Bureau of Statistics, Washington, D. C.,
May 20th, 1876.

(Signed) EDWARD YOUNG,
Chief of Bureau.

Statistics of production of raw silk in the United States at irregular periods.

Year.	Value.
1821	$171,000
1834	450,800
1835	290,000
1840	250,000
1843	1,400,000
1850	54,215
1860	47,000
1870	90,000

Imports, Re-Exports and net dutiable Imports of Raw Silk, with rates of duty, and estimated amount of duty, from 1843 to 1875, inclusive.

Fiscal Years ended June 30.	Imports of Raw Silk.		Re-Exports of Raw Silk.	Net Imports.	Rate of Duty.	Amount of Duty (Estimated.)
	Free of Duty.	Dutiable.				
1843	....	$53,350	$3,353	$49,997	50c. per lb.	$8,299
1844	....	172,953	7,102	165,851	"	28,668
1845	....	208,454	4,362	204,092	"	30,581
1846	....	216,647	23,999	192,648	"	31,413
1847	....	161,624	42,251	119,373	15 %	17,906
1848	....	340,769	19,858	320,911	"	48,137
1849	....	366,238	55,515	310,723	"	46,608
1850	....	386,281	63,026	323,255	"	48,488
1851	....	448,198	43,856	404,342	"	60,651
1852	....	360,836	7,143	353,693	"	53,054
1853	....	712,092	282	711,810	"	106,771
1854	....	1,085,261	2,956	1,082,305	"	162,345
1855	....	742,251	63,279	678,972	"	101,846
1856	....	991,234	4,255	986,979	"	148,047
1857	....	953,734	4,163	949,571	"	142,436
1858	$1,300,065	*242,130	94,092	1,448,103	Free.	24,213
1859	1,330,890	*88,267	19,978	1,599,179	"	28,826
1860	1,235,976	*104,700	177,881	1,162,795	"	10,470
1861	1,411,416	*67,378	124,104	1,354,690	"	6,737
1862	413,972	*75,554	21,412	468,114	"	7,555
1863	897,661	*120,807	14,112	1,004,356	"	12,080
1864	1,932,766	*125,198	31,501	2,026,463	"	12,519
1865	1,040,809	*153,061	480,193	713,677	"	15,306
1866	3,437,900	....	198,429	3,239,471	"	....
1867	2,469,001	....	26,276	2,442,725	"	....
1868	2,520,404	....	245,657	2,274,747	"	....
1869	3,318,496	....	57,031	3,261,465	"	....
1870	3,017,958	....	43,031	2,974,927	"	....
1871	5,739,592	....	189,783	5,549,809	"	....
1872	5,625,620	....	133,370	5,492,250	"	....
1873	6,460,621	....	45,892	6,414,729	"	....
1874	3,854,008	....	29,065	3,824,943	"	....
1875	4,504,306	....	32,910	4,471,396		....

* Via Cape of Good Hope, paying 10 per cent. duty.

Bureau of Statistics, Washington, D. C.,
May 20th, 1876.

Signed, EDWARD YOUNG,
Chief of Bureau.

Export of American Manufactured Silks, chiefly Sewing-Silk and Machine Twist, in the years 1870–75.

Year.	Value.
1870	$11,648
1871	27,580
1872	62,521
1873	65,560
1874	40,878
1875	71,534

STATEMENT showing the Imports, Re-exports and net dutiable Imports of Silk Manufactures, with rates and estimated amount of duty, from 1821 to 1842, inclusive.

Fiscal Years ended Sept. 30th.	IMPORTS OF SILK MANUFACTURES.							Dutiable Silk Manufactures Re-exported.	Dutiable Net Imports.	Rate of Duty.	Amount of Duty Estimated.	Fiscal Years ended Sept. 30th.
	FREE OF DUTY.		DUTIABLE.									
			PIECE GOODS.		OTHER MANUFACTURES.							
	Other than India Shawls, Shades, etc.	Other Manufactures.	From India.	From Other places.	From India.	From Other places.	Total Dutiable.					
1821							$4,486,924	$1,057,233	$3,429,691	30 %	$1,028,907	1821
1822							6,840,928	1,016,262	5,824,666	"	1,747,400	1822
1823							6,713,771	1,512,449	5,201,322	"	1,560,397	1823
1824			$790,756	$1,241,882	$22,415	$5,148,281	7,203,334	1,816,325	5,387,009	20 & 25 %*	1,118,260	1824
1825			3,500,884	3,253,318	193,823	3,323,502	10,271,527	1,706,651	8,564,876	"	1,897,711	1825
1826			2,839,694	2,480,902	400,173	2,384,068	8,104,837	1,226,584	6,878,253	"	1,537,644	1826
1827			1,483,238	2,960,201	63,019	2,038,787	6,545,245	2,615,636	3,929,609	"	863,234	1827
1828			2,726,127	2,840,871	103,627	1,937,989	7,608,614	1,226,584	6,382,030	20 & 30 %*	1,559,381	1828
1829			1,809,391	3,015,405	203,693	2,020,139	7,048,628	920,958	6,127,670	"	1,426,842	1829
1830			1,367,092	2,824,918	31,224	1,550,776	5,774,010	918,979	4,855,031	"	1,110,838	1830
1831			1,803,239	6,155,739	53,766	2,891,649	10,904,393	1,041,620	9,862,773	"	2,158,256	1831
1832			2,564,262	4,000,010	132,080	2,451,370	9,147,722	1,269,441	7,878,281	5 & 10 %*	651,231	1832
1833			1,562,263	6,195,980	47,157	1,368,799	9,174,199	1,261,133	7,913,066	"	598,624	1833
1834			1,493,893	716,765	31,241	367,450	2,609,349	1,056,489	1,552,860	Free & 10 %*	265,521	1834
1835	$562,826	$14,421,758	1,223,971		39,227	350,201	1,613,399	259,975	1,353,424	"	240,402	1835
1836	974,857	19,357,039	1,747,106		83,542	699,633	2,530,381	208,152	2,322,129	"	428,110	1836
1837	297,461	10,816,718	2,293,296		261,886	445,810	3,000,992	647,460	2,353,532	"	360,180	1837
1838	171,030	8,106,675	1,176,455		34,237	323,941	1,534,633	138,622	1,396,011	"	214,108	1838
1839	345,490	18,685,295	1,738,509		50,650	818,884	2,608,043	230,354	2,377,689	"	450,678	1839
1840	309,858	7,979,100	963,441		23,314	251,275	1,238,030	653,897	584,133	"	167,182	1840
1841	358,663	14,018,573	485,641		17,359	376,671	879,671	169,277	710,394	"	161,440	1841
1842			541,506	8,060,409	23,418	790,042	9,415,375	256,621	9,158,754	20 %	1,852,351	1842

* The higher rate of duty is on Silk Manufactures imported from beyond the Cape of Good Hope.

Bureau of Statistics, Washington, May 20, 1876.

EDWARD YOUNG, *Chief of Bureau.*

Imports, Re-exports and net dutiable imports of Silk Manufactures, with Rates and [illegible] Duty from 1843 to 1875, inclusive.

Fiscal Years ended June 30.	IMPORTS OF SILK MANUFACTURES DUTIABLE.				Dutiable Silk Manufactures Re-Exported.	Dutiable Net Imports.	Rate of Duty.	Amount of Duty.	Fiscal Years ended June 30.
	Piece Goods.	Hosiery.	Other Manufactures.	Total.					
1843	$238,809	....	$2,424,592	$2,663,401	$205,777	$2,457,624	30% & $2.50* per lb.	$743,431	1843
1844	....	....	8,312,669	8,312,669	238,051	8,074,618	" "	2,442,572	1844
1845	....	....	9,740,867	9,740,867	262,425	9,478,442	" "	2,867,229	1845
1846	....	....	10,692,118	10,692,118	210,144	10,481,974	" *25%	3,118,388	1846
1847	4,534,487	201,759	1,650,485	6,386,731	203,846	6,182,885	" "	1,839,408	1847
1848	10,762,801	427,703	3,367,334	14,557,838	314,853	14,242,985	" "	4,237,288	1848
1849	7,588,822	468,393	5,751,514	13,808,729	388,572	13,420,157	" "	3,992,493	1849
1850	14,459,560	616,217	2,578,951	17,654,728	297,019	17,357,709	" "	5,163,918	1850
1851	22,178,379	785,832	2,451,285	25,415,496	505,475	24,910,021	" "	7,379,594	1851
1852	16,823,528	599,673	4,156,462	21,579,663	611,140	20,968,523	" "	6,211,925	1852
1853	22,470,911	1,124,680	6,850,134	30,445,725	611,275	29,834,450	" "	8,838,456	1853
1854	25,296,519	1,001,299	10,007,129	36,304,947	874,284	35,430,663	" "	10,496,334	1854
1855	20,069,957	459,093	5,480,711	26,009,761	973,264	25,036,497	" "	7,417,062	1855
1856	25,200,651	611.298	5,749,830	31,561,779	574,539	30,987,240	" "	9,180,020	1856
1857	21,067,369	839,299	7,473,897	29,380,565	157,186	29,223,379	24% & 19%*	6,867,494	1857
1858	16,121,395	417.168	4,932,925	21,471,488	254,959	21,216,529	"	4,985,884	1858
1859	21,182,188	460.034	6,438,144	28,080,366	249,598	27,830,768	"	6,540,231	1859
1860	24,876,075	546,845	7,538,200	32,961,120	298,034	32,663,086	"	7,675,825	1860
1861	18,339,068	344.365	5,002,918	23,686,351	298,564	23,387,787	30%	7,016,336	1861
1862	4,306,605	....	3,281,771	7,588,376	201,109	7,387,267	40%	2,954,907	1862
1863	6,457,512	....	6,433,248	12,890,760	276,785	12,613,975	"	5,045,590	1863
1864	11,926,658	....	8,670,965	20,597,623	164,172	20,433,451	"	8,173,380	1864
1865	3,606,601	205,737	5,584,170	9,396,508	415,634	8,980,874	60% & 50%*	5,253,811	1865
1866	14,395,488	....	13 960,418	28,355,906	209,329	28,145,577	"	16,465,163	1866
1867	8,161,665	....	11,616,543	19,778,208	246,086	19,532,122	"	11,426,291	1867
1868	7,151,576	....	10,626,051	17,777,627	114,524	17,663,103	"	10,332,916	1868
1869	10,916,898	44.931	11,371,771	22,333,600	138,943	22,194,657	"	12,731,833	1869
1870	12,624,353	33.906	11,245,789	23,904,048	221,235	23,682,813	"	13,925,347	1870
1871	18,209,742	186.397	13,944,862	32,341,001	111,016	32,230,985	"	18,097,342	1871
1872	20,295,251	106,924	16,046,443	36,448,618	283,577	36,165,041	"	20,381,070	1872
1873	17,509,442	54.168	12,326,425	29,890,035	864,357	29,025,678	"	17,283,315	1873
1874	15,618,976	73.618	8,304,186	23,996,780	481,675	23,515,105	"	14,198,533	1874
1875	18,261,673	84.943	6,034,307	24,380,923	273,258	24,107,665	"	14,037,998	1875
	$440,652,959	$9,694,282	$250,047,114	$700,394,355	$11,530,705	$688,863,650		$277,421,384	

* The lower rate of Duty is on goods "not otherwise provided for," silk chief value.

Bureau of Statistics,
Washington, May 20, 1876.

(Signed),

EDWARD YOUNG,
Chief of Bureau.

STATEMENT OF THE RATES OF DUTY ON SILK IMPORTS, RAW SILK AND MANUFACTURES OF SILK,

Since the organization of the United States Government under the Federal Constitution, in the Year 1789.

Compiled by the Secretary of the Silk Association of America from the Special Report of 1874, on the Customs Tariff Legislation of the United States, by Dr. Edward Young, chief of the U. S. Bureau of Statistics at Washington.

The first tariff Act, July 4, 1789, was the second act of any kind passed after the organization of the United States Government under the Federal Constitution. The following is its preamble, in the first section: "*Whereas, it is necessary for the support of Government, for the discharge of the debts of the United States, and the encouragement and the protection of manufactures, that duties be laid on goods, wares, and merchandises imported, &c.*"

BY THE TARIFF ACTS OF

Date		Rate		
Aug. 10, 1790,	Silk manufactures paid	7½	per cent. ad valorem rate of duty.	
May 2, 1792,	" " "	10	" " "	
March 3, 1797,	" " "	12½	" " "	
" 16, 1804,	" " "	15	" " "	
July 1, 1812,	" " "	30	" "	[War with Great Britain.]
May 22, 1824,*	" " "	20	From beyond Cape of Good Hope 25 per cent.	
" 19, 1828,	" " "	20	" " " " 30 "	

Sectional excitement, the South against the North, was the cause of a general reduction of duties in 1832. By Act

July 14, 1832, Duty on Silk manufactures from this side of Cape of Good Hope, was reduced to.......................... 5 per cent.
From beyond Cape of Good Hope, to.................. 10 "

" " A duty of 40 per cent. was levied upon sewing-silk, and 12½ per cent. on raw silk.

March 2, 1833, Mr. Clay's Compromise Act abolished the duties on "Manufactures of silk, or of which silk shall be the component material of chief value, coming from *this side* of the Cape of Good Hope, except sewing-silk." Raw silk remained at 12½ per cent. The act further provided for a reduction every two years, on the 1st January 1836, 1838 and 1840 respectively, of one-tenth part of the excess of duty over 20 per cent., on *all* foreign imports; a reduction on the 1st January, 1842, of one-half the remainder of such excess, and from and after the 31st of December, 1842, the residue of such excess to be deducted. All but the latter provision was enforced, the rate on sewing silk being reduced to 26 per cent. .... } 10 per cent.

Sept. 11, 1841, Silk manufactures and raw silk, whether from beyond or from this side of the Cape of Good Hope, were advanced to } 20 per cent.

Date		Manufactures			Raw silk
Aug. 30, 1842,†	Silk manufactures paid	30	per cent.	n. o. p. f.‡.........	$2.50 per lb.
July 30, 1846,§	" " "	30	"	n. o. p. f...........	25 per cent.
March 3, 1857,‖	" " "	24	"	n. o. p. f...........	19 "
March 2, 1861,	" " "	30	"	n. o. p. f...........	30 "
Aug. 5, 1861,	" " "	40	"	n. o. p. f...........	40 "
June 30, 1864,	" " "	60	"	n. o. p. f...........	50 "
Feb. 8, 1875,	all silk goods containing over 75 per cent. in value of silk, irrespective of commercial designation............	60	"	n. o. p. f...........	50 "

* It appears that raw silk was subject to an ad valorem duty of 15 per cent., under *unenumerated articles* by the Tariff Act of April 27, 1816, which imposed a duty of 15 per cent. "on all articles not free, and not subject to any other rate of duty." The first revenue actually received by the Government from raw silk is stated by Dr. Young to have been in 1823. The duty on raw silk continued at 15 per cent. until it was reduced to 12½ per cent. by the Act of July 14, 1832.

† By Act of Aug. 30, 1842, a duty of 50 cents per pound of 16 oz. was levied on Raw Silk, *comprehending all silks in the gum, whether in hanks, reeled, or otherwise.*

‡ Not otherwise provided for. Silk chief value.

§ Raw silk again subject to an ad valorem duty of 15 per cent. by Act of July 30, 1846.

‖ " made free by Act of March 3, 1857.

SILK MOVEMENT THROUGHOUT THE WORLD IN OR ABOUT 1874.

COUNTRIES.	Production of Raw Silk in 1874.		Exports of Raw Silk in 1874.		Imports of Raw Silk in 1874.	
	Pounds.	Values.	Pounds.	Values.	Pounds.	Values.
China	23,232,000	$92,928,000	8,492,000	$33,968,000		
Japan	4,950,000	19,800,000	1,533,400	6,133,600		
Italy	9,875,000	79,000,000	7,338,980	58,711,840	1,419,000	$5,676,000
Switzerland	381,194	3,049,552				
Austria, Hungary	514,600	4,116,800			350,000	2,800,000
Spain and Portugal	314,000	2,198,000	297,000	2,079,000		
Turkey in Europe	1,320,000	7,920,000	792,000	4,752,000		
Russia, the Caucasus, &c.	2,420,000	14,520,000	966,800	5,800,800	1,518,000	5,373,800
Persia, Turkestan, &c.	1,100,000	6,050,000	55,000	302,500		
India	8,800,000	26,400,000	1,069,200	3,741,200		
Anam, Cambodia and Cochin China	500,000	2,000,000	220,000	880,000		
France	5,207,800	41,662,400	1,183,920	9,461,360		80,800,000
Great Britain					3,752,540	18,763,000
United States					1,159,420	4,504,306

COUNTRIES.	Production of Manufactured Silk in 1874.	Exports of Manufactured Silk in 1874.	Imports of Manufactured Silk in 1874.
France	$116,400,000	$95,400,000	$12,693,570
Italy, estimated		35,000,000	
Great Britain		17,730,725	49,276,320
Germany	38,000,000	19,300,000	
Switzerland	16,000,000	13,400,000	
Austria	12,000,000	4,712,000	
Russia	10,600,000		
Belgium	15,130,000	11,248,095	
Sweden and Norway	320,000		
United States	21,120,428	40,878	23,996,782

This table is deficient in having some blanks which no available information enables us to fill. Such are the production of manufactured silks in Italy and in Great Britain; the exports of manufactured silks from Russia, which are known to be of considerable amount, and the importation of manufactured silks into the same country from France and Italy. But notwithstanding these imperfections, it is believed to be the closest approximation yet made to a full statement of the aggregate movement of silk throughout the world.

GENERAL STATEMENT OF SILK CONDITIONED IN EUROPE IN THE YEARS 1869–'75.

FRANCE.

CITIES.	1875	1874	1873	1872	1871	1870	1869
	Lbs.	Lbs.	Lbs	Lbs.	Lbs.	Lbs.	Lbs.
Lyons	7,278,878	6,486,580	5,385,326	7,111,697	6,350,599	4,905,520	6,840,986
St. Etienne	1,794,800	1,317,556	1,210,282	1,290,651	1,491,938	1,000,735	1,161,158
Aubenas	994,806	663,786	875,544	1,214,255	854,512	823,390	1,044,825
Avignon	598,202	391,035	402,266	512,663	438,549	443,924	496,459
Paris	509,320	....	....	....	....	....	....
Privas	243,562	....	200,491	267,669	209,258	191,820	213,449
Nimes	44,936	....	56,008	93,093	114,020	73,133	61,207
Total	11,464,504	8,858,957	8,129,917	10,490,028	9,458,876	7,438,522	9,818,084

ITALY.

CITIES.	1875	1874	1873	1872	1871	1870	1869
	Lbs.	Lbs.	Lbs.	Lbs.	Lbs.	Lbs.	Lbs.
Milan	6,830,217	5,727,694	5,524,472	5,822,336	4,874,163	3,671,858	3,811,271
Turin	2,062,902	2,107,954	1,816,547	1,767,098	1,872,877	1,154,140	1,155,083
Bergamo	409,954	347,517	318,720	362,133	475,405	285,211	318,380
Lecco	302,704	259,996	233,207	222,480	231,024	141,673	174,139
Como	288,293	231,926	320,669	341,467	348,540	208,144	197,010
Florence	117,616	155,453	126,364	82,977	193,758	66,073	99,736
Udine	113,258	112,260	86,562	113,638	121,564	67,777	81,496
Brescia	45,879	47,885	42,238	59,119	68,485	38,786	35,164
Ancona	37,372	39,676	36,744	29,622	....	....	....
Pesaro	9,318	19,198	10,974	....	....	....	....
Total	10,217,513	9,049,559	8,516,497	8,800,870	8,185,816	5,633,662	5,872,279

SWITZERLAND.

CITIES.	1875	1874	1873	1872	1871	1870	1869
	Lbs.	Lbs.	Lbs.	Lbs.	Lbs.	Lbs.	Lbs.
Zürich	1,282,254	1,144,366	1,005,143	1,033,688	1,060,734	904,220	761,271
Basel	639,332	437,813	415,134	429,229	514,319	384,643	282,825
Total	1,921,586	1,582,179	1,420,277	1,462,917	1,575,053	1,288,863	1,044,096

CITIES.	1875	1874	1873	1872	1871	1870	1869
	Lbs.	Lbs.	Lbs.	Lbs.	Lbs.	Lbs.	Lbs.
Crefeld	925,843	949,722	904,529	912,938	967,982	762,278	725,758
Elberfeld	444,324	361,412	340,283	364,768	381,067	283,087	270,540
Total..........	1,370,167	1,311,134	1,244,812	1,277,706	1,349,049	1,045,365	996,298

AUSTRIA

CITY.	1875	1874	1873	1872	1871	1870	1869
	Lbs.	Lbs.	Lbs.	Lbs.	Lbs.	Lbs.	Lbs.
Vienna..........	224,427	225,920	241,870	332,050	375 539	317,221	307,735

ENGLAND.

CITY.	1875	1874	1873	1872	1871	1870	1869
	Lbs.	Lbs.	Lbs.	Lbs.	Lbs.	Lbs.	Lbs.
London	198,379	221,257	240,337	321,535	397,885	226,678	174,913

SPAIN.

CITY.	1875	1874	1873	1872	1871	1870	1869
	Lbs.	Lbs.	Lbs.	Lbs.	Lbs.	Lbs.	Lbs.
Valencia..........	120,164	81,820	90,342	....	....	....	....

SUMMARY STATEMENT OF SILK CONDITIONED IN EUROPE IN THE YEARS 1869-'75.

COUNTRIES.	1875	1874	1873	1872	1871	1870	1869
	Lbs.	Lbs.	Lbs.	Lbs.	Lbs.	Lbs.	Lbs.
France	11,464,504	8,858,957	8,129,917	10,490,028	9,458,876	7,438,522	9,818,084
Italy	10,217,513	9,049,559	8,516,497	8,800,870	8,185,816	5,633,662	5,872,279
Switzerland	1,921,586	1,582,179	1,420,277	1,462,917	1,575,053	1,288,863	1,044,096
Germany..........	1,370,167	1,311,134	1,244,812	1,277,706	1,349,049	1,045,365	996,298
Austria	224,427	225,920	241,870	332,050	375,539	317,221	307,735
England	198,379	221,257	240,337	321,535	397,885	226,678	174,913
Spain..........	120,164	81,820	90,342	....	....	....	....
Total..........	25,516,740	21,330,826	19,884,052	22,685,106	21,342,218	15,950,311	18,213,405

PRODUCTION OF SPUN SILK IN EUROPE, 1873.

STATISTICS of the Production of Spun Silk, from silk waste, pierced and imperfect cocoons, Arrindy cocoons,* &c., &c., in the European States, in the years 1872 and 1873.

Countries in which the Spun Silk was produced.	Amount produced in 1872.	Amount produced in 1873.
	Pounds.	Pounds.
France	1,980,000	1,540,000
England	1,980,000	2,000,000
Switzerland	1,800,000	1,760,000
Germany	1,100,000	1,144,000
Austria	330,000	330,000
Russia	33,000	33,000
All Europe	7,223,000	6,807,000

M. Rondot, in his report, states that France, in addition to her own production of these spun silks, imports annually about 470,000 kilogrammes = 1,038,700 pounds, from Switzerland, England and Austria; about three-fifths of the amount being furnished by Switzerland. He states, moreover, that owing to the reduction in the price of silk and the decline in the use of passementerie, the ouantity of spun silk produced would be much less in 1874 and 1875.

PRODUCTION OF RAW SILK THROUGHOUT THE WORLD.

The following statement is believed to be a tolerably near approximation to the yearly production of raw silk in the several silk-producing countries of the world at the present time:

China and Chinese Empire	$92,928,000
Japan	19,800,000
Persia, Turkistan, &c	6,250,000
Syria and Asia Minor	8,500,000
Italy	59,250,000
France	31,246,800
Turkey in Europe	7,920,000
Spain and Portugal	1,884,000
Greece	1,087,000
Morocco	300,000
Austria-Hungary	3,087,600
India	35,200,000
America	100,000
	$267,553,400

* The Arrindy cocoons are those made by the *Bombyx cynthia* which feeds on the leaves of the Castor Oil Plant (*Ricinus communis.*)

AMERICAN SILK MANUFACTURERS AT THE CENTENNIAL INTERNATIONAL EXHIBITION,

PHILADELPHIA, 1876.

Compiled from the Official Catalogue of the U. S. Centennial Commission.

MAIN EXHIBITION BUILDING.

DEPARTMENT 11.—MANUFACTURES.

CLASSIFICATION.

Silk and Silk Fabrics, and Mixtures in which Silk is the predominating Material.

CLASS 242.—Cocoons and raw silk as reeled from the cocoon; thrown or twisted silks in the gum.

CLASS 243.—Thrown or twisted silks, boiled off or dyed, in hanks, skeins, or on spools.

CLASS 244.—Spun silk yarns and fabrics, and the materials from which they are made.

CLASS 245.—Plain woven silks, lutestrings, sarsnets, satins, serges, foulards, tissues for hat and millinery purposes, etc.

CLASS 246.—Figured silk piece goods, woven or printed, Upholstery silks, etc.

CLASS 247.—Crapes, velvets, gauzes, cravats, handkerchiefs, hosiery, knit goods, laces, scarfs, ties, veils, all descriptions of cut and made up silks.

CLASS 248.—Ribbons, plain, fancy, and velvet.

CLASS 249.—Bindings, braids, cords, galloons, ladies' dress trimmings, upholsterers', tailors', military, and miscellaneous trimmings.

The exhibit is situated at the eastern entrance of the Main Exhibition Building, occupying a space 117 feet along the central avenue or nave.

The location of objects is shown by a letter and figure indicating the nearest column of the building. The column H is the eighth range of columns proceeding southward from the northern wall of the building; the columns being lettered consecutively from A to U. The easternmost column of the building is 79. The American Silk Department is located between columns 77–73, and along column H.

The Class of the classification to which each exhibit belongs is indicated by the figures at the end of the line.

EXHIBITORS.

STEARNS, JNO. N., & Co., New York, N. Y. H 77.

Brocade Silks 246
Silk Handkerchiefs 247

DEXTER, LAMBERT & Co., New York, N. Y. H 73.

Silk Piece Goods 245
Ribbons 248
Dress Trimmings 249

BELDING BROS. & Co., Rockville, Conn. H 76.
Twisted Silk in gum, Raw Silk, Cocoons............... 242
Machine Twists; Sewings, Embroidery and Saddlers' Silks; Buttonhole Twist................................ 243

HEMINWAY, M. & SONS' SILK Co., New York, N. Y. H 73.
Spool, Embroidery and Saddlers' Silk; Machine and Buttonhole Twist, etc.............................. 243

HOLLAND MANUFACTURING Co., Willimantic, Conn. H 74.
Silk Machine Twist and Sewing Silk.................. 243

AUB, HACKENBURG & Co., Philadelphia, Pa. H 76.
Raw Silk and Cocoons............................ 242
Machine and Buttonhole Twist, Sewing and Spool Silk... 243

HOVEY, F. S., Philadelphia, Pa. H 76.
Sewing-Silks and Machine Twists..................... 243

BRAINERD, ARMSTRONG & Co., New York, N. Y. H 75.
Spool and Skein Silks, black and colors 243

WEIDMANN & GREPPO, Paterson, N. J. H 76.
Dyed Silks, blacks and colors........................ 246

MOREL, CHAS., & SONS, Philadelphia, Pa. H 76.
Skein Silks, dyed.................................. 243

WRIGHT, WM. P., Philadelphia, Pa. H 76.
Oiled Silks and Muslins............................ 245

AMERICAN SILK LABEL MANUFACTURING Co., New York, N.Y. H 77.
Names of Signers of Declaration of Independence, Labels and other designs, woven in silk..................... 246

E. DE BOISSIERE, Silkville, Williamsburgh, Kansas. H 76.
Raw Silk and Cocoons 242
Silk Velvet Ribbons............................... 248

MACHINERY HALL.

DEPARTMENT V.—MACHINERY.

CLASSIFICATION.

CLASS 520.—MACHINES FOR THE MANUFACTURE OF SILK GOODS.

EXHIBITORS.

NONOTUCK SILK Co., Florence, Mass. D 41.
Machinery for throwing and finishing sewing-silk, twist, and embroidery; machine for printing spools............ 520

DANFORTH LOCOMOTIVE AND MACHINE Co., Paterson, N. J. D 28 and 41. Machinery for throwing silk........................ 520

CUTTER, JOHN D. & Co., New York, N. Y. B 30.
Jacquard silk loom in operation. Mechanism for measuring silk while spooling it.............................. 520

HOLLAND MANUFACTURING Co., Willimantic, Conn. D 34.
Machinery for throwing organzine, winding and spooling silk twist, measuring and testing the strength of silk and other threads.................................. 520

WRIGLEY, JOHN, Paterson, N. J. D 28.
Jacquard loom, changeable for power or hand........... 520

KNOWLES & BRO., Worcester, Mass. D 51.
Looms for silk dress goods, ribbons, webbings, etc........ 520

PHŒNIX SILK MANUFACTURING Co., Paterson, N. J. D 4 and 32.
Jacquard looms, weaving silk dress goods, and book marks.

WOMEN'S PAVILION.

SILK EXHIBITORS.

ITSCHNER, WERNER, & Co., Philadelphia, Pa.—
Jacquard and Ribbon weaving in operation.

HORSTMANN, WM. H. & SONS, Philadelphia, Pa.—
Manufacturers of Military, Regalia, Church and Theatrical Goods, Banners, Flags, &c.

AGRICULTURAL HALL.

EXHIBITOR.

NEUMANN, JOSEPH, San Francisco, Cal.—
California Raw Silk, Cocoons, Silk-Worms feeding, silk reeling, flags, &c.

LIST OF JUDGES FOR GROUP IX.

Silk and Wool Fabrics, including Materials and Machinery.

* ELLIOTT C. COWDIN, of New York, *Chairman.*
* Consul GUSTAV GEBHARD, of Elberfeld, Germany, *Secretary.*
HENRY MITCHELL, - - - - - - of Bradford, England.
JOHN L. HAYES, - - - - - - of Cambridge, Mass.
* JOHN G. NEESER, - - - - - - - - of Switzerland.
* AUG. BEHMER, - - - - - - - - - of Egypt.
* KENZO HAYAMI, - - - - - - - - - of Japan.
* M. CHATEL, - - - - - - - - - of France.
* CHARLES LEBOUTILLIER, - - - - - of Philadelphia.
Dr. MAX WEIGERT, - - - - - - - - of Germany.
CARL ARNBERG, - - - - - - - - - of Sweden.
THEODORE BOCHNER, - - - - - - - of Austria.
C. J. ELLIS, - - - - - - - - - of Philadelphia.
J. D. LANG, - - - - - - - - of Vassalboro', Me.

* Those marked with an asterisk are assigned to silk fabrics and machinery.

EXTRACTS FROM THE RULES RELATING TO AWARDS.

Awards shall be based upon written reports attested by the signatures of their authors.

Reports and Awards shall be based upon inherent and comparative merit. The elements of merit shall be held to include considerations relating to originality, invention, discovery, utility, quality, skill, workmanship, fitness for the purpose intended, adaptation to public wants, economy, and cost.

Reports recommending awards shall be made and signed by a Judge in each Group, stating the grounds of the proposed award, and such reports shall be accepted, and the acceptance signed by a majority of the Judges in such Group.

Awards will be finally decreed by the United States Centennial Commission, in compliance with the Act of Congress, of June 1, 1872, and will consist of a special report of the Judges on the subject of the Award, together with a Diploma and a uniform Bronze Medal.

Signed,

A. T. GOSHORN, *Director General.*

F. A. WALKER, *Chief of Bureau of Awards.*

DIRECTORY OF SILK MANUFACTURE IN THE UNITED STATES.

1876.

SILK DEPARTMENT,

INCLUDING IMPORTERS OF RAW SILK, BROKERS, DEALERS, AND SILK MANUFACTURERS.

NEW YORK CITY.

IMPORTERS OF RAW SILK.

C. A. Auffmordt & Co.	10 Greene
A. Begoden	12 Old Slip
Jesse S. Blydenburgh	66 Pine
Cary & Co.	90 „
John Caswell & Co.	87 Front
H. Fogg & Co.	32 Burling Slip
Gossler & Co.	134 Pearl
Hadden & Co.	33 Chambers
Heinemann & Casey. (In liquidation)	58 Pine
Hewlett & Torrance	69 Wall
A. A. Low & Bros.	31 Burling Slip
William F. Milton & Co.	159 Maiden Lane
Morewood & Co.	34 South
Oelrichs & Co.	2 Bowling Green
Olyphant & Co., of China	104 Wall
J. C. Phillips & Co.	130 Water
William Ryle, and dealer in Thrown Silks	33 Mercer
William H. Smith & Son	77 William
Swire Bros.; A. H. Gibbes, Agent	68 Wall
Vogel, Hagedorn, & Co.; Benjamin D. Smith	120 Front
John T. Walker	81 Pine
Wetmore, Cryder, & Co.	74 South
Wood, Payson, & Colgate	64 Pine

BROKERS IN RAW SILK.

D. O'Donoghue & Co.	48 Howard
George M. Haywood	191 Church

Rowland Johnson . . . . 54 Beaver
B. Richardson & Son . . . . 5 Mercer
Nathan H. Johnson . . . . . . 119 Market Street, Philadelphia

---

SILK MANUFACTURERS, AND DEALERS IN SILK MANUFACTURES.

NEW YORK.

Arnold & Banning. Twills, &c. Salesroom, 56 Lispenard Street.

Bache & Bidmead. Elastic Webs. Factory and salesroom, 155 and 157 11th Avenue.

Bernstein & Mack. Ladies' Dress Trimming and Passementerie. Factory, 214 to 222 West 26th Street; salesroom, 479 Broadway.

Samuel Bertschy & Co. Ribbons, Ladies' Dress Trimmings, &c. Factory, cor. 10th Avenue and 46th Street; salesroom, 460 Broome Street.

C. F. Blake. Ribbons. Fulton Street, Brooklyn.

William Blau. Tassels and Fur Trimmings. Factory and salesroom, 88 Prince Street.

Boston & Schmid. Coach Laces, Fringes, and Tassels. Factory and salesroom, 5 West Fourth Street.

Brainerd, Armstrong, & Co. Sewing Silk and Twist. 469 Broadway; 301 Market Street, Philadelphia; 13 German Street, Baltimore.

Edward G. Brown. Upholstery Trimmings. Factory and salesroom, 787 and 789 Broadway.

John T. Camp & Co. Ladies' Dress Trimmings. Factory and salesroom, 19 Mercer Street.

B. L. Cohen. Ladies' Dress Trimmings. Factory and salesroom, 5 Howard Street.

Collett & Hugel. Fringes, Gimps, and Cords. Factory and salesroom, 26 Union Square.

William H. Copcutt & Co. Tram, Spool Silks, Sewing Silk, and Twist. Mills, Yonkers; salesroom, 350 Canal Street.

James Dalton. Hair Nets. Factory and salesroom, 61 Hudson Street.

Deppeler & Kammerer. Ladies' Dress Trimmings. Factory and salesroom, 108 Grand Street.

George Dietzel. Hair Goods and Ladies' Dress Trimmings. Factory and salesroom, 398 Broome Street.

F. Dreisacker & Co. Cloak Trimmings and Buttons. Factory and salesroom, 491 Broadway.

Julius Dreyfuss. Dress Trimmings. Factory and salesroom, 146 Eldridge Street.

Adolph S. Ellison. Dress Trimmings. 46 Walker Street.

Fisher & Taff. Ladies' Dress and Cloak Trimmings. Factory and salesroom, 8 Howard Street.

Louis Franke. Organzine, Tram, Twist, and Fringe Silk, Braid and Silk Fringes, Sash Ribbons, Braided Cord, Tubular Braid, &c. Braiding works and silk mill, Paterson; Trimming factory, 444 Broome Street, New York; salesroom, 480 Broadway.

Frankenheimer & Co. Upholstery Trimmings. Factory and salesroom, 810 Broadway.

Hugo Funke. Ribbons. Mills, College Point; salesroom, 343 Canal Street.

German Braid Company. Silk Braids. Brooklyn, E. D.

Henry Gimpel & Co. Ladies' Dress Trimmings, Cords, and Tassels. Factory and salesroom, 403 Broadway.

Frederick Gminder & Co. Ladies' Dress Trimmings, Cords, and Tassels. Factory and salesroom, 56 Walker Street.

Louis Greenbaum. Cords and Tassels. Factory, 447 to 453 West 26th Street; salesroom, 248 Canal Street.

P. Hagan. Dress Trimmings. Factory and salesroom, 180 Bowery.

M. Haiges. Dress Trimmings. Rochester.

Henry Hartwig & Co. Upholstery Trimmings. Factory and salesroom, 340 Bowery.

Frederick Haubner & Co. Upholstery Trimmings. Factory and salesroom, 606 Eighth Avenue.

Thomas F. Hayes. Ladies' Dress and Cloak Trimmings. Factory and salesroom, 77 University Place.

James Heidenreick. Silk Dyer. 423 and 425 West 35th Street, and 422, 424 36th Street.

Jacob Heinemann. Ladies' Dress Trimmings, Cords, Tassels, &c. 28 Howard Street.

Helmke & Co. Ladies' Dress Trimmings. Factory and salesroom, 731 Broadway.

William H. H. K. C. Higgins. Agent for Hobley Bros., Williamsburgh and Uncas Ribbon Co., Preston, Conn. Dealer in Ribbons and Ladies' Dress Trimmings. Salesroom, 107 Grand Street.

Isaac Hilton. Ladies' Dress Trimmings. Factory and salesroom, 128 River Street, Troy.

Hobley Bros. William H. H. K. C. Higgins, Agent. Belt Ribbons, Ladies' Dress and Cloak Trimmings, &c. Factory, Williamsburgh; salesroom, 107 Grand Street.

F. Hoffman. Furrier Trimmings. Factory and salesroom, 356 Bowery.

Horstmann Bros. & Allien. Military Equipments, Regalia, Silk Bunting, Theatrical Goods, &c. Factory, Philadelphia; salesroom, 7 Bond Street.

George Howard. Fancy Goods, Twills, &c. Roman Scarfs a specialty. Factory and salesroom, 343 West 24th Street.

C. W. Jackson & Co. Dress Trimmings. Factory and salesroom, 114 East 14th Street.

A. G. Jennings. Guipure, Blonde and Brussels Laces, Grenadine Veiling, &c. Factory, "Nottingham Lace Works," Park Avenue and Hall Street, Brooklyn; salesroom, 428 Broome Street.

Alexander King & Co. Dealers in Organzine, Tram, Fringes, Twist and Sewing Silks. Salesroom, 52 White Street.

Kormann & Stepath. Ladies' Dress Trimmings. Factory and salesroom, 42 Walker Street.

Rudolph Krumsick. Cords, Tassels, and Fur Trimmings. Factory and salesroom, 7 Mercer Street.

M. Leiter. Ribbons and Upholstery Gimps. Factory and salesroom, 59 to 65 Goerck Street.

F. Leschhorn & Co. Ladies' Dress and Cloak Trimmings. Factory and salesroom, 21 Howard Street.

Robert Levy & Co. Eureka Cord and Tassel Co. Cords and Tassels. Factory and salesroom, 204 West Houston Street.

J. Lovatt's Sons. Sewing Silk and Twist. Factory and salesroom, Tarrytown.

S. McLure. Dress Trimmings. Factory and salesroom, 251 Fulton Street, Brooklyn.

William Macfarlane. Gum Silk, Sewing Silk and Twist. Mills and salesroom, Yonkers, "Nepperhan Silk Works."

Macfarlane & Co. Agents for Macfarlane Bros., Mansfield, Conn. Sewing Silk and Twist. Salesroom, 43 Walker Street.

J. Maidhof & Co. Ladies' Dress Trimmings. Factory and salesroom, 455 and 457 Broadway.

John Marr. Hair-nets, Lace Goods, Jacquard Weaving. Factory and salesroom, 144 Centre Street.

Charles N. Martin. Sewing Silk and Twist. Salesroom, 319 Canal Street.

A. Maynard & Co. Upholstery Trimmings. Factory and salesroom, 100 South 6th Street, Brooklyn, E. D.

L. Meyer & Co. Dress Trimmings. Factory and salesroom, 424 Broome Street.

A. Moll. Braids. Factory and salesroom, 233 and 235 5th Street, Brooklyn, E. D.

George S. Moulton & Co. Gros Grain Ribbons, Hat Bands, &c. Salesrooms, 100 and 102 Worth Street, and 73 Chauncy Street, Boston.

Ernst Müller. Ladies' Dress Trimmings. Factory and salesroom, 820 Broadway.

J. Nawl. Cords and Braids. Brooklyn.

William Neustaedter. Dealer in Tram, Organzine, and Spun Silk. Salesroom, 46 Walker Street.

Jacob New. Ribbons. Factory, 422 to 428 West 38th Street; salesroom, 458 Broome Street.

New York Silk Manufacturing Co. Gros Grain Ribbons, Beltings, and Hat Bandings. Factory and salesroom, 291 West 11th Street. L. Bloom, Sole Agent.

Nordheim & Harris. Dress and Upholstery Trimmings. Factory and salesroom, 7 Washington Place.

Maurice O'Brien. Upholstery Trimmings and Fringes. Factory and salesroom, 94 Bowery.

Oneida Community, Oneida. Sewing Silk and Twist. Mills and salesroom, Oneida.

Morris Opper. Dress Trimmings. Factory and salesroom, 684 Broadway.

A. L. Phillips & Co. Hatters' and Furriers' Trimmings. Factory and salesroom, 54 Mercer Street.

S. Pick. Dress and Cloak Trimmings. Factory and salesroom, 595 Broadway.

Reitmeyer & Dusenberry. Manufacturers and Importers of Silk Worsted, Linen and Cotton Fringes and Trimmings, Hatters' Trimmings, &c. Factory, 324 to 332 Delancey Street, and 31 to 41 Tompkins Street; salesroom, 29 Howard Street.

Roemer & Co. Upholstery Trimmings and Fringes. Factory and salesroom, 729 Broadway.

Reuben Ryle & Co. Agents for Sterrett, Ryle, & Murphy, Paterson, N. J. Tram, Organzine, Spool Silks, and Ribbons. Salesroom, 19 Mercer Street.

Sanquoit Silk Manufacturing Co. L. R. Stelle, President. Richard Rossmässler, Treasurer. Tram, Organzine, and Fringe Silks. Factory and salesroom, Sanquoit, near Utica; and 319 to 323 Garden Street, Philadelphia.

C. A. Schmidt. Upholstery Trimmings and Fringes. Factory and salesroom, 85 Chambers and 67 Reade Streets.

J. Silbermann & Co. Bonnet and Belt Ribbons, Dress Trimmings, Cords, Tassels, &c. Factory, 452 to 456 10th Avenue; salesroom, 21 Mercer Street.

George B. Skinner & Co. Tram, Organzine, and Fringe Silk, Sewing and Twist. Mills, Yonkers; salesroom, 59 Walker Street.

John N. Stearns & Co. Organzine, Dress, and Fancy Silks, Poplins, Serges, Pongees, &c., &c. Factory, 213 to 221 East 42d Street; salesroom, 43 Mercer Street.

R. Steinhardt. Ribbons. Factory, 162 to 164 West 27th Street; salesroom, 89 Grand Street.

L. Sutro. Ladies' Dress and Fur Trimmings. Factory and salesroom, 35 Wooster Street.

R. Weinberg. Upholstery Trimmings and Fringes. Factory and salesroom, 814 Broadway.

William Weiss. Ladies' Dress Trimmings, Buttons, and Ornaments. Factory and salesroom, 424 Broome Street.

P. H. & W. Williams. Fringes, Tassels, Gimps, &c. Factory and salesroom, 875 Broadway.

NEW JERSEY.

R. H. Adams. Ribbons and Fancy Silks. Factory and salesroom, Paterson.

C. B. Auer & Co. Neckties, Bindings, &c. Mills, Paterson, "Oldham Mills;" salesroom, 18 Mercer Street, New York. M. H. Chapin & Co.

Frederick Baare. Plain and Fancy Silks, Ribbons. Factory, Paterson; salesroom, 21 Mercer Street, New York. G. W. Geer, Agent.

P. & J. Bannagan. Tram, Organzine, Fringe, and Fancy Silks. Mills, Paterson; salesroom, 123 Mercer Street, New York.

Barnes & Co. Tram, Organzine, and Braids. Mill, "Beaver Mill," Paterson.

Boonton Silk Factory. J. A. Van Orden, President; S. L. Garrison, Secretary; James Stansfield, Manager. Piece Goods. Boonton.

J. H. Booth & Co. Tram, Organzine, and Fringe Silks. Mills, cor. Market and Spruce Streets, Paterson.

C. Chaffonjon. Broad Silks, Serges, Satin de Chêne, &c. Mills, Hudson City, "Favorite Silk Manufactory."

Dale Manufacturing Co. Thomas N. Dale, President; C. H. Kimball, Treasurer. Stokes, Caldwell, & Co., Agents. Tram, Organzine, Sewing Silk, and Twist, Scarfs, Tie Silks, Cords, and all classes of Silk Braids and Bindings. Mills, Paterson; salesroom, 70 Franklin Street, New York.

Joseph Day. Ribbons. Factory and salesroom, Paterson.

Day Manufacturing Co. A. A. Hopper, President; Edward Arnold, Treasurer; Arnold & Banning, Agents. Dress and Fancy Silks, &c. Mills, Paterson; salesroom, 56 Lispenard Street, New York.

Dexter, Lambert, & Co. Twill Silks, Tie Silks, Ribbons, and Ladies' Dress Trimmings. Mills, Paterson. Agents, C. A. Auffmordt & Co., 10 to 14 Greene Street, New York.

Polydor Dorgeval & Co. Dyers in the Piece, and Finishers. 59 Bridge Street, Paterson.

John Dunlop. Sewing Silk and Twist. Mills, Paterson, "Union Silk Works;" salesroom, 51 Leonard Street, New York.

W. R. Edwards. Handkerchiefs, Fancy Silks, &c. Factory and salesroom, Paterson.

Excelsior Manufacturing Co. John D. Cutter. Sewing Silk, Twist, and Fish Lines. Factory, Grant Locomotive Works, Paterson; salesroom, 92 Church Street, New York.

Joseph Fletcher. Twills, &c. Factory and salesroom, 109 Tyler Street, Paterson.

H. H. Freeman & Co. Piece Silks and Sewing Silks. Mills, Paterson; salesroom, 103 Franklin Street, New York.

Giametti & Co. Throwsters. Factory and salesroom, Haledon.

Givernaud Bros. Gum Silks, Dress and Fancy Silks. Factory and salesroom, Hoboken; office, 48 Howard Street, New York.

F. Grassan. Upholstery Trimmings. Factory and salesroom, Washington Street, Hoboken.

Grimshaw Bros. Twills, &c. Mills, cor. Market and Spruce Streets, Paterson.

Hamil & Booth. Tram, Organzine, and Fringe Silks, Ribbons, Fancy Silks, &c. Mills, Paterson, "Passaic Silk Works" and "Hamil" Mill; salesroom, 461 Broome Street, New York.

I. P. Hulser & Co. Fancy Silks. Factory, Paterson; salesroom, 324 West 37th Street, New York.

Manhattan Loom Company. John Burns & Co. Ribbons, Silks, &c. Mills, Paterson; salesroom, 491 Broadway, New York.

J. P. McKay. Dress, Plain, and Fancy Silks, Scarfs, &c. Mills and salesroom, Paterson.

Caspar Meisch. Hat Bindings. Factory and salesroom, Paterson.

S. M. Meyenberg. Ribbons, Veils, Ties, &c. Factory, Paterson; salesroom, 40 Lispenard Street, New York.

Morlot, Stettheimer, & Co. Silk Dyers ("Passaic Silk Dye Works"), and Ribbons. Mills, Paterson; salesroom, 98 Grand Street, New York. Elliott C. Cowdin & Co.

Pelgram & Meyer. Ribbons, Piece Goods, &c. Mills, Paterson; salesroom, 456 Broome Street, New York.

Phœnix Silk Manufacturing Co. Benjamin B. Tilt, President; W. H. K. Bibby, Secretary. B. B. Tilt & Son, Agents. Silk Piece Goods, Handkerchiefs, Ribbons, &c., Trams, Organzines, &c. Mills, Paterson; salesroom, 477 Broome Street, New York, and in Boston and Philadelphia.

John Ryle & Sons. Tram, Organzine, and Spool Silks, Dress and Fancy Silks, &c. The Murray Mills, Paterson; salesroom, 100 Worth Street, New York.

J. Jackson Scott. Sewing Silk and Twist, and Silk Dyer. Factory and salesroom, Paterson.

See & Sheehan. Silk Dyers. Dye Works, Paterson; office, 461 Broome Street, New York.

A. Siedendorf. Upholstery Trimmings. Factory and salesroom, Hoboken.

Herman Simon. Dress and Fancy Silks. Factory and salesroom, Town of Union.

Singer Manufacturing Co. Inslee A. Hopper, President, Machine Twist. Mills, Newark; salesrooms, Union Square and 16th Street, New York; 69 Hanover Street, Boston; 13 North Charles Street, Baltimore; 186 King Street, Charleston, S. C.; 89 Canal Street, New Orleans; 605 North Fourth Street, St. Louis, Mo.; 105 Kearney Street, San Francisco; 111 State Street, Chicago; and in all the principal cities of America and Europe.

Wright Smith. Millinery Silks. Paterson.

A. Soleliac & Sons. Ribbons, Plain and Fancy Silks. Factory, Dale Mills, Paterson; salesroom, 90 and 92 Grand Street, New York. Kiefer & Co., Agents.

Sterett, Ryle, & Murphy. Agents, Reuben Ryle & Co. Ribbons. Factory, Paterson. Salesroom, 19 Mercer Street, New York.

C. Spangenberg. Upholstery Trimmings. Factory and salesroom, Garden Street, Hoboken.

William Strange & Co. Ribbons, Handkerchiefs, Millinery Silks, &c., Trams, Organzines, &c. Mills, Paterson. Salesroom, Strange & Bro. 455 Broome Street, New York. Paris house, E. B. Strange & Bro.

William Ther & Sons. Elastic Webbing. Factory and salesroom, New Brunswick.

J. Vacher. Serges, Satins, &c. Factory and salesroom, Haledon.

Weidmann & Greppo. Silk Dyers. Dye Works, cor. Paterson and Ellison Streets, Paterson. Black Dyeing a specialty. Office, 400 Broadway, New York.

Wortendyke Manufacturing Co. Tram, Organzine, and Fringe Silks. Mills, Wortendyke; Salesroom, 52 White Street, New York. Alexander King & Co.

PENNSYLVANIA.

PHILADELPHIA.

Aub, Hackenburg, & Co. Sewing Silk and Twist. Factory, 244 to 248 North Front Street; salesrooms, 20 North 3d Street; 216 Church Street, New York; 20 German Street, Baltimore; 69 West 3d Street, Cincinnati.

G. F. Bechmann. Upholstery Trimmings. Factory and salesroom, 116 North 3d Street.

Columbia Mutual Silk Co. Tram, Organzine, and Fringe Silks, Ribbons, Fancy Silks, &c. Mills and salesroom, 319 to 323 Garden Street.

Cunningham & Hill. Upholstery Trimmings. Factory and salesroom, 204 Church Street.

M. C. Cuttle. Silk Dyer. Germantown Road above Lehigh Avenue.

Davenport Bros. Upholstery Trimmings. Factory and salesroom, cor. Mosher and York Streets.

H. L. Freyer. Ladies' Dress Trimmings. Factory, 25 South 8th Street; salesroom, 727 Jaine Street.

E. H. Godschalk. Ladies' Dress Trimmings. Fringes, Cords, Tassels, &c. Factory and salesroom, cor. 12th and Buttonwood Streets; salesroom in New York, 71 Franklin Street.

John Goldthorp. Upholstery Trimmings, Cords, Tassels, &c. Factory and salesroom, 1111 Chestnut Street.

J. C. Graham. Ladies' Dress and Cloak Trimmings of every description. Factory and salesroom, 525 and 527 Cherry Street.

S. R. & F. Hansell. Upholstery and Shade Trimmings of every description. Factory, 9th Street and Columbia Avenue; salesroom, 21 North 4th Street.

L. M. Harned & Co. Upholstery Goods, Shade Trimmings, Cords and Tassels. Factory and salesroom, 139 North 6th Street.

Hensel, Colladay, & Co. Ladies' Dress Trimmings of every description. Factory and salesroom, 22 to 24 North 4th Street.

B. Hooley & Son. Tram, Organzine, Floss, and Fringe Silks, Sewing Silk, and Twist. "Keystone Silk Mills;" salesroom, 226 Market Street.

William H. Horstmann & Sons. Gum Silks, Ladies' Dress and Cloak Trimmings of every description, Ribbons, Fringes, Floss, Upholstery Trimmings, Coach and Carriage Laces and Trimmings, Jacquard Weaving. [Military Equipments, Regalia, Theatrical Goods, Silk Bunting, Sashes, Scarfs, &c. Horstmann Bros. & Allien, 7 Bond Street, New

York.] Factory and salesroom, cor. 5th and Cherry Streets, Philadelphia; salesroom, 410 Broadway, New York.

F. S. Hovey. Sewing Silks and Twist. Salesroom, 248 Chestnut Street.

W. Itschner & Co. Ribbons. Mills, Tioga Station, Germantown; salesrooms, 233 Chestnut Street; 462 Broome Street, New York.

T. Jones & Son. Silk Dyer. Dye Works, 110 and 112 Putnam Street.

J. & A. Kemper. Ladies' Dress Trimmings. Factory and salesroom, 33 South 4th Street.

Rudolph Klauder & Co. Dyer of Silk, Wool, and Worsted. "Quaker City Dye and Print Works," cor. Howard and Oxford Streets.

Henry C. Lees. Upholstery Trimmings. Factory and salesroom, 303 Chestnut Street.

M. W. Lipper & Co. Ladies' Dress and Cloak Trimmings, and Ladies' Neck-wear. "Keystone Braid Mills;" salesrooms, 144 and 146 North 5th Street; 338 Broadway, New York; and 49 Summer Street, Boston.

Charles Morel. Silk Dyer. 2219 Richmond Street.

G. A. Perks & Co. Upholstery Trimmings. Factory and salesroom, 34 South 2d Street.

Philadelphia Silk Manufacturing Co. John Carnahan, President; A. M. Sutton, Treasurer and Manager. Gros Grain Ribbons, Beltings, and Hat Bindings. Factory and salesroom, 60 to 66 Canal Street.

Joseph Roehm. Dealer in Sewing Silk and Twist. Office, 47 South 4th Street.

Sanquoit Silk Manufacturing Co. L. R. Stelle, President; Richard Rossmässler, Treasurer. Tram, Organzine, and Fringe Silks. Factory and salesroom, 319 to 323 Garden Street; and at Sanquoit, near Utica, N. Y.

The Scranton Silk Co. Henry A. Atkins, President; Frederick Harvey, Superintendent; Arnold B. Fenner, Treasurer. Alexander King & Co., Sole Agents. Organzine and Tram. Mills, Scranton. Joseph K. Harvey, Agent. Salesroom, 52 White Street, New York.

MARYLAND.

BALTIMORE.

M. Hecht & Co. Ladies' and Gents' Neck-wear, and Dress Trimmings. Factory and salesroom, 43 German Street.

G. Tallerman & Co. Ladies' Dress and Cloak Ornaments, and Upholstery Trimmings. 231 Frederick Avenue.

William P. Towles & Bro. Ribbons, Neckties, Scarfs, Trimmings, Suspenders, &c. 145 Baltimore Street.

CONNECTICUT.

O. Atwood. Sewing Silk and Twist. Mills and salesroom, New London.

Atwood & Richmond. Machine Twist. Mills and salesroom, Brooklyn.

Belding Bros. & Co. Sewing Silk and Twist. Mills, Rockville; salesrooms, 510 Broadway, New York; 56 Summer Street, Boston; 56 West 4th Street, Cincinnati; 198 East Madison Street, Chicago; 601 North 4th Street, St. Louis; 6th, cor. Arch Street, Philadelphia. L. C. Hall, Jr., & Co., Agents for Philadelphia house.

I. H. Booth. Coach Laces. New Haven.

C. L. Bottum & Co. Sewing Silk and Twist. Mills, Willimantic; salesroom, 79 Chambers Street, New York.

L. D. Brown & Son. Sewing Silk and Twist. Mills, Middletown; salesroom, 439 Broadway, New York. H. H. Albro, Agent.

O. S. Chaffee & Son. Sewing Silk and Twist. Mills and salesrooms, Mansfield Centre and Willimantic.

Cheney Bros. Tram, Organzine, and Spun Silk, Sewing Silk and Twist, Dress and Fancy Silks, Sash, Bonnet, and Belt Ribbons, Marcellines, Florentines, Foulards, Pongees, Twills, Handkerchiefs, Flags, &c. Mills, Hartford and South Manchester; salesrooms, 477 Broome Street, New York, and 19 Franklin Street, Boston.

A. A. & H. E. Conant. Sewing Silk and Twist. Mills and salesroom, Willimantic.

Connah & Turner. Tram, Organzine, Sewing Silk, and Twist. Mills, Turnerville; salesroom, 269 Canal Street, New York.

C. H. Farnham. Dealer in Sewing Silk and Twist. Salesroom, Willimantic.

Charles R. Garratt. Belt Ribbons, Bonnet Ribbons. Factory, Golden Hill, Bridgeport, Conn.; salesroom, 469 Broadway, New York. Brainerd, Armstrong, & Co.

P. G. & J. S. Hanks. Sewing Silk and Twist. Mills and salesroom, Gurleyville.

J. H. Hayden. Sewing Silk and Twist. Mills and salesroom, Windsor Locks.

M. Heminway & Sons' Silk Co. Sewing Silk and Twist. Mills, Watertown; salesrooms, 78 Reade Street and 99 Church Street, New York.

Holland Manufacturing Co. Ira Dimock, Manager. Sewing Silk and Twist. Mills, Willimantic; salesroom, 435 Broadway, New York.

Tobias Kohn. Sewing Silks, Braids, and Trimmings. "Novelty Weaving and Braiding Works," Hartford; salesrooms, 42 Market Street, Hartford; Arnold & Banning, 56 Lispenard Street, New York; 42 Bedford Street, Boston; 30 Bank Street, Philadelphia; 7 German Street, Baltimore; 163 5th Aveuue, Chicago.

John N. Leonard. Sewing Silk and Twist. Mills and salesroom, Rockville.

Macfarlane Bros. Sewing Silk, Machine and Button-hole Twist. Mills, Mansfield Centre; salesroom, Macfarlane & Co., 43 Walker Street, New York.

B. K. Mills & Co. Coach Laces, Fringes, Tassels, &c. Factory and salesroom, 56 and 58 Cannon Street, Bridgeport.

J. S. Morgan. C. L. Bottum & Co., Agents. Sewing Silk and Twist. Mills, South Coventry; salesroom, 79 Chambers Street, New York.

Norfolk Silk Co. Sewing Silk and Twist. Mills and salesroom, Norfolk. Salesroom, Baldwin, Lovell, & Co., 107 8th Avenue, New York.

Oneida Community. Sewing Silk and Twist. Mills and salesroom, Wallingford, and Oneida, N. Y.

Charles H. Pardee. Coach Laces. New Haven.

E. B. Smith. Belding Bros. & Co., Agents. Sewing Silk and Twist. Mills, Gurleyville; salesroom, 510 Broadway, New York.

Uncas Ribbon Co. E. Oldfield, Superintendent; William H. H. K. C. Higgins, Treasurer. Ribbons. Factory, Preston, near Norwich; salesroom, William H. H. K. C. Higgins, 107 Grand Street, New York.

MASSACHUSETTS.

Barr, Rider, & Co. Dealers in Sewing Silks. Salesroom, 21 Summer Street, Boston.

Boston Elastic Fabric Co. Suspender Webs, Garter Webs, Frills, Cords, and Braids. Mills, Chelsea; salesrooms, 175 Devonshire Street, Boston; 102 Chambers Street, New York.

Burr, Brown, & Co. Upholstery Trimmings. Factory and salesroom, 85 Devonshire and 289 Washington Streets, Boston.

Henry Day. Ribbons. Factory and salesroom, 19 Franklin Street, Boston.

Isaac Farwell, Jr., & Co. Sewing Silk and Twist. Mills, Newton; salesroom, 32 Avon Street, Boston.

O. Fiedler & Co. Ladies' Dress Trimmings. Factory and salesroom, 36 Winter Street, Boston.

Fiedler, Moeldner, & Co. Dress and Cloak Trimmings. Factory, 473 to 477 Tremont Street; salesroom, 36 Winter Street, Boston.

A. W. French & Co. Dealers in Gum Silks. Salesroom, 28 Winter Street, Boston.

Glendale Manufacturing Co. Stoddard, Lovering & Co., Agents. Rubber Elastics, Bands, &c. Mills, Easthampton; salesroom, 121 Duane Street, New York.

G. H. Mansfield & Co. Fish Lines. Factory and salesroom, Canton.

V. J. Messinger & Co. Dealers in Sewing Silk and Twist, and all kinds of Twisted Silk. Salesroom, 23 Dock Square, Boston.

Milliken Bros. Dealers in Sewing Silk and Twist, Ribbons, and Ladies' Dress Trimmings. 56 Summer Street, Boston.

Nonotuck Silk Co. Ira Dimock, President; A. T. Lilly, Treasurer. Sewing Silk and Twist. Mills, Florence and Leeds; salesrooms, 2 Bedford Street, Boston; 147 State Street, Chicago; 88 West 3d Street, Cincinnati; 66 and 68 Thomas Street, New York. E. W. Eaton, Agent.

Saunders Silk Co. E. Saunders, President; R. Gardner, Treasurer. Sewing Silk and Twist. Mills, Pittsfield, Mass.; salesroom, 77 Franklin Street, New York.

Seavey, Foster, & Bowman. Sewing Silk and Twist. Mills, Canton; salesrooms, 7 Mercer Street, New York; 40 Summer Street, Boston; 6 Washington Street, Chicago; 323 Arch Street, Philadelphia.

William Skinner. Organzine, Sewing Silk and Twist, and Silk Braids. "Unquomonk Silk Mills," Holyoke, Mass.; salesroom, 327 Broadway, New York. J. R. Peck, Manager, New York.

Streeter, Merrick, & Co. Machine Twist. Mills and salesroom, Shelburne Falls.

L. D. Suydam. Dealer in Sewing Silks. Salesroom, 8 Hamilton Place, Boston.

Warner & Lathrop. Sewing Silk, Machine Twist, Tailors' Twist, &c. Mills and salesroom, Northampton.

H. L. Whitney. Dealer in Sewing Silks. Salesroom, Boston.

Thomas Wilkins & Co. Dealers in Sewing Silks. Salesroom, Green Street, near Bowdoin, Boston.

Ziegler & Downs. Sewing Silk and Twist. Factory at Boston Highlands; office, 5 Chauncy Street, Boston.

NEW HAMPSHIRE.

Charles W. Kelsea & Co. Sewing Silk and Twist. Mills and salesroom, Antrim.

VERMONT.

J. F. Stearns. Sewing Silk and Twist. Mills and salesroom, Brattleboro'.

KANSAS.

E. de Boissiere. Silkworms' Eggs, Cocoons, Mulberry Trees, Ribbons, and Ladies' Dress Trimmings. Mills, Silkville, Williamsburgh, Franklin County.

MISSOURI.

Schact & Bro. Upholstery Trimmings. Market Street, St. Louis.

ILLINOIS.

Ederer & Peters. Upholstery Trimmings. 61 Washington Street, Chicago.

A. B. Fiedler. Upholstery Trimmings. 56 State Street, Chicago.

E. A. Jacobs. Upholstery, Dress, and Military Trimmings. 106 to 110 South State Street, Chicago.

OHIO.

F. Brogelmann. Upholstery Trimmings. 204 Vine Street, Cincinnati.

John Franz. Fringes, Tassels, Cords, and Gimps. 25 Oregon Street, Cleveland.

F. Hoffmeister. Fringes, Gimps, Tassels, &c. 152 West 4th Street, Cincinnati.

Hoffmeister & Deneal. Fringes, Dress Trimmings, &c. Factory and salesroom, 104 5th Street, Cincinnati.

CALIFORNIA.

The California Silk Manufacturing Co. Rodgers, Meyer, & Co. Tram, Organzine, Sewing Silk, and Twist. Mills, South San Francisco. Agents, William McDonald & Co. Salesroom, 13 Post Street.

Joseph Neumann, Silk Culturist of San Francisco, and Manufacturer of Silk Flags, &c. 909½ Market Street.

Pacific Factory. William Englander. Silk Fringes and Gimps. Factory and salesroom, 751 Market Street, San Francisco.

Union Pacific Silk Manufacturing Co. George C. Bode, President. Ribbons. Mills, San Francisco.

INDEX OF NAMES.*

* The Directory of Silk Manufacturers, the Business Announcements, and names in the History that are not connected with the Silk Industry in America, are not included in this Index.

Business Announcements.

INDEX
TO BUSINESS ANNOUNCEMENTS.

BRAINERD, ARMSTRONG & CO.,

Manufacturers of

SEWING

SILK,

MACHINE

TWIST

Manufacturers of

BUTTONHOLE

TWIST,

EMBROIDERY

SILK.

SALESROOMS:

469 Broadway, N.Y. 301 Market St., Philadelphia. 13 German St., Baltimore, Md.

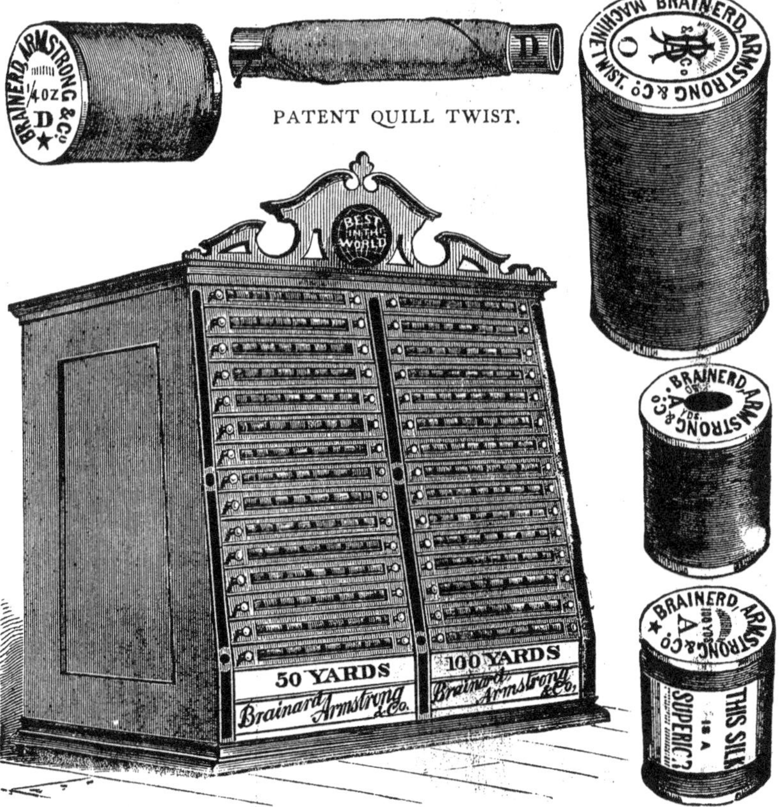

PATENT QUILL TWIST.

NEW ENGLAND

Cotton Manufacturers' Association.

BOARD OF GOVERNMENT.

1876.

President.

E. A. STRAW, Manchester, N. H.

Vice-Presidents.

A. D. LOCKWOOD, Providence, R. I.	EDWARD ATKINSON, Boston, Mass.

Directors.

Chas. Nourse, Woonsocket, R. I.	John Kilburn, Salem, Mass.
Thos. J. Borden, Fall River, Mass.	A. G. Cumnock, Lowell, Mass.
Wm. P. Haines, Biddeford, Me.	Cyrus I. Barker, Lewiston, Me.

Secretary and Treasurer,

AMBROSE EASTMAN, Boston, Mass.

Office of the Association, Room 53 Sears Building, Boston.

NATIONAL ASSOCIATION OF WOOL MANUFACTURERS,

FOUNDED, NOVEMBER 30, 1864.

President.

J. WILEY EDMANDS, ... Boston, Massachusetts.

Vice-Presidents.

J. W. STITT, . . . New York, N. Y.

LUCIUS P. PORTER, New Brunswick, N. J.

GEORGE ROBERTS, Hartford, Conn.

Treasurer.

SAMUEL FAY, ... Boston, Mass.

Secretary.

JOHN L. HAYES, . . . Boston, Mass.

Directors.

MAINE.

J. H. BURLEIGH, . . South Berwick.
S. O. BROWN, . . . Dover.

MASSACHUSETTS.

E. R. MUDGE, . . . Boston.
A. C. RUSSELL, . . Great Barrington.
AMORY MAYNARD, . Maynard.
C. P. TALBOT, . . . Billerica.
THEODORE POMEROY, . Pittsfield.
CHARLES L. HARDING, Boston.
JAMES A. SMITH, . . Cherry Valley.
ERASTUS B. BIGELOW, . Boston.

NEW YORK.

STEPHEN SANFORD, . . Amsterdam.
R. H. THURMAN, . . Troy.
THOMAS FITZINGER, . Waterloo.
SAMUEL HARRIS, . . Catskill.
F. H. FARNHAM, . . Troy.
ANDREW ROOT, . . . Cohoes.
H. S. RANKEN, . . . Troy.

PENNSYLVANIA.

R. D. NESMITH, . . Johnstown.
GEORGE BULLOCK, . . Johnstown.
CHARLES SPENCER, . . Germantown.
CLEMENT H. SMITH (of Wm. Wood & Co.), Philadelphia.
GEORGE P. EVANS, . . Philadelphia.

ILLINOIS.

GEORGE S. BOWEN, . Chicago.

NEW HAMPSHIRE.

D. H. BUFFUM, . . . Great Falls.
DANIEL HOLDEN, . . Concord.
ALMON HARRIS, . . Fisherville.
JOHN HALL, ... East Rochester.
SAMUEL R. PAYSON, . Manchester.

VERMONT.

SOLOMON WOODWARD, . Woodstock.
JOSEPH SAWYER, (Burlington Woolen Co.), Winooski Falls.

RHODE ISLAND.

J. T. FISK, ... Pascoag.
A. L. SAYLES, . . . Pascoag.
DARIUS GOFF, . . . Pawtucket.

CONNECTICUT.

GEORGE MAXWELL, . Rockville.
GEORGE W. CAPRON, . South Coventry.
SABIN L. SAYLES, . . Dayville.
C. C. CLARK, . . . Rockville.

NEW JERSEY.

WILLIAM DUNCAN, . Franklin.
DAVID OAKES, . . . Bloomfield.
JONATHAN EARLE, . . New Brunswick.

OHIO.

ALTON POPE, . . . Cleveland.

MINNESOTA.

PARIS GIBSON, . . . Minneapolis.

Standing Committees.

Finance.

J. WILEY EDMANDS, . . Boston, Mass.
C. FITTON, ... Rockville, Conn.
J. W. STITT, ... New York, N. Y.
JAMES A. SMITH, . . . Cherry Valley, Mass.

Statistics.

GEORGE WM. BOND, . . Boston, Mass.
J. V. BARKER, ... Pittsfield, Mass.
E L. STIMSON, ... Cohoes, N. Y.
JOHN T. WARING, . . . Yonkers, N. Y.

Raw Material.

J. W. BLAKE, ... Boston. Massachusetts
J. J. ROBINSON, . . . Rockville, Conn.
S. J. SOLMS, ... Philadelphia, Pa.
A. LAWRENCE EDMANDS, Boston, Mass.

Machinery.

GEORGE L. DAVIS, . . North Andover, Mass.
C. FITTON, ... New Britain, Conn.
J. K. KILBOURN, . . . New Britain, Conn.
THOMAS F. EDDY, . . Fall River, Mass.
SAMUEL HARRIS, . . . Catskill, N. Y.
ROBERT MIDDLETON, . Utica, N. Y.

OFFICE, 11 PEMBERTON SQUARE, BOSTON MASS.

OFFICERS OF THE AMERICAN IRON AND STEEL ASSOCIATION FOR 1875.

OFFICE AT 265 SOUTH FOURTH STREET, PHILADELPHIA.

President.

SAMUEL J. REEVES, No. 410 Walnut Street, Philadelphia.

Vice-Presidents.

JOSEPH WHARTON, Philadelphia.
ABRAM S. HEWITT, 17 Burling Slip, New York.
S. M. FELTON, 216 South Fourth Street, Philadelphia.
JAMES I. BENNETT, Pittsburgh.
JAMES PARK, Jr., Pittsburgh.

Secretary.

JAMES M. SWANK, 265 South Fourth Street, Philadelphia.

Treasurer.

CHARLES WHEELER, Philadelphia.

Executive Committee.

S. J. Reeves, 410 Walnut St., Philadelphia.
A. S. Hewitt, 17 Burling Slip, New York.
C. S. Kauffman, Columbia, Penn.
J. B. Moorhead, 230 S. 3d St., Philadelphia.
James Park, Jr., Pittsburgh, Penn.
Percival Roberts, 265 S. 4th St., Phila.
James I. Bennett, Pittsburgh, Penn.
Joseph Wharton, Philadelphia.
Alfred Hunt, Bethlehem, Penn.
E. Y. Townsend, 218 S. 4th St., Phila.
Charles Wheeler, Philadelphia.
Chas. Stewart Wurts, 218 S. 4th St. Phila.
A. B. Stone, Cleveland, Ohio.
Edward Harrison, St. Louis, Mo.

Board of Managers.

J. J. Hagerman, Milwaukee, Wis.
A. S. Hewitt, 17 Burling Slip, New York.
Samuel Thomas, Hokendauqua, Penn.
John H. Reed, Boston, Mass.
James Park, Jr., Pittsburgh, Penn.
Joseph Kinsey, Cincinnati, Ohio.
C. S. Kauffman, Columbia, Penn.
Thomas S. Blair, Pittsburgh, Penn.
A. B. Stone, Cleveland, Ohio.
B. F. Jones, Pittsburgh, Penn.
J. T. Wilder, Chattanooga, Tenn.
Charles Wheeler, Philadelphia.
A. W. Humpheys, 42 Pine Street, N. Y.
Horace Abbott, Baltimore, Md.
S. J. Reeves, 410 Walnut St., Philadelphia.
J. M. Lord, Indianapolis, Ind.
Thomas Beaver, Danville, Penn.
E. Y. Townsend, 218 S. 4th St., Philadelphia.
James I. Bennett, Pittsburgh, Penn.
Alfred Hunt, Bethlehem, Penn.
Percival Roberts, 265 S. 4th St., Phila.
James Rogers, Essex, N. Y.
Joseph Wharton, Philadelphia.
Louis Scofield, Atlanta, Ga.
R. E. Blankenship, Richmond, Va.
Geo. D. Hall, St. Louis, Mo.
Chester Griswold, Troy, N. Y.
E. B. Pratt, Buffalo, N. Y.
Abram Patterson, Port Kennedy, Penn.
R. C. Hannah, Chicago, Ill.

THE DALE SILK MILL, PATERSON, NEW JERSEY.

L. D. Brown & Son,

MANUFACTURERS OF ALL KINDS OF

Machine Twist and Sewing Silk.

ESTABLISHED 1850.

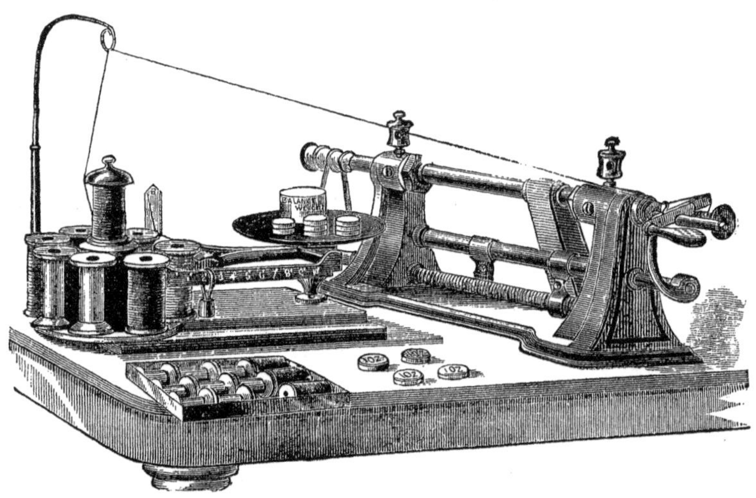

This Cut represents our Spooling and Weighing Apparatus, patented June 4, 1872, by the use of which accurate weight for each and every spool is insured, thereby securing uniformity in measurement. (See page 73.)

Mills at	Trade Marks:	Salesrooms:
MIDDLETOWN,	L. D. BROWN & SON, Middletown Mills, Paragon, Conn. Valley.	439 BROADWAY,
Conn.		New York.

The attention of manufacturers is called to our PURE DYE brands which are excelled by none. Samples and Price List sent on application.

www.ingramcontent.com/pod-product-compliance
Lightning Source LLC
La Vergne TN
LVHW020227110826
845151LV00003B/844

* 9 7 8 1 4 2 5 5 3 1 7 6 8 *